APPLICATIONS FOR ENROLLMENT OF CHICKASAW NEWBORN ACT OF 1905 VOLUME I

TRANSCRIBED BY
JEFF BOWEN

NATIVE STUDY
Gallipolis, Ohio
USA

Copyright © 2013
by Jeff Bowen

ALL RIGHTS RESERVED
No part of this publication may be reproduced
or used in any form or manner whatsoever
without previous written permission from the
copyright holder or publisher.

Originally published:
Baltimore, Maryland
2013

Reprinted by:

Native Study LLC
Gallipolis, OH
www.nativestudy.com
2020

Library of Congress Control Number: 2020917160

ISBN: 978-1-64968-063-1

Made in the United States of America.

Other Books and Series by Jeff Bowen

1901-1907 Native American Census Seneca, Eastern Shawnee, Miami, Modoc, Ottawa, Peoria, Quapaw, and Wyandotte Indians (Under Seneca School, Indian Territory)

1932 Census of The Standing Rock Sioux Reservation with Births And Deaths 1924-1932

Census of The Blackfeet, Montana, 1897- 1901 Expanded Edition

Eastern Cherokee by Blood, 1906-1910, Volumes I thru XIII

Choctaw of Mississippi Indian Census 1929-1932 with Births and Deaths 1924-1931   Volume I
Choctaw of Mississippi Indian Census 1933, 1934 & 1937, Supplemental Rolls to 1934 & 1935 with Births and Deaths 1932-1938, and Marriages 1936-1938 Volume II

Eastern Cherokee Census Cherokee, North Carolina 1930-1939 Census 1930-1931 with Births And Deaths 1924-1931 Taken By Agent L. W. Page Volume I
Eastern Cherokee Census Cherokee, North Carolina 1930-1939 Census 1932-1933 with Births And Deaths 1930-1932 Taken By Agent R. L. Spalsbury   Volume II
Eastern Cherokee Census Cherokee, North Carolina 1930-1939 Census 1934-1937 with Births and Deaths 1925-1938 and Marriages 1936 & 1938 Taken by Agents R. L. Spalsbury And Harold W. Foght Volume III

Seminole of Florida Indian Census, 1930-1940 with Birth and Death Records, 1930-1938

Texas Cherokees 1820-1839 A Document For Litigation 1921

Choctaw By Blood Enrollment Cards 1898-1914 Volumes I thru XVII

Starr Roll 1894 (Cherokee Payment Rolls) Districts: Canadian, Cooweescoowee, and Delaware Volume One
Starr Roll 1894 (Cherokee Payment Rolls) Districts: Flint, Going Snake, and Illinois   Volume Two
Starr Roll 1894 (Cherokee Payment Rolls) Districts: Saline, Sequoyah, and Tahlequah; Including Orphan Roll Volume Three

Cherokee Intruder Cases Dockets of Hearings 1901-1909 Volumes I & II

Indian Wills, 1911-1921 Records of the Bureau of Indian Affairs Books One thru Seven;
Native American Wills & Probate Records 1911-1921

Other Books and Series by Jeff Bowen

Turtle Mountain Reservation Chippewa Indians 1932 Census with Births & Deaths, 1924-1932

Chickasaw By Blood Enrollment Cards 1898-1914 Volume I thru V

Cherokee Descendants East An Index to the Guion Miller Applications Volume I
Cherokee Descendants West An Index to the Guion Miller Applications Volume II (A-M)
Cherokee Descendants West An Index to the Guion Miller Applications Volume III (N-Z)

Applications for Enrollment of Seminole Newborn Freedmen, Act of 1905

Eastern Cherokee Census, Cherokee, North Carolina, 1915-1922, Taken by Agent James E. Henderson   Volume I (1915-1916)
Volume II (1917-1918)
Volume III (1919-1920)
Volume IV (1921-1922)

Complete Delaware Roll of 1898

Eastern Cherokee Census, Cherokee, North Carolina, 1923-1929, Taken by Agent James E. Henderson   Volume I (1923-1924)
Volume II (1925-1926)
Volume III (1927-1929)

Applications for Enrollment of Seminole Newborn Act of 1905 Volumes I & II

North Carolina Eastern Cherokee Indian Census 1898-1899, 1904, 1906, 1909-1912, 1914 Revised and Expanded Edition

1932 Hopi and Navajo Native American Census with Birth & Death Rolls (1925-1931) Volume 1 - Hopi
1932 Hopi and Navajo Native American Census with Birth & Death Rolls (1930-1932) Volume 2 - Navajo

Western Navajo Reservation Navajo, Hopi and Paiute 1933 Census with Birth & Death Rolls 1925-1933

Cherokee Citizenship Commission Dockets 1880-1884 and 1887-1889 Volumes I thru V

Visit our website at **www.nativestudy.com** to learn more about these and other books and series by Jeff Bowen

This series is dedicated to the descendants of the Chickasaw newborn listed in these applications.

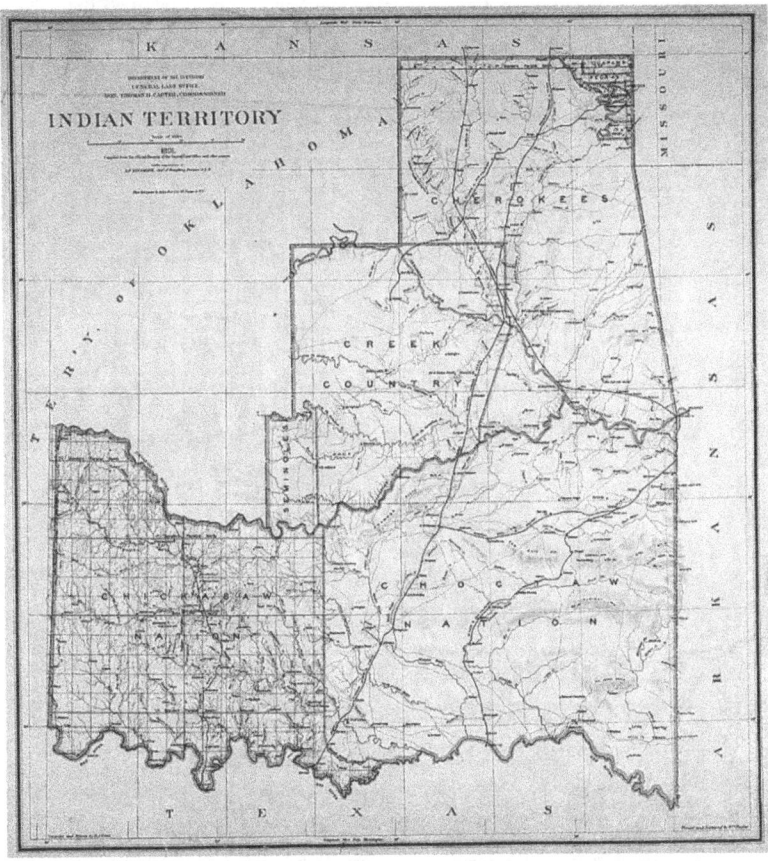

This map of Indian Territory shows how large the Choctaw and Chickasaw Nations' land base was that contained huge deposits of asphalt and coal. Just the size and territory involved was flooded with the "Grafters".

DEPARTMENT OF THE INTERIOR,
Commission to the Five Civilized Tribes.

Rules and Regulations Governing the Selection of Allotments and the Designation of Homesteads in the Choctaw and Chickasaw Nations.

1. Selections of allotments and designations of homesteads for adult citizens and selections of allotments for adult freedmen must be made in person except as herein otherwise provided.
2. Applications to have land set apart and homesteads designated for duly identified Mississippi Choctaws must be made personally before the Commission to the Five Civilized Tribes. Fathers may apply for their minor children and if the father be dead the mother may apply. Husbands may apply for wives. Applications for orphans, insane persons and persons of unsound mind may be made by duly appointed guardian or curator, and for aged and infirm persons and prisoners by agents duly authorized thereunto by power of attorney, in the discretion of said Commission.
3. At the time of the selection of allotment each citizen and duly identified Mississippi Choctaw shall designate as a homestead out of said selection land equal in value to one hundred and sixty acres of the average allottable land of the Choctaw and Chickasaw Nations, as nearly as may be.
4. Each Choctaw and Chickasaw freedman, at the time of selection shall designate as his or her allotment of the lands of the Choctaw and Chickasaw Nations, land equal in value to forty acres of the average allottable land of the Choctaw and Chickasaw Nations.
5. Citizens, freedmen and identified Mississippi Choctaws who are married, whether they have attained their majority or not, will be regarded as of age for the purpose of making selections.
6. Selections may be made by citizen and freedman parents for unmarried male children under twenty-one years of age and for unmarried female children under eighteen years of age, and a male citizen or freedman may make selection for his wife, if she is entitled to make selection, unless she shall, at the time or previously thereto, protest in writing.
7. Where the father of an unmarried minor citizen, freedman or identified Mississippi Choctaw is a non-citizen, the citizen, freedman or identified Mississippi Choctaw mother of such children must make selection in person in behalf of said children.
8. Selections of allotments and designations of homesteads for minor citizens and selections of allotments for minor freedmen may be made by the citizen father or mother or freedman father or mother, as the case may be, or by a guardian, curator, or an administrator having charge of their estate, in the order named.
9. Selections of allotments and designations of homesteads for citizen, and freedmen, prisoners, convicts, aged and infirm persons and soldiers and sailors of the United States on duty outside of Indian Territory, may be made by duly appointed agents under power of attorney, and for incompetents by guardians, curators, or other suitable person akin to them.
10. Selections may be made and homesteads designated by duly identified Mississippi Choctaws, who have, within one year after the date of their identification as such, made satisfactory proof of bona fide settlement within the Choctaw-Chickasaw country, at any time within six months after the date of their said identification.
11. Persons authorized to make selections by power of attorney, as provided in rules 2 and 9 hereof, must be the husband or wife, or a relative not further removed than a cousin of the first degree of the person for whom such selection is made.
12. It shall be the duty of the Commission to the Five Civilized Tribes to see that selections of allotments and designations of homesteads for the classes of persons mentioned in rules 2, 6, 7, 8 and 9 hereof, are made for the best interests of such persons.
13. Selections of allotments for citizens, freedmen and identified Mississippi Choctaws who have died subsequent to September 25, 1902, and before making a selection of allotment, shall be made by a duly appointed administrator or executor. If, however, such administrator or executor be not duly and expeditiously appointed, or fails to act promptly when appointed, or for any other cause such selections be not so made within a reasonable and practicable time, the Commission to the Five Civilized Tribes shall designate the lands thus to be allotted.
14. In determining the value of a selection the appraised value of the land selected shall be increased by the appraised value of such pine timber on such land as has heretofore been estimated by the Commission to the Five Civilized Tribes.
15. Selections of allotments may be made only by citizens and freedmen whose enrollment has been approved by the Secretary of the Interior, and by persons duly identified by the Commission to the Five Civilized Tribes as Mississippi Choctaws, and by none others.
16. When a selection of land has been made by a citizen, freedman or identified Mississippi Choctaw, and the land so selected is claimed by a person whose rights as a citizen or freedman have not been finally determined, contest for the land so selected may be instituted by the person claiming the land, formal application for the land being first made as is required by the Rules of Practice in Choctaw and Chickasaw allotment contest cases.

THE COMMISSION TO THE FIVE CIVILIZED TRIBES.
TAMS BIXBY, Chairman.

Muskogee, Indian Territory, March 24, 1903.

The above statement published prior to 1905, was established for what was supposed to be a set of guidelines when it came to allotments. But with supplemental agreements and Congressional legislation, time frames as well as rules and regulations often changed and were not the same for every tribe.

INTRODUCTION

The *Applications for Enrollment of Chickasaw Newborn Act of 1905*, National Archive film M-1301, Rolls 455-458, are found under the heading of Applications for Enrollment of the Commission to the Five Civilized Tribes. For this series, I have transcribed the application forms filled out by individuals applying for enrollment in the Five Civilized Tribes under the Dawes Commission. These applications contain considerably more information than stated on the census cards found in series M-1186. M-1301 possesses its own numerical sequence, separate from M-1186. To find each party's roll number you would have to reference M-1186.

The Chickasaw as well as the Choctaw allotments were likely some of the most sought after properties in Indian Territory. There was supposed to be a 25-year restriction on the sale or lease of any Indian lands so as to insure that the owners wouldn't be swindled, but that isn't what happened. This fact is borne out in the Dawes Commission General Allotment Act, of February 8, 1887, Section 5, which "Provides that after an Indian person is allotted land, the United States will hold the land 'in trust [1] for the sole use and benefit of the Indian' (or his heirs if the Indian landowner dies) for a period of 25 years. (Land held in trust by the United States government cannot be sold or in anyway alienated by the Indian landowner, since the United States government considers the underlying ownership of the land held by itself and not the tribe. After the period of trust ends, the Indian landowner is free to sell the land and is free from any encumbrance from the United States.)"[1] Instead, Native Americans were exploited by the devious. The Chickasaw and Choctaw Districts both had huge asphalt and coal deposits, so there was pressure from outsiders to acquire them from the minute they were discovered. After repeated attacks throughout the years and many legislative changes, President "Roosevelt finally signed the Five Tribes Bill at noon on April 26, 1906, the forces seeking to end all restrictions were disappointed. Section 19 removed restrictions from the sale of all inherited land but directed that no full-bloods could sell their land for twenty-five years. The Act also prohibited leases for more than one year without the approval of the Secretary of the Interior."[2]

Angie Debo described the opportunists that wanted these Native American allotments as, "Grafters". The parents of the newborns enumerated within this series would no sooner receive the approval for their child's allotment than there would be someone there with cash in hand holding a new deed or lease for the parents to sign their child's birthright away. Angie Debo said it best, "As the business incapacity of the allottees became apparent, a horde of despoilers fastened themselves upon their property." According to Debo, "The term 'grafter' was applied as a matter of course to dealers in Indian land, and was frankly accepted by them. The speculative fever also affected Government employees so that it was almost impossible to prevent them from making personal investments."[3]

---

[1] General Allotment Act, Act of Feb. 8, 1887 (24 Stat. 388, ch. 119, 25 USCA 331)
[2] The Dawes Commission and the Allotment of the Five Civilized Tribes, 1893-1914 by Kent Carter, pg. 173
[3] And Still the Waters Run, Angie Debo, p. 92.

INTRODUCTION

According to the Department of Interior in 1905, "It is estimated that there will be added to the final rolls of the citizens and freedmen of the Choctaw and Chickasaw nations the names of 2,000 persons, including 1,500 new-born children to be enrolled under the provisions of the act of Congress approved March 3, 1905."[4]

The quote below explains, in detail, the requirements for qualifying as a newborn Chickasaw, "By the act of Congress approved March 3, 1905 (H.R. 17474), entitled 'An act making appropriations for the current and contingent expenses of the Indian Department and for fulfilling treaty stipulations with various Indian tribes for the fiscal year ending June 30, 1906, and for other purposes,' it was provided as follows:

'That the Commission to the Five Civilized Tribes is hereby authorized for sixty days after the date of the approval of this act to receive and consider applications for enrollment of infant children born prior to September twenty-fifth, nineteen hundred and two, and who were living on said date, to citizens by blood of the Choctaw and Chickasaw tribes of Indians whose enrollment has been approved by the Secretary of the Interior prior to the date of the approval of this act; and to enroll and make allotments to such children.'

'That the Commission to the Five Civilized Tribes is authorized for sixty days after the date of the approval of this act to receive and consider applications for enrollment of children born subsequent to September twenty-fifth, nineteen hundred and two, and prior to March fourth, nineteen hundred and five, and who were living on said latter date, to citizens by blood of the Choctaw and Chickasaw tribes of Indians whose enrollment has been approved by the Secretary of the Interior prior to the date of the approval of this act; and to enroll and make allotments to such children.'

"Notice is hereby given that the Commission to the Five Civilized Tribes will, up to and inclusive of midnight, May 2, 1905, receive applications for the enrollment of infant children born prior to September 25, 1902, and who were living on said date, to citizens by blood of the Choctaw and Chickasaw tribes of Indians whose enrollment has been approved by the Secretary of the Interior prior to March 3, 1905."[5]

Following is the scope of these transcriptions: Besides the applications themselves, researchers will find the identities of other individuals within these applications -- doctors, lawyers, mid-wives, and other relatives -- that may help with your genealogical research.

Jeff Bowen
Gallipolis, Ohio
NativeStudy.com

---

[4] Annual Reports of the Department of the Interior For the Fiscal Year Ended June 30, 1905, p. 609.
[5] Annual Reports of the Department of the Interior For the Fiscal Year Ended June 30, 1905, p. 593.

Applications for Enrollment of Chickasaw Newborn
Act of 1905 Volume I

Chic. N.B - 1
    (Tandy C. Walker, Jr.
    Born April 29, 1903)
    (Maimie Walker
    Born January 14, 1905)

BIRTH AFFIDAVIT.

DEPARTMENT OF THE INTERIOR.
COMMISSION TO THE FIVE CIVILIZED TRIBES.

IN RE APPLICATION FOR ENROLLMENT, as a citizen of the Chickasaw Nation, of Tandy C Walker, Jr, born on the 29 day of April, 1903

Name of Father: J. C. Walker   a citizen of the Chickasaw Nation.
Name of Mother: Lucy Walker   a citizen of the United States Nation.

        Postoffice   Stonewall, I.T.

AFFIDAVIT OF MOTHER.

UNITED STATES OF AMERICA, Indian Territory,
    Southern   DISTRICT.

    I, Lucy Walker, on oath state that I am Twenty-five years of age and a citizen by ...., of the United States ~~Nation~~; that I am the lawful wife of J. C. Walker, who is a citizen, by Blood of the Chickasaw Nation; that a male child was born to me on 29 day of April, 1903, that said child has been named Tandy C Walker Jr, and is now living.

                            Lucy Walker

Witnesses To Mark:

    Subscribed and sworn to before me this 27 day of Mch, 1905.

                            W. F. Harrison
                            Notary Public.

Applications for Enrollment of Chickasaw Newborn
Act of 1905   Volume I

AFFIDAVIT OF ATTENDING PHYSICIAN OR MID-WIFE.

UNITED STATES OF AMERICA, Indian Territory, }
Southern   DISTRICT.

    I,   Geo H Truax   , a   Physician   , on oath state that I attended on Mrs.   Lucy Walker   , wife of   J.C. Walker   on the   April[sic]   day of 29[sic] , 1903; that there was born to her on said date a   male   child; that said child is now living and is said to have been named Tandy C Walker Jr

                             Geo. H. Truax M.D.

Witnesses To Mark:
{

    Subscribed and sworn to before me this 27th day of   Mch   , 1905.

                             W.F. Harrison
                               Notary Public.

BIRTH AFFIDAVIT.

DEPARTMENT OF THE INTERIOR.
COMMISSION TO THE FIVE CIVILIZED TRIBES.

    IN RE APPLICATION FOR ENROLLMENT, as a citizen of the   Chickasaw   Nation, of Tandy C Walker, Jr   , born on the   29th day of   April   , 1903

Name of Father: J. C. Walker   a citizen of the   Chickasaw   Nation.
                                                            Intermarried
Name of Mother: Lucy Walker   a citizen of the United States Nation.

                     Postoffice   Stonewall, I.T.

AFFIDAVIT OF MOTHER.

UNITED STATES OF AMERICA, Indian Territory, }
Southern   DISTRICT.

    I,   Lucy Walker   , on oath state that I am Twenty-five   years of age and a citizen by ...., of the   United States ~~Nation~~; that I am the lawful wife of   J. C. Walker   , who is a citizen, by   Blood   of the   Chickasaw   Nation; that a male   child was born to me on   29th day of   April   , 1903, that said child has been named   Tandy C Walker Jr   , and is now living.

                                 Lucy Walker

Applications for Enrollment of Chickasaw Newborn
Act of 1905 Volume I

Witnesses To Mark:
{

    Subscribed and sworn to before me this 26th day of Jan , 1905.

                                      W. F. Harrison
                                      Notary Public.

AFFIDAVIT OF ATTENDING PHYSICIAN OR MID-WIFE.

UNITED STATES OF AMERICA, Indian Territory, }
    Southern   DISTRICT. }

    I, Geo H Truax , a Physician , on oath state that I attended on Mrs. Lucy Walker , wife of J.C. Walker on the 29th day of April , 1903; that there was born to her on said date a male child; that said child is now living and is said to have been named Tandy C Walker Jr

                                    Geo. H. Truax M.D.

Witnesses To Mark:
{

    Subscribed and sworn to before me this 26th day of Jan , 1905.

                                      W.F. Harrison
                                      Notary Public.

BIRTH AFFIDAVIT.   *No 2*

DEPARTMENT OF THE INTERIOR.
COMMISSION TO THE FIVE CIVILIZED TRIBES.

    IN RE APPLICATION FOR ENROLLMENT, as a citizen of the Chickasaw Nation, of Maimie Walker , born on the 14th day of January , 1905

Name of Father: J. C. Walker   a citizen of the Chickasaw Nation.
Name of Mother: Lucy Walker   a citizen of the United States Nation.

                          Postoffice   Stonewall, I.T.

Applications for Enrollment of Chickasaw Newborn
Act of 1905 Volume I

AFFIDAVIT OF MOTHER.

UNITED STATES OF AMERICA, Indian Territory, }
  Southern   DISTRICT.

I, Lucy Walker , on oath state that I am Twenty-five years of age and a citizen by Blood , of the United States Nation; that I am the lawful wife of J. C. Walker , who is a citizen, by Blood of the Chickasaw Nation; that a Female child was born to me on 14th day of Jan , 1905, that said child has been named Maimie Walker , and is now living.

           Lucy Walker

Witnesses To Mark:
{

Subscribed and sworn to before me this 26th day of Jan , 1905.

           W. F. Harrison
           Notary Public.

AFFIDAVIT OF ATTENDING PHYSICIAN OR MID-WIFE.

UNITED STATES OF AMERICA, Indian Territory, }
  .... DISTRICT.

I, P. C. Bradley , a Physician , on oath state that I attended on Mrs. Lucy Walker , wife of J.C. Walker on the 14th day of Jan , 1905; that there was born to her on said date a Female child; that said child is now living and is said to have been named Maimie Walker

           P.C. Bradley M.D.

Witnesses To Mark:
{

Subscribed and sworn to before me this 14th [sic] day of Jan , 1905.

           W.F. Harrison
           Notary Public.

Applications for Enrollment of Chickasaw Newborn
Act of 1905   Volume I

BIRTH AFFIDAVIT.

DEPARTMENT OF THE INTERIOR.
COMMISSION TO THE FIVE CIVILIZED TRIBES.

IN RE APPLICATION FOR ENROLLMENT, as a citizen of the   Chickasaw   Nation, of Maimie Walker , born on the 14   day of Feb[sic] , 1905

Name of Father: J. C. Walker   a citizen of the Chickasaw Nation.
Name of Mother: Lucy   a citizen of the United States Nation.

Postoffice   Stonewall, I.T.

AFFIDAVIT OF MOTHER.

UNITED STATES OF AMERICA, Indian Territory,
Southern   DISTRICT.

I, Lucy Walker , on oath state that I am Twenty-five years of age and a citizen by ...., of the   United States ~~Nation~~; that I am the lawful wife of   J. C. Walker , who is a citizen, by   Blood   of the   Chickasaw   Nation; that a Female   child was born to me on 14th   day of Feb , 1905, that said child has been named Maimie Walker , and is now living.

Lucy Walker

Witnesses To Mark:
{

Subscribed and sworn to before me this 27th day of Mch , 1905.

W. F. Harrison
Notary Public.

AFFIDAVIT OF ATTENDING PHYSICIAN OR MID-WIFE.

UNITED STATES OF AMERICA, Indian Territory,
Southern   DISTRICT.

I, P. C. Bradley   , a   Physician   , on oath state that I attended on Mrs. Lucy Walker , wife of J.C. Walker   on the 14 day of Feb , 1905; that there was born to her on said date a   Female   child; that said child is now living and is said to have been named Maimie Walker

P.C. Bradley M.D.

Witnesses To Mark:
{

Applications for Enrollment of Chickasaw Newborn
Act of 1905   Volume I

Subscribed and sworn to before me this 27 day of Mch   , 1905.

W.F. Harrison
Notary Public.

BIRTH AFFIDAVIT.

DEPARTMENT OF THE INTERIOR.
COMMISSION TO THE FIVE CIVILIZED TRIBES.

    IN RE APPLICATION FOR ENROLLMENT, as a citizen of the   Chickasaw   Nation, of Maimie Walker   , born on the 14   day of Jan   , 1905

Name of Father: J.C. Walker   a citizen of the   Chickasaw   Nation.
Name of Mother: Lucy Walker   a citizen of the United States Nation.

Postoffice   Stonewall I.T.

AFFIDAVIT OF MOTHER.

UNITED STATES OF AMERICA, Indian Territory,   }
   Southern   DISTRICT.

    I, Lucy Walker   , on oath state that I am 25   years of age and a citizen by ——————— , of the United States Nation; that I am the lawful wife of J.C. Walker   , who is a citizen, by blood   of the   Chickasaw   Nation; that a   female   child was born to me on 14   day of   January   , 1905; that said child has been named   Maimie Walker   , and was living March 4, 1905.

Lucy Walker

Witnesses To Mark:
{

Subscribed and sworn to before me this 25 day of   May   , 1905

W.F. Harrison
Notary Public.

Applications for Enrollment of Chickasaw Newborn
Act of 1905 Volume I

AFFIDAVIT OF ATTENDING PHYSICIAN OR MID-WIFE.

UNITED STATES OF AMERICA, Indian Territory,
Southern DISTRICT.

I, P.C. Bradley, a Physician, on oath state that I attended on Mrs. Lucy Walker, wife of J.C. Walker on the 14 day of January, 1905; that there was born to her on said date a female child; that said child was living March 4, 1905, and is said to have been named Maimie Walker

P.C. Bradley MD

Witnesses To Mark:
{

Subscribed and sworn to before me this 25 day of May, 1905

W.F. Harrison
Notary Public.

9 N.B. 1.

Muskogee, Indian Territory, June 1, 1905.

J. C. Walker,
Stonewall, Indian Territory.

Dear Sir:

Receipt is hereby acknowledged of the affidavits of Lucy Walker and P. C. Bradley, M.D., to the birth of Maimie Walker, daughter of J. C. and Lucy Walker, January 14, 1905, and the same have been filed with our records in the matter of the enrollment of said child.

Respectfully,

Chairman.

Applications for Enrollment of Chickasaw Newborn
Act of 1905 Volume I

9-NB-1.

Muskogee, Indian Territory, May 20, 1905.

J. C. Walker,
    Stonewall, Indian Territory.

Dear Sir:

    There is enclosed you herewith for execution application for the enrollment of your infant child, Maimie Walker, born January 14, 1905.

    In the affidavits of January 14, and 26, 1905, heretofore filed with the Commission, the date of the birth of the child is given as January 14, 1905, while in the affidavits of March 27, 1905, the date of birth is given as February 14, 1905. The date in the former affidavit is apparently correct, but as these do not show the child living on March 4, 1905, it will be necessary that you execute the enclosed application.

    In having these affidavits executed care should be exercised to see that all names are written in full, as they appear in the body of the affidavit, and in the event that either of the persons signing the affidavit are unable to write, signatures by mark must be attested by two witnesses. Each affidavit must be executed before a Notary Public and the notarial seal and signature of the officer must be attached to each separate affidavit.

                                Respectfully,

VR 20-2.   Chairman.

Chic. N.B - 2
    (Bessie Trentham
    Born August 24, 1904)

Applications for Enrollment of Chickasaw Newborn
Act of 1905 Volume I

BIRTH AFFIDAVIT.

DEPARTMENT OF THE INTERIOR.
COMMISSION TO THE FIVE CIVILIZED TRIBES.

IN RE APPLICATION FOR ENROLLMENT, as a citizen of the Chickasaw Nation, of Bessie Trentham, born on the 24th day of August, 1904

Name of Father: Henderson Trentham   a citizen of the Chickasaw Nation.
Name of Mother: Belle Smith Trentham   a citizen of the Chickasaw Nation.

Postoffice   Coalgate Ind. Ter.

AFFIDAVIT OF MOTHER.

UNITED STATES OF AMERICA, Indian Territory,
Central   DISTRICT.

I, Belle Smith Trentham, on oath state that I am 30 years of age and a citizen by Intermarriage, of the Chickasaw Nation; that I am the lawful wife of Henderson Trentham, who is a citizen, by blood of the Chickasaw Nation; that a female child was born to me on 24th day of August, 1904; that said child has been named Bessie Trentham, and was living March 4, 1905.

Belle Smith Trentham

Witnesses To Mark:

Subscribed and sworn to before me this 25th day of March, 1905.

Geo. A. Fooshee
Notary Public.

AFFIDAVIT OF ATTENDING PHYSICIAN OR MID-WIFE.

UNITED STATES OF AMERICA, Indian Territory,
Central   DISTRICT.

I, Giles W. Harkins, a Physcian[sic], on oath state that I attended on Mrs. Belle Smith Trentham, wife of Henderson Trentham on the 24th day of August, 1904; that there was born to her on said date a female child; that said child was living March 4, 1905, and is said to have been named Bessie Trentham

Giles W. Harkins, M.D.

Witnesses To Mark:

Applications for Enrollment of Chickasaw Newborn
Act of 1905   Volume I

Subscribed and sworn to before me this 25th day of   March   , 1905

          Geo. A. Fooshee
          Notary Public.

                Chickasaw 20

       Muskogee, Indian Territory, March 30, 1905.

Fooshee & Brunson,
  Attorneys at Law,
    Coalgate, Indian Territory.

Gentlemen:

  Receipt is hereby acknowledged of your letter of March 25, transmitting affidavits of Belle Smith Trentham and Giles W. Harkins to the birth of Bessie Trentham, infant daughter of Henderson and Belle Smith Trentham August 24, 1904, and the same have been filed with our records as an application for the enrollment of said child.

        Respectfully,

        Chairman.

Chic. N.B - 3
  (Walter Colbert
  Born April 1, 1904)

BIRTH AFFIDAVIT.

DEPARTMENT OF THE INTERIOR.
COMMISSION TO THE FIVE CIVILIZED TRIBES.

  IN RE APPLICATION FOR ENROLLMENT, as a citizen of the   Chickasaw   Nation, of   Walter Colbert   , born on the   1st day of   April   , 1904

Name of Father: Walton Colbert   a citizen of the Chickasaw Nation.
Name of Mother: Louisa Colbert   a citizen of the Chickasaw Nation.

      Postoffice   Franks

Applications for Enrollment of Chickasaw Newborn
Act of 1905 Volume I

AFFIDAVIT OF MOTHER.

UNITED STATES OF AMERICA, Indian Territory, }
Southern DISTRICT. }

I, Louisa Colbert, on oath state that I am 38 years of age and a citizen by blood, of the Chickasaw Nation; that I am the lawful wife of Walton Colbert, who is a citizen, by blood of the Chickasaw Nation; that a male child was born to me on 1st day of April, 1904; that said child has been named Walter, and was living March 4, 1905.

            Louisa Colbert

Witnesses To Mark:
{

Subscribed and sworn to before me this 30 day of April, 1905

            W.H. Burdeshaw
              Notary Public.

AFFIDAVIT OF ATTENDING PHYSICIAN OR MID-WIFE.

UNITED STATES OF AMERICA, Indian Territory, }
Sou DISTRICT. }

I, Lucy Brown, a midwife, on oath state that I attended on Mrs. Louisa Colbert, wife of Walton Colbert on the 1st day of April, 1904; that there was born to her on said date a male child; that said child was living March 4, 1905, and is said to have been named Walter

            her
          Lucy x Brown
Witnesses To Mark: mark
 { Galloway Lewis
 { Jackson Lewis

Subscribed and sworn to before me this 30 day of Mch, 1905

            W.H. Burdeshaw
              Notary Public.

Applications for Enrollment of Chickasaw Newborn
Act of 1905 Volume I

9-21

Muskogee, Indian Territory, April 5, 1905.

Walton Colbert,
    Franks, Indian Territory.

Dear Sir:

    Receipt is hereby acknowledged of the affidavits of Louisa Colbert and Lucy Brown to the birth of Walter Colbert, son of Walton and Louisa Colbert, April 1, 1904, and the same have been filed with our records as an application for the enrollment of said child.

    Respectfully.

    Commissioner in Charge.

Chic. N.B - 4
    (May Hawkins
    Born October 5, 1904)

BIRTH AFFIDAVIT.   #116

IN RE-APPLICATION FOR ENROLLMENT, as a citizen of the Chickasaw Nation, of May Hawkins , born on the 5 day of October , 1904

Name of Father: Morris H Hawkins   a citizen of the Chickasaw Nation.
Name of Mother: Mary Hawkins   a citizen of the Intermarried Nation.

Postoffice   Maxwell IT

AFFIDAVIT OF MOTHER.

UNITED STATES OF AMERICA, INDIAN TERRITORY, }
    Southern   District.

    I, Mary Hawkins , on oath state that I am 28 years of age and a citizen by Intermarried , of the Chickasaw Nation; that I am the lawful wife of Morris H Hawkins , who is a citizen, by blood of the Chickasaw Nation; that a female child was born to me on 5 day of October , 1904 , that said child has been named May Hawkins , and is now living.

Applications for Enrollment of Chickasaw Newborn
Act of 1905 Volume I

                            her
                        Mary x Hawkins
Witnesses To Mark: mark
{ U B Standridge
{ J H Standridge

Subscribed and sworn to before me this 24 day of Feb , 1905.

                        Alfred Summers
                            Notary Public.

AFFIDAVIT OF ATTENDING PHYSICIAN OR MID-WIFE.

UNITED STATES OF AMERICA, INDIAN TERRITORY,
Southern District.

I, R A Standridge , a Midwife , on oath state that I attended on Mrs. Mary Hawkins , wife of Morris H Hawkins on the 5 day of October , 190 4; that there was born to her on said date a female child; that said child is now living and is said to have been named May Hawkins

                          her
                        R A x Standridge
Witnesses To Mark: mark
{ U B Standridge
{ J H Standridge

Subscribed and sworn to before me this 24 day of Feb , 1905.

                        Alfred Summers
                            Notary Public.

BIRTH AFFIDAVIT.

DEPARTMENT OF THE INTERIOR.
COMMISSION TO THE FIVE CIVILIZED TRIBES.

IN RE APPLICATION FOR ENROLLMENT, as a citizen of the Chickasaw Nation, of May Hawkins , born on the 5th day of October , 1904

Name of Father: Morris H Hawkins   a citizen of the Chickasaw Nation.
Name of Mother: Mary Hawkins   a citizen of the Chickasaw Nation.

                    Postoffice   Maxwell, Indian Territory

Applications for Enrollment of Chickasaw Newborn
Act of 1905 Volume I

AFFIDAVIT OF MOTHER.

UNITED STATES OF AMERICA, Indian Territory,
Southern   DISTRICT.

I, Mary Hawkins, on oath state that I am twenty eight (28) years of age and a citizen by Marriage, of the Chickasaw Nation; that I am the lawful wife of Morris H Hawkins, who is a citizen, by blood of the Chickasaw Nation; that a female child was born to me on 5th day of October, 1904; that said child has been named May Hawkins, and was living March 4, 1905.

Mary Hawkins

Witnesses To Mark:
 UB Standridge
 F Summers

Subscribed and sworn to before me this 29 day of March, 1905

Alfred Summers
Notary Public.

AFFIDAVIT OF ATTENDING PHYSICIAN OR MID-WIFE.

UNITED STATES OF AMERICA, Indian Territory,
Southern   DISTRICT.

I, ..., a mid-wife, on oath state that I attended on Mrs. Mary Hawkins, wife of Morris H Hawkins on the 5th day of October, 1904; that there was born to her on said date a female child; that said child was living March 4, 1905, and is said to have been named May Hawkins

R.A. Standridge

Witnesses To Mark:
 UB Standridge
 F. Summers

Subscribed and sworn to before me this 29 day of March, 1905

Alfred Summers
Notary Public.

Applications for Enrollment of Chickasaw Newborn
Act of 1905 Volume I

BIRTH AFFIDAVIT.

DEPARTMENT OF THE INTERIOR.
COMMISSION TO THE FIVE CIVILIZED TRIBES.

IN RE APPLICATION FOR ENROLLMENT, as a citizen of the Chickasaw Nation, of May Hawkins, born on the 5th day of October, 1904

Name of Father: Morris H Hawkins   a citizen of the Chickasaw Nation.
Name of Mother: Mary Hawkins   a citizen of the Chickasaw Nation.

Postoffice   Maxwell, Ind Ter

AFFIDAVIT OF MOTHER.

UNITED STATES OF AMERICA, Indian Territory,
Southern   DISTRICT.

I, Mary Hawkins, on oath state that I am 28 years of age and a citizen by ...., of the United States Nation; that I am the lawful wife of Morris H Hawkins, who is a citizen, by blood of the Chickasaw Nation; that a female child was born to me on 5th day of October, 1904; that said child has been named May Hawkins, and was living March 4, 1905.

                                       her
                              Mary x Hawkins

Witnesses To Mark: mark
  Ed Tyson
  Florence Summers

Subscribed and sworn to before me this 26 day of May, 1905

                            Alfred Summers
                                Notary Public.

AFFIDAVIT OF ATTENDING PHYSICIAN OR MID-WIFE.

UNITED STATES OF AMERICA, Indian Territory,
Southern   DISTRICT.

I, ..., a ...., on oath state that I attended on Mrs. Mary Hawkins, wife of Morris H Hawkins on the 5th day of October, 1904; that there was born to her on said date a female child; that said child was living March 4, 1905, and is said to have been named May Hawkins

                                       her
                          Ruth Adlin x Standridge
                                mark

Applications for Enrollment of Chickasaw Newborn
Act of 1905 Volume I

Witnesses To Mark:
{ Ed Tyson
{ Florence Summers

Subscribed and sworn to before me this 26 day of May , 1905

Alfred Summers
Notary Public.

Chickasaw 25.

Muskogee, Indian Territory, April 4, 1905.

Morris H. Hawkins,
Maxwell, Indian Territory.

Dear Sir:

Receipt is hereby acknowledged of the affidavits of Mary Hawkins and R. A. Standridge to the birth of May Hawkins, daughter of Morris H. and Mary Hawkins, October 5, 1904, and the same have been filed with our records as an application for the enrollment of said child.

Respectfully,

Commissioner in Charge.

9-NB-4.

Muskogee, Indian Territory, May 20, 1905.

Morris H. Hawkins,
Maxwell, Indian Territory.

Dear Sir:

There is enclosed you herewith for execution application for the enrollment of your infant child, May Hawkins, born October 5, 1904.

Referring to the affidavits of February 24, 1905, heretofore filed with the Commission, purported to be executed by Mary Hawkins and R. A. Standridge, it appears that both of these names, as well as the witnesses to their marks, have been signed by the notary public, while it appears from the affidavits of March 29, 1905, that both, Mary Hawkins and R. A. Standridge, are able to write.

Applications for Enrollment of Chickasaw Newborn
Act of 1905 Volume I

    In executing the enclosed affidavits have all the parties who are able to write to sign their own name, if unable to write, signatures by mark must be attested by two witnesses who are able to write. Care should be exercised to see that all the names are written in full, as they appear in the body of the affidavit. Each affidavit must be executed before a Notary Public and the notarial seal and signature of the officer must be attached to each separate affidavit.

Respectfully,

VR 19-5.   Chairman.

9-N.B. 4.

Muskogee, Indian Territory, June 2, 1905.

Morris H. Hawkins,
    Maxwell, Indian Territory.

Dear Sir:

    Receipt is hereby acknowledged of the affidavits of Mary Hawkins and Rutha Adlin Standridge to the birth of May Hawkins, daughter of Morris H. and Mary Hawkins, October 5, 1904, and the same have been filed with our records in the matter of the enrollment of said child.

Respectfully,

Commissioner in Charge.

Chic. N.B - 5
    (Opal Truax
    Born May 10, 1903)

BIRTH AFFIDAVIT.

DEPARTMENT OF THE INTERIOR.
COMMISSION TO THE FIVE CIVILIZED TRIBES.

    IN RE APPLICATION FOR ENROLLMENT, as a citizen of the   Chickasaw   Nation, of   Opal Truax   , born on the 20th day of May , 1903

Name of Father: George H Truax   a citizen of the   Chickasaw Nation.
Name of Mother: Mary C. Truax   a citizen of the   Chickasaw Nation.

Applications for Enrollment of Chickasaw Newborn
Act of 1905   Volume I

Postoffice   Stonewall, Ind. Ter.

AFFIDAVIT OF MOTHER.

UNITED STATES OF AMERICA, Indian Territory, }
Southern   DISTRICT.

I, Mary C Truax , on oath state that I am Forty years of age and a citizen by Blood , of the Chickasaw Nation; that I am the lawful wife of George H. Truax , who is a citizen, by Intermarriage of the Chickasaw Nation; that a Female child was born to me on the 20th day of May , 1903, that said child has been named Opal Truax , and is now living.

Mary C Truax

Witnesses To Mark:
{

Subscribed and sworn to before me this 21 day of Jan , 1905.

W.F. Harrison
Notary Public.

AFFIDAVIT OF ATTENDING PHYSICIAN OR MID-WIFE.

UNITED STATES OF AMERICA, Indian Territory, }
Southern   DISTRICT.

Midwife

I, Porter Hall , a ~~Attendant~~ , on oath state that I attended on Mrs. Mary C. Truax , wife of George H Truax on the 20th day of May , 1903; that there was born to her on said date a Female child; that said child is now living and is said to have been named Opal Truax

Porter Hall

Witnesses To Mark:
{

Subscribed and sworn to before me this 21 day of Jan , 1905.

W.F. Harrison
Notary Public.

Applications for Enrollment of Chickasaw Newborn
Act of 1905   Volume I

BIRTH AFFIDAVIT.

DEPARTMENT OF THE INTERIOR.
COMMISSION TO THE FIVE CIVILIZED TRIBES.

IN RE APPLICATION FOR ENROLLMENT, as a citizen of the Chickasaw Nation, of Opal Truax, born on the 20th day of May, 1903

Name of Father: George Henry Truax   a citizen of the Chickasaw Nation.
Name of Mother: Mary C Truax   a citizen of the Chickasaw Nation.

Postoffice   Stonewall Ind Ter

AFFIDAVIT OF MOTHER.

UNITED STATES OF AMERICA, Indian Territory,
Southern DISTRICT.

I, Mary C Truax, on oath state that I am Forty years of age and a citizen by Blood, of the Chickasaw Nation; that I am the lawful wife of George Henry Truax, who is a citizen, by Intermarriage of the Chickasaw Nation; that a Female child was born to me on 20th day of May, 1903; that said child has been named Opal Truax, and was living March 4, 1905.

Mary C Truax

Witnesses To Mark:

Subscribed and sworn to before me this 27 day of Mch, 1905

W.F. Harrison
Notary Public.

AFFIDAVIT OF ATTENDING PHYSICIAN OR MID-WIFE.

UNITED STATES OF AMERICA, Indian Territory,
Southern DISTRICT.

I, Porter Hall, a midwife, on oath state that I attended on Mrs. Mary C. Truax, wife of George Henry Truax on the 20th day of May, 1903; that there was born to her on said date a Female child; that said child was living March 4, 1905, and is said to have been named Opal Truax

Porter Hall

Witnesses To Mark:

Applications for Enrollment of Chickasaw Newborn
Act of 1905   Volume I

Subscribed and sworn to before me this 27   day of   Mch   , 1905

W.F. Harrison
Notary Public.

———

9-38

Muskogee, Indian Territory, March 31, 1905.

George H. Truax,
   Stonewall, Indian Territory.

Dear Sir:

Receipt is hereby acknowledged of your letter of March 27, 1905, enclosing the affidavits of Mary C. Truax and Porter Hall to the birth of Opal Truax, daughter of George Henry and Mary C. Truax May 20, 1903, and the same have been filed with our records as an application for the enrollment of said child.

Respectfully,

Chairman.

———

Chic. N.B - 6
   (Jessie Underwood
   Born October 22, 1903)

BIRTH AFFIDAVIT.
DEPARTMENT OF THE INTERIOR.
COMMISSION TO THE FIVE CIVILIZED TRIBES.

IN RE APPLICATION FOR ENROLLMENT, as a citizen of the   Chickasaw   Nation, of   Jessie Underwood   , born on the 22   day of   Oct , 1903

Name of Father: Wesley Underwood   a citizen of the Chickasaw Nation.
Name of Mother: Sallie Sealy Underwood   a citizen of the Chickasaw Nation.

Postoffice   Madill, Ind. Ter.

Applications for Enrollment of Chickasaw Newborn
Act of 1905   Volume I

AFFIDAVIT OF MOTHER.

UNITED STATES OF AMERICA, Indian Territory, }
Southern   DISTRICT.

I, Sallie Sealy Underwood, on oath state that I am 22 years of age and a citizen by blood, of the Chickasaw Nation; that I am the lawful wife of Wesley Underwood, who is a citizen, by blood of the Chickasaw Nation; that a male child was born to me on 22 day of October, 1903; that said child has been named Jessie Underwood, and was living March 4, 1905.

                    Sallie Underwood

Witnesses To Mark:
{ C. P. Florence
{ E. A. Morgan

Subscribed and sworn to before me this 17 day of March, 1905

                    F. E. Kennemer
                    Notary Public.

AFFIDAVIT OF ATTENDING PHYSICIAN OR MID-WIFE.

UNITED STATES OF AMERICA, Indian Territory, }
Southern   DISTRICT.

I, Nancy Underwood, a mid wife, on oath state that I attended on Mrs. Sallie Underwood, wife of Wesley Underwood on the 22 day of Oct., 1903; that there was born to her on said date a male child; that said child was living March 4, 1905, and is said to have been named Jessie Underwood

                    her
                Nancy x Underwood
Witnesses To Mark: mark
{ Thomas James
{ J.D. Moon

Subscribed and sworn to before me this 20 day of March, 1905

                    J.C. Little
                    Notary Public.

Applications for Enrollment of Chickasaw Newborn
Act of 1905   Volume I

9-39

Muskogee, Indian Territory, March 27, 1905.

Rider & Kennemer,
    Attorneys at Law,
        Madill, Indian Territory.

Gentlemen:

    Receipt is hereby acknowledged of your letter of March 21, 1905, enclosing affidavits of Sallie Underwood (Sealy) and Nancy Underwood to the birth of Jessie Underwood, son of Wesley and Sallie Underwood, October 22, 1903, and the same have been filed with our records as an application for the enrollment of said child.

Respectfully,

Chairman.

Chic. N.B - 7
    (Leo Mayfield Grayson
    Born May 28, 1904)

BIRTH AFFIDAVIT.
DEPARTMENT OF THE INTERIOR.
COMMISSION TO THE FIVE CIVILIZED TRIBES.

    IN RE APPLICATION FOR ENROLLMENT, as a citizen of the Chickasaw Nation, of Leo Mayfield Grayson, born on the 28 day of May, 1904

Name of Father: James J. Grayson   a citizen of the Chickasaw Nation.
Name of Mother: Laura Grayson   a citizen of the U. S. ~~Nation~~.

Postoffice   Pontotoc I.T.

Applications for Enrollment of Chickasaw Newborn
Act of 1905   Volume I

AFFIDAVIT OF MOTHER.

UNITED STATES OF AMERICA, Indian Territory,
Southern   DISTRICT.

I,   Laura Grayson   , on oath state that I am   25   years of age and a citizen by................., of the   United States   ~~Nation~~; that I am the lawful wife of   James J Grayson   , who is a citizen, by Blood   of the   Chickasaw   Nation; that a Male   child was born to me on   28th day of   May   , 1904; that said child has been named   Leo Mayfield Grayson   , and was living March 4, 1905.

Laura Grayson

Witnesses To Mark:
{

Subscribed and sworn to before me this   21st day of   April   , 1905

M.S. Bradford
Notary Public.

AFFIDAVIT OF ATTENDING PHYSICIAN OR MID-WIFE.

UNITED STATES OF AMERICA, Indian Territory,
Southern   DISTRICT.

I,   Lue Griffin   , a   Mid wife   , on oath state that I attended on Mrs.   Laura Grayson   , wife of   James J Grayson   on the 28" day of   May   , 1904; that there was born to her on said date a   male   child; that said child was living March 4, 1905, and is said to have been named Leo Mayfield Grayson

Lue Griffin

Witnesses To Mark:
{

Subscribed and sworn to before me this   21st day of   April   , 1905

M.S. Bradford
Notary Public.

Applications for Enrollment of Chickasaw Newborn
Act of 1905 Volume I

CERTIFICATE OF RECORD OF MARRIAGE

UNITED STATES OF AMERICA,
   INDIAN TERRITORY, } sct.
      SOUTHERN DISTRICT.

I, C. M. CAMPBELL, Clerk of the United States Court, in the Territory and District aforesaid Do HEREBY CERTIFY, that the License for and Certificate of Marriage of

MR   Jas. Grayson   and
M   Laura Griffin

were filed in my office in said Territory and District the 20" day of August A.D., 190 3 and duly recorded in Book G of Marriage Record, Page 364

WITNESS my hand and Seal of said Court, at Ardmore, this 20" day of August A.D. 190 3

      C. M. Campbell
                 CLERK.

Return this License to the United States Clerk at Ardmore, that it may be recorded, when it will be mailed to the proper address.

      Ardmoreite Steam Print.

DEPARTMENT OF THE INTERIOR,
COMMISSION TO THE FIVE CIVILIZED TRIBES.
FILED
APR 25 1905
Tams Bixby CHAIRMAN.

No person is authorized to perform the Marriage Ceremony in the Indian Territory unless the proper credentials have first been recorded in the Clerk's office.

MARRIAGE LICENSE.

№ 1069

United States of America,
  Indian Territory, } ss
    Southern District.

To Any Person Authorized by Law to Solemnize Marriage, Greeting:

Applications for Enrollment of Chickasaw Newborn
Act of 1905 Volume I

𝔜ou are hereby Commanded to solemnize the Rite and publish the Banns of Matrimony between Mr. James Grayson of Connerville in the Indian Territory, aged 22 years, and Miss Laura Griffin of Pontotoc in the Indian Territory, aged 24 years, according to law; and do you officially sign and return this license to the parties therein named.

𝔚itness my hand and official Seal, this 15" day of August A. D. 190 3

C. M. Campbell
Clerk of the United States Court.

Certificate of Marriage.

United States of America
Indian Territory, } ss
Southern District.

I, F.C. Mabery a Minister of the Gospel do hereby certify that on the 16 day of Aug A. D. 190 3 , I did duly and according to law, as commanded in the foregoing License, solemnize the Rite and publish the Banns of Matrimony between the parties therein named.

𝔚itness my hand this 16 day of August A. D. 190 3

My credentials are recorded in the office of the Clerk of the United States Court, Indian Territory, Southern District, at Ardmore, Book A , Page 125

F.C. Mabery a Minister
of the Gospel

NOTE. (a)- This License and Certificate of Marriages must be returned to the office of the Clerk of the United States Court in the Indian Territory, at Ardmore, within sixty days from the date thereof, or the party to whom the License was issued will be liable in the amount of ONE HUNDRED DOLLARS ($100).

BIRTH AFFIDAVIT.

IN RE-APPLICATION FOR ENROLLMENT, as a citizen of the Chickasaw Nation, of Leo Mayfield Grayson , born on the 28 day of May , 1904

Name of Father: James J Grayson   a citizen of the Chickasaw Nation.
Name of Mother: Laura Grayson   a citizen of the U. S. Nation.

Postoffice Pontotoc I.T.

Applications for Enrollment of Chickasaw Newborn
Act of 1905 Volume I

AFFIDAVIT OF MOTHER.

UNITED STATES OF AMERICA, INDIAN TERRITORY, }
Central District.

I, Laura Grayson, on oath state that I am 25 years of age and a citizen by ...., of the U. S. Nation; that I am the lawful wife of James J Grayson, who is a citizen, by Blood of the Chickasaw Nation; that a male child was born to me on 28 day of May, 1904, that said child has been named Leo Mayfield Grayson, and is now living.

                     Laura Grayson

Witnesses To Mark:
{ Maggie Cravatt
{ Mary Wallace

Subscribed and sworn to before me this 28 day of Feb, 1905.

                   E.J. Ball
                        Notary Public.

AFFIDAVIT OF ATTENDING PHYSICIAN OR MID-WIFE.

UNITED STATES OF AMERICA, INDIAN TERRITORY, }
Central District.

I, Lou Griffin, a Midwife, on oath state that I attended on Mrs. Laura Grayson, wife of James J Grayson on the 28 day of May, 190 4; that there was born to her on said date a male child; that said child is now living and is said to have been named Leo Mayfield Grayson

                     Lou Griffin

Witnesses To Mark:
{ Maggie Cravatt
{ Mary Wallace

Subscribed and sworn to before me this 28 day of Feb, 1905.

                   E.J. Ball
                        Notary Public.

Applications for Enrollment of Chickasaw Newborn
Act of 1905   Volume I

9-41

Muskogee, Indian Territory, March 18, 1905.

James J. Grayson,
    Pontotoc, Indian Territory.

Dear Sir:

    Receipt is hereby acknowledged of the affidavits of Laura Grayson and Lou Griffin to the birth of Leo Mayfield Grayson infant son of James J. and Laura Grayson, May 28, 1904, and the same have been filed with our records as an application for the enrollment of said child.

                  Respectfully,

                                Chairman.

9 N.B. 7

Muskogee, Indian Territory, April 12, 1905.

James J. Grayson,
    Pontotoc, Indian Territory.

Dear Sir:

    There is inclosed you herewith for execution application for the enrollment of your infant child, Leo Mayfield Grayson, born May 28, 1904.

    The affidavits heretofore filed with the Commission show the child was living on February 28, 1904. It is necessary, for the child to be enrolled, that he was living on March 4, 1905.

    The affidavits also show the child claims through you. It is, therefore, necessary that the license and the certificate of your marriage to the applicants[sic] mother, Laura Grayson, be forwarded with the return of the inclosed application.

    In having these affidavits executed care should be exercised to see that all names are written in full, as they appear in the body of the affidavit, and in the event that either of the persons signing the affidavit are unable to write, signatures by mark must be attested by two witnesses. Each affidavit must be executed before a Notary Public and the notarial seal and signature of the officer must be attached to each separate affidavit.

                  Respectfully,

LM 12-8   Commissioner in Charge.

Applications for Enrollment of Chickasaw Newborn
Act of 1905   Volume I

9 NB 7

Muskogee, Indian Territory, April 26, 1905.

James J. Grayson,
Pontotoc, Indian Territory.

Dear Sir:

Receipt is hereby acknowledged of the affidavit of Laura Grayson and Lue Griffin to the birth of Leo Mayfield Grayson, son of James J. and Laura Grayson, May 28, 1904, and the same have been filed with our records in the matter of the enrollment of said child.

Receipt is also acknowledged of the marriage license and certificate between James J. Grayson and Laura Griffin, and the same has been filed with our records in the matter of the enrollment of said child.

Respectfully,

Chairman.

9-41
9-NB-7

Muskogee, Indian Territory, February 27, 1906.

Mrs. Laura Grayson,
Pontotoc, Indian Territory.

Dear Madam:

Receipt is hereby acknowledged of your letter of February 21, 1906, in which you state that August 16, 1903, you married James J. Grayson a citizen of the Chickasaw Nation and that your citizen child is named Leo Mayfield Grayson.

In reply to your letter you are advised that your child Leo Mayfield Grayson has been enrolled as a new born citizen of the Chickasaw Nation and his enrollment as such approved by the Secretary of the Interior, June 25, 1905. You are advised, however, that under the act of Congress approved July 1, 1902, no person who married a citizen of the Choctaw or Chickasaw Nation subsequent to September 25, 1902, the date of the ratification of said act, is entitled to enrollment and allotment in the Choctaw or Chickasaw Nations[sic].

Applications for Enrollment of Chickasaw Newborn
Act of 1905   Volume I

Respectfully,

Acting Commissioner.

Chic. N.B - 8
*(Eathem Lee Durant
Born June 2, 1904)*

BIRTH AFFIDAVIT.

DEPARTMENT OF THE INTERIOR.
COMMISSION TO THE FIVE CIVILIZED TRIBES.

IN RE APPLICATION FOR ENROLLMENT, as a citizen of the Chickasaw Nation, of Eathem Lee Durant, born on the 2nd day of June, 1904

Name of Father: Jacob Durant   a citizen of the Chickasaw Nation.
Name of Mother: Maggie Durant   a citizen of the Chickasaw Nation.

Postoffice   Scipio, I.T.

AFFIDAVIT OF MOTHER.

UNITED STATES OF AMERICA, Indian Territory, }
Central   DISTRICT.

I, Maggie Durant, on oath state that I am 17 years of age and a citizen ~~by~~ ...., of the United States ~~Nation~~; that I am the lawful wife of Jacob Durant, who is a citizen, by blood of the Chickasaw Nation; that a male child was born to me on 2nd day of June, 1904; that said child has been named Eathem Lee Durant, and was living March 4, 1905.

Maggie Durant

Witnesses To Mark:
{

Subscribed and sworn to before me this 20th day of March, 1905.

Wirt Franklin
Notary Public.

Applications for Enrollment of Chickasaw Newborn
Act of 1905   Volume I

AFFIDAVIT OF ATTENDING PHYSICIAN OR MID-WIFE.

UNITED STATES OF AMERICA, Indian Territory, }
   Central   DISTRICT.

    I, Mary Durant, a————————, on oath state that I attended on Mrs. Maggie Durant, wife of Jacob Durant on the 2nd day of June, 1904; that there was born to her on said date a male child; that said child was living March 4, 1905, and is said to have been named Eathem Lee Durant

Mary Durant

Witnesses To Mark:
{

    Subscribed and sworn to before me this 20th day of March, 1905.

Wirt Franklin
Notary Public.

Tobucksy County, Aug. 9, 1903.

    Residents of the Choctaw Nation, a man named J. B. Durant came to me to be united in marriage according to law, and I have united them in marriage, the woman named Maggie Duke. These came before me and I united them according to the ordinance of God.

    I am an humble servant of God.

(Signed) A. F. Wade.

Witnesses:

  1 E. B. Wright
  2 Francis Wright.

    Jefferson D. Ward, interpreter to the Commission to the Five Civilized Tribes at the Choctaw Land Office, on oath state that the above and foregoing is a full, true and correct translation from the Choctaw into the English language of what purports to be the original marriage certificate issued by A. F. Wade to J. B. Durant and Maggie Duke, dated August 9, 1903.

Jefferson D. Ward

Subscribed and sworn to before me this April 1, 1905.

W.H. Angell
Notary Public.

Applications for Enrollment of Chickasaw Newborn
Act of 1905   Volume I

9-61

Muskogee, Indian Territory, April 6, 1905.

Jacob Durant,
    Scipio, Indian Territory.

Dear Sir:

    There is returned to you herewith what purports to be a marriage certificate between J. B. Durant and Maggie Duke, in the Choctaw language. A certified copy of said certificate has been made and filed with our records. *(Illegible...) of the enrollment of your child Eathem Lee Durant.*

                              Respectfully,

                                            Commissioner in Charge.

AB 2-6

Chic. N.B - 9
    (Andrew J. Taylor
    Born January 5, 1903)

DEPARTMENT OF THE INTERIOR,
COMMISSION TO THE FIVE CIVILIZED TRIBES.

    Record in the matter of the application for enrollment as a citizen by blood of the Chickasaw Nation of:

            ANDREW J. TAYLOR   9-NB-9.

Applications for Enrollment of Chickasaw Newborn
Act of 1905   Volume I

W.J.
9-NB-9

DEPARTMENT OF THE INTERIOR,
COMMISSION TO THE FIVE CIVILIZED TRIBES.

In the matter of the application for the enrollment of Andrew J. Taylor as a citizen by blood of the Chickasaw Nation.

---oOo---

It appears from the record herein that on March 10, 1905 there was filed with the Commission application for the enrollment of Andrew J. Taylor as a citizen by blood of the Chickasaw Nation.

It further appears from the record in this case and the records of the Commission that the applicant was born on January 5, 1903; that he is a son of Minnie Taylor, a recognized and enrolled citizen by blood of the Chickasaw Nation whose name (as Minnie Ayakatubby) appears as number 27 upon the final roll of citizens by blood of the Chickasaw Nation, approved by the Secretary of the Interior December 12, 1902, and Luther Taylor, a citizen of the United States; and that said applicant died on August 2, 1903.

The Act of Congress approved March 3, 1905 (Public No. 212) among other things provides:

"That the Commission to the Five Civilized Tribes is authorized for sixty days after the date of the approval of this act to receive and consider applications for enrollment of children born subsequent to September twenty-fifth, nineteen hundred and two, and prior to March fourth, nineteen hundred and five, and who were living on said latter date, to citizens by blood of the Choctaw and Chickasaw tribes of Indians whose enrollment has been approved by the Secretary of the Interior prior to the date of the approval of this act; and to enroll and make allotments to such children."

It is, therefore, hereby ordered that the application for the enrollment of Andrew J. Taylor as a citizen by blood of the Chickasaw Nation be dismissed in accordance with the order of the Commission of March 31, 1905.

COMMISSION TO THE FIVE CIVILIZED TRIBES.

Tams Bixby
Chairman.

Muskogee, Indian Territory,
JUN 16 1905

Applications for Enrollment of Chickasaw Newborn
Act of 1905 Volume I

DEPARTMENT OF THE INTERIOR.
COMMISSION TO THE FIVE CIVILIZED TRIBES.

In the matter of the death of Andrew J Taylor   a citizen of the   Chickasaw Nation, who formerly resided at or near   Olney   , Ind. Ter., and died on the   2   day of   August   , 1903

AFFIDAVIT OF RELATIVE.

UNITED STATES OF AMERICA, Indian Territory,}
Central   DISTRICT.

I,   Minnie Taylor   , on oath state that I am   19   years of age and a citizen by Blood   , of the   Chickasaw   Nation; that my postoffice address is   Olney   , Ind. Ter.; that I am   mother   of   Andrew J Taylor   who was a citizen, by   Blood   , of the   Chickasaw   Nation and that said   Andrew J Taylor   died on the   2   day of   August   , 1903

Minnie Taylor

Witnesses To Mark:
{ G Y Austin
{ J E Austin

Subscribed and sworn to before me this   18   day of   April   , 1905.

W.O. Austin
Notary Public.

AFFIDAVIT OF ACQUAINTANCE.

UNITED STATES OF AMERICA, Indian Territory,}
Central   DISTRICT.

I,   Culberson Seeley   , on oath state that I am   30   years of age, and a citizen by Blood   of the   Chickasaw   Nation; that my postoffice address is   Olney   , Ind. Ter.; that I was personally acquainted with   Andrew J Taylor   who was a citizen, by   Blood, of the   Chickasaw   Nation; and that said   Andrew J Taylor   died on the   2   day of   August   , 1903   his
Culberson x Seeley
Witnesses To Mark: mark
{ G Y Austin
{ M L Brown

Applications for Enrollment of Chickasaw Newborn
Act of 1905   Volume I

Subscribed and sworn to before me this   18   day of   April   , 1905.

W.O. Austin
Notary Public.

BIRTH AFFIDAVIT.

DEPARTMENT OF THE INTERIOR,
COMMISSION TO THE FIVE CIVILIZED TRIBES.

IN RE *Application for Enrollment,* as a citizen of the   Chickasaw   Nation, of   Andrew J Taylor   , born on the   5   day of   Jany   , 1903

Name of Father: Luther Taylor   a citizen of the   U.S.   Nation.
Name of Mother: Minnie Taylor   a citizen of the   Chickasaw   Nation.

Post-Office: Waldon, I.T.

AFFIDAVIT OF MOTHER.

UNITED STATES OF AMERICA, }
   INDIAN TERRITORY.
Southern   District.

   I,   Minnie Taylor   , on oath state that I am   18   years of age and a citizen by   blood   , of the   Chickasaw   Nation; that I am the lawful wife of   Luther Taylor   , who is a citizen, by .... of the U. S. ~~Nation~~; that a   male   child was born to me on   5   day of   January   , 1903 , that said child has been named   Andrew J Taylor   , and ~~is now living~~. *died Aug. 2 –1903*

Minnie Taylor

WITNESSES TO MARK:
{ W. H. Hackleman
{ C.T. Barlar

   Subscribed and sworn to before me this   30   day of   October   , 1903

My Commission Expires   H G Trosper Jr
   Nov 23 1905   NOTARY PUBLIC.

Applications for Enrollment of Chickasaw Newborn
Act of 1905   Volume I

AFFIDAVIT OF ATTENDING PHYSICIAN OR MID-WIFE.

UNITED STATES OF AMERICA,
 INDIAN TERRITORY.
 Southern   District.

I, R.C. Meloy, M.D.   , a   Physician   , on oath state that I attended on Mrs. Minnie Taylor   , wife of   Luther Taylor   on the   5   day of   January , 1903; that there was born to her on said date a   male   child; that said child is now living and is said to have been named   Andrew J Taylor

R.C. Meloy

WITNESSES TO MARK:
 W. H. Hackleman
 C.T. Barlar

Subscribed and sworn to before me this   30   day of   October   , 1903

My Commission Expires   H G Trosper Jr
    Nov 23 1905   *NOTARY PUBLIC.*

9-9

Muskogee, Indian Territory, December 17, 1904.

Luther Taylor,
   Olney, Indian Territory.

Dear Sir:

Receipt is hereby acknowledged of your letter of the 13th instant, stating that the maiden name of the mother of Andrew J. Taylor was Minnie Ayakatubby and that she was enrolled at Lebanon, Indian Territory, about five years ago and that you were married to her at Oklahoma City, April 5, 1901.

You are advised that there was recently received at this office the affidavits of Minnie Taylor and H. C. Meloy relative to the birth of Andrew J. Taylor January 5, 1903, which it is presumed has been forwarded to this office as an application for enrollment of this child as a citizen by blood of the Chickasaw Nation.

You are further advised that the act of Congress approved July 1, 1902, which was ratified by the citizens of the Choctaw and Chickasaw Nations September 25, 1902, among other things provides that no child born to a citizen or freedman of the Choctaw or Chickasaw Nation subsequent to the date of said ratification shall be entitled to enrollment in the Choctaw or Chickasaw Nation.

Applications for Enrollment of Chickasaw Newborn
Act of 1905   Volume I

Respectfully,
SIGNED

Tams Bixby
Chairman.

9 N. B. 9

Muskogee, Indian Territory, April 12, 1905.

Luther Taylor,
Waldon, Indian Territory.

Dear Sir:

It appears from the application for the enrollment of your infant child, Andrew J. Taylor, heretofore filed with the Commission, that he died August 2, 1903, It will, therefore, be necessary for you to furnish proof of his death for which there is inclosed you herewith blank to have executed and return to the Commission at the earliest practicable date.

Respectfully,
SIGNED

T. B. Needles.

D.C.   Commissioner in Charge.

9-NB-9.

Muskogee, Indian Territory, April 25, 1905.

Minnie Taylor,
Olney, Indian Territory.

Dear Madam:

Receipt is hereby acknowledged of your affidavit and the affidavit of Culberson Seeley, to the death of your son, Andrew J. Taylor, August 2, 1903, and the same have been filed with our records as evidence of the death of the above named citizen. of death of said child.

Respectfully,
SIGNED

Tams Bixby
Chairman.

Applications for Enrollment of Chickasaw Newborn
Act of 1905   Volume I

9-NB-9

Muskogee, Indian Territory, June 16, 1905.

Luther Taylor,   **COPY**
    Waldon, Indian Territory.

Dear Sir:

    Inclosed herewith you will find a copy of the order of this Commission, dated June 16, 1905, dismissing the application for the enrollment of your infant child, Andrew J. Taylor, as a citizen by blood of the Chickasaw Nation.

                              Respectfully,

                              SIGNED

                                   Tams Bixby
Registered.   Chairman.
Incl. 9-NB-9.

---

9 NB 9

Muskogee, Indian Territory, June 16, 1905.

Mansfield, McMurray & Cornish,
    Attorneys for Choctaw and Chickasaw Nations,
        South McAlester, Indian Territory.

Gentlemen:

    Inclosed herewith you will find a copy of the order of this Commission, dated June 14, 1905, dismissing the application for the enrollment of Andrew J. Taylor, as a citizen by blood of the Chickasaw Nation.

                              Respectfully,
                              SIGNED

                                  Tams Bixby
                                   Chairman.
Incl. 9-NB-9

Applications for Enrollment of Chickasaw Newborn
Act of 1905 Volume I

Chic. N.B - 10
(Carrie Hayes
Born July 19, 1904)

UNITED STATS OF AMERICA,
INDIAN TERRITORY,
SOUTHERN DISTRICT.

William R. Hayes, being duly sworn, states on oath that he is the father of Carrie Hayes and that he elects the Chickasaw Nation as the nation in which he desires to have the said child enrolled.

William R. Hayes

Subscribed and sworn to before me this 20 day of April 1905.

My Commission Expires Jan. 30, 1907.   J.C. Little
                                              Notary Public.

UNITED STATS OF AMERICA,
INDIAN TERRITORY,
SOUTHERN DISTRICT.

Agnes Hayes, being duly sworn states on oath that she is the wife of William R. Hayes and the mother of Carrie Hayes; that she is a citizen of the Chickasaw Nation and that she elects to have the said infant child, Carrie Hayes, enrolled as a member of the Chickasaw Tribe.

Agnes Hayes

Subscribed and sworn to before me this 20th day of April, 1905.

My Commission Expires Jan. 30, 1907.   J.C. Little
                                              Notary Public.

BIRTH AFFIDAVIT.   *No. 50*
DEPARTMENT OF THE INTERIOR.
COMMISSION TO THE FIVE CIVILIZED TRIBES.

IN RE APPLICATION FOR ENROLLMENT, as a citizen of the   Chickasaw   Nation, of Carrie Hayes , born on the 19th day of July , 1904

Name of Father: William R. Hayes   a citizen of the Seminole Nation.
Name of Mother: Agnes Hayes   a citizen of the Chickasaw Nation.

Postoffice   Roff, Indian Territory.

Applications for Enrollment of Chickasaw Newborn
Act of 1905   Volume I

AFFIDAVIT OF MOTHER.

UNITED STATES OF AMERICA, Indian Territory, }
   Southern   DISTRICT.

I,   Agnes Hayes   , on oath state that I am   Twenty-five   years of age and a citizen by   blood   , of the   Chickasaw   Nation; that I am the lawful wife of William R. Hayes   , who is a citizen, by   blood   of the   Seminole   Nation; that a   Female   child was born to me on   the 19th day of   July 1904   , 1......, that said child has been named   Carrie Hayes   , and is now living.

                              Agnes Hayes
Witnesses To Mark:
{

   Subscribed and sworn to before me this   10   day of   December   , 1904

                              Jno P. Crawford
                                 Notary Public.

AFFIDAVIT OF ATTENDING PHYSICIAN OR MID-WIFE.

UNITED STATES OF AMERICA, Indian Territory, }
   Southern   DISTRICT.

                     of age
   I,   Leah Leader, about   years   , a   Midwife   , on oath state that I attended on Mrs.   Agnes Hayes   , wife of   William R Hayes   on the   19th day of   July , 1904; that there was born to her on said date a   Female   child; that said child is now living and is said to have been named Carrie Hayes
                                 her
                           Leah x Leader
Witnesses To Mark: mark
  { Jno. P. Crawford
    (Name Illegible)

   Subscribed and sworn to before me this   10   day of   December   , 1904

                              Jno P. Crawford
                                 Notary Public.

Applications for Enrollment of Chickasaw Newborn
Act of 1905 Volume I

BIRTH AFFIDAVIT.

DEPARTMENT OF THE INTERIOR.
COMMISSION TO THE FIVE CIVILIZED TRIBES.

IN RE APPLICATION FOR ENROLLMENT, as a citizen of the Chickasaw Nation, of Carrie Hayes, born on the 19th day of July 1904, 1........

Card 209 Roll 724

Name of Father: William R Hayes   a citizen of the Seminole Nation.
Name of Mother: Agnes Hayes   a citizen of the Chickasaw Nation.

Postoffice   Roff, Indian Territory

AFFIDAVIT OF MOTHER.

UNITED STATES OF AMERICA, Indian Territory, }
Southern Judicial   DISTRICT. }

I, Agnes Hayes, on oath state that I am 26 years of age and a citizen by blood, of the Chickasaw Nation; that I am the lawful wife of William R Hayes, who is a citizen, by blood of the Seminole Nation; that a Female child was born to me on 19th day of July, 1904, 1........; that said child has been named Carrie Hayes, and was living March 4, 1905.

                                           Agnes Hayes

Witnesses To Mark:
{

Subscribed and sworn to before me this 28 day of March, 1905

                                            J. C. Little
                                            Notary Public.

AFFIDAVIT OF ATTENDING PHYSICIAN OR MID-WIFE.

UNITED STATES OF AMERICA, Indian Territory, }
Southern Judicial   DISTRICT. }

I, Leah Leader, a Mid-wife, on oath state that I attended on Mrs. Agnes Hayes, wife of William R. Hayes on the 19th day of July 1904; , 1........; that there was born to her on said date a Female child; that said child was living March 4, 1905, and is said to have been named Carrie Hayes

                                                  her
                                            Leah x Leader
                                                mark

Applications for Enrollment of Chickasaw Newborn
Act of 1905   Volume I

Witnesses To Mark:
   { Tom D McKeown
   { Melton Leader

   Subscribed and sworn to before me this 28th day of March   , 1905

Tom D. McKeown
Notary Public.

9-74

Muskogee, Indian Territory, March 20, 1905.

Agnes Hayes,
   Roff, Indian Territory.

Dear Madam:

   Receipt is hereby acknowledged of your letter of March 14, 1905, in which you state that you made application for the enrollment of your daughter Carrie Hayes born July 19, 1904, and handed the same to Honorable T. C. Walker to file with this Commission; you ask if that application has been filed with this office if it will be necessary for you to forward new affidavits.

   In reply to your letter you are informed that there is inclosed herewith a blank application for the enrollment of an infant child and you are advised that you should have the same executed and returned to this office within sixty days from March 3, 1905, the date of the approval of the act authorizing he Commission to receive applications for the enrollment of infant children.

Respectfully,

B. C.   Chairman.

Chickasaw 74.

Muskogee, Indian Territory, April 5, 1905.

William R. Hayes,
   Roff, Indian Territory.

Dear Sir:

   Receipt is hereby acknowledged of the affidavits of Agnes Hayes and Leah Leader to the birth of Carrie Hayes, daughter of William R. and Agnes Hayes, July 19,

Applications for Enrollment of Chickasaw Newborn
Act of 1905   Volume I

1904, and the same have been filed with our records as an application for the enrollment of said child.

Respectfully,

Commissioner in Charge.

9 N.B. 10

Muskogee, Indian Territory, April 12, 1905.

William R. Hayes,
Roff, Indian Territory.

Dear Sir:

Referring to the application for the enrollment of your infant child, Carrie Hayes, it appears that you are a citizen by blood of the Seminole Nation, while your wife is a citizen by blood of the Chickasaw Nation.

Your attention is called to the provision of the Act of Congress approved June 28, 1898, as follows:

"The several Tribes may, by agreement, determine the right of persons who for any reason may claim citizenship in two or more tribes, and to allotment of lands and distribution of moneys belonging to each tribe; but if no such agreement be made, then such claimant shall be entitled to such rights in one tribe only, and may elect in which tribe he will take such right; but if he fail or refuse to make such selection in due time, he shall be enrolled in the tribe with whom he has resided, and there be given such allotment and distributions, and not elsewhere."

It will therefore be necessary for you and your wife to appear before a Notary Public or other officer authorized to administer oaths, and by affidavit elect in which nation you desire to have said child enrolled, forwarding same, when properly executed, to the Commission.

Respectfully,

Commissioner in Charge.

Applications for Enrollment of Chickasaw Newborn
Act of 1905 Volume I

9-N.B. 10.

Muskogee, Indian Territory, April 26, 1905.

William R. Hayes,
  Roff, Indian Territory.

Dear Sir:

  Receipt is hereby acknowledged of the affidavit of Agnes Hayes electing to have your child Carrie Hayes enrolled as a citizen of the Chickasaw Nation, and the same has been filed with our records in the matter of the enrollment of said child.

Respectfully,

Chairman.

Chic. N.B - 11
  (Billy Arpealer
  Born July 17, 1903)

BIRTH AFFIDAVIT.

DEPARTMENT OF THE INTERIOR.
COMMISSION TO THE FIVE CIVILIZED TRIBES.

  IN RE APPLICATION FOR ENROLLMENT, as a citizen of the   Chickasaw   Nation, of   Billy Arpealer   , born on the 17th   day of July   , 1903

Name of Father: William Arpealer   a citizen of the Chickasaw   Nation.
Name of Mother: Rena Pusley   a citizen of the Chickasaw   Nation.

Postoffice   Arpelar, I.T.

AFFIDAVIT OF MOTHER.

UNITED STATES OF AMERICA, Indian Territory, ⎫
  Central   DISTRICT.   ⎭

  I,   Rena Pusley   , on oath state that I am   about 35   years of age and a citizen by   blood   , of the   Chickasaw   Nation; that I am *not* the lawful wife of

43

Applications for Enrollment of Chickasaw Newborn
Act of 1905   Volume I

William Arpealer, who is a citizen, by blood of the Chickasaw Nation; that a male child was born to me on the 17th day of July, 1903; that said child has been named Billy Arpealer, and was living March 4, 1905.

                                      her
                              Rena x Pusley

Witnesses To Mark: mark
{ Columbus Campelube
{ W. H. Stanton

Subscribed and sworn to before me this 16th day of March, 1905

                                        Wirt Franklin
                                        Notary Public.

AFFIDAVIT OF ATTENDING PHYSICIAN OR MID-WIFE.

UNITED STATES OF AMERICA, Indian Territory, }
   Central   DISTRICT. }

I, William Arpealer, a———, on oath state that I attended on Mrs. Rena Pusley with whom, ~~wife of~~ I am living on the 17th day of July, 1903; that there was born to her on said date a male child; that said child was living March 4, 1905, and ~~is said to have~~ *has* been named Billy Arpealer and that I am the father of said child

                                    his
                            William x Arpealer

Witnesses To Mark: mark
{ Columbus Campelube
{ W. H. Stanton

Subscribed and sworn to before me this 16th day of March, 1905

                                      Wirt Franklin
                                      Notary Public.

BIRTH AFFIDAVIT.

DEPARTMENT OF THE INTERIOR.
COMMISSION TO THE FIVE CIVILIZED TRIBES.

    IN RE APPLICATION FOR ENROLLMENT, as a citizen of the Chickasaw Nation, of Billy Arpealer, born on the 17th day of July, 1903

Name of Father: William Arpealer (Chick.blood.254) a citizen of the Chickasaw Nation.
Name of Mother: Rena Pusley   a citizen of the Chickasaw Nation.

Applications for Enrollment of Chickasaw Newborn
Act of 1905   Volume I

Postoffice   Arpelar, I.T.

AFFIDAVIT OF MOTHER.

UNITED STATES OF AMERICA, Indian Territory, }
Central   DISTRICT.   }

I,   Rena Pusley   , on oath state that I am 35   years of age and a citizen by blood   , of the   Chickasaw   Nation; that I am the lawful wife of   William Arpealer   , who is a citizen, by blood   of the   Chickasaw   Nation; that a male   child was born to me on   the 17th day of   July   , 1903; that said child has been named   Billy Arpealer   , and was living March 4, 1905.

                                Her
                            Rena (x) Pusley

Witnesses To Mark: mark
  { Joe B Williams
    Henry L Baker

Subscribed and sworn to before me this 17th   day of   April   , 1905

                            Henry L Baker
                            Notary Public.

AFFIDAVIT OF ATTENDING PHYSICIAN OR MID-WIFE.

UNITED STATES OF AMERICA, Indian Territory, }
Central   DISTRICT.   }

I,   Nellie Nelson   , a   Midwife   , on oath state that I attended on Mrs.   Rena Pusley   , wife of   William Arpealer   on the 17th day of July   , 1903; that there was born to her on said date a   male   child; that said child was living March 4, 1905, and is said to have been named Billy Arpealer

                              Her
                         Nellie (x) Nelson

Witnesses To Mark: mark
  { Joe B Williams
    Henry L Baker

Subscribed and sworn to before me this 17th day of   April   , 1905

                            Henry L Baker
                            Notary Public.

Applications for Enrollment of Chickasaw Newborn
Act of 1905 Volume I

9-87

Muskogee, Indian Territory, March 21, 1905.

Rena Pusley,
    Arpealer[sic], Indian Territory.

Dear Madam:

    Receipt is hereby acknowledged of the affidavits of Rena Pusley and William Arpealer to the birth of Billy Arpealer[sic], Indian Territory son of William Arpealer and Rena Pusley, July 17, 1903, and the same have been filed with our records as an application for the enrollment of said child.

                  Respectfully,

                            Chairman.

---

9 N.B. 11

Muskogee, Indian Territory, April 12, 1905.

William Arpealer,
    Arpelar, Indian Territory.

Dear Sir:

    Referring to the application heretofore forwarded to the Commission for the enrollment of Billy Arpealer it is noted that you filled out the affidavit of the attending physician or midwife. If there was no one in attendance at the birth of said child, it will be necessary for you to secure the affidavits of two persons who have actual knowledge of the fact, that the child was born, the date of his birth, that he was living on March 4, 1905, and that Rena Pusley is his mother.

    Please give this matter your immediate attention.

                  Respectfully,

                            Commissioner in Charge.

Applications for Enrollment of Chickasaw Newborn
Act of 1905   Volume I

Chic. N.B - 12
(Elmer E. Jones
Born October 1, 1902)

BIRTH AFFIDAVIT.

Department of the Interior,
COMMISSION TO THE FIVE CIVILIZED TRIBES.

IN RE APPLICATION FOR ENROLLMENT, as a citizen of the   Chickasaw   Nation, of   Elmer E. Jones   , born on the   1st   day of   October   , 1902
United States

Name of Father: Bill Jones   a citizen of the   Chickasaw Nation.
Name of Mother: Susan Jones   a citizen of the   Chickasaw Nation.

Post-Office: Owl, I.T.

AFFIDAVIT OF MOTHER.

UNITED STATES OF AMERICA, }
INDIAN TERRITORY,
Central   District.

I,   Susan Jones   , on oath state that I am   35   years of age and a citizen by   blood , of the   Chickasaw   Nation; that I am the lawful wife of   Bill Jones   , who is a citizen, by ~~blood~~   of the   United States   ~~Nation~~; that a male   child was born to me on   1st   day of   October   , 1902, that said child has been named   Elmer E. Jones   , and is now living.

her
Susan x Jones
WITNESSES TO MARK: mark
{ J.A. Hains
  R.M. Wilson

Subscribed and sworn to before me this   19"   *day of*   November   , *1902*

D.H. Linebaugh
Notary Public.

47

Applications for Enrollment of Chickasaw Newborn
Act of 1905   Volume I

AFFIDAVIT OF ATTENDING PHYSICIAN OR MID-WIFE.

UNITED STATES OF AMERICA,
  INDIAN TERRITORY,
  Central   District.

I,   Sarah J. Darken   , ~~attended~~   , on oath state that I attended on Mrs.   Susan Jones , wife of   Bill Jones   on the   1st day of   October   , 190 2; that there was born to her on said date a   male   child; that said child is now living and is said to have been named   Elmer E. Jones

SJ Darken

WITNESSES TO MARK:

Subscribed and sworn to before me this   19"   day of   November   , 1902

D.H. Linebaugh
Notary Public.

BIRTH AFFIDAVIT.

DEPARTMENT OF THE INTERIOR.
COMMISSION TO THE FIVE CIVILIZED TRIBES.

IN RE APPLICATION FOR ENROLLMENT, as a citizen of the   Chickasaw   Nation, of   Elmer E. Jones   , born on the   1st   day of   Oct   , 1902

Name of Father: Bill Jones   a citizen of the   U. S.   Nation.
Name of Mother: Susan Jones   a citizen of the   Chickasaw   Nation.

Postoffice   Owl, Ind. Ter.

AFFIDAVIT OF MOTHER.

UNITED STATES OF AMERICA, Indian Territory,
.... DISTRICT.

I,   Susan Jones   , on oath state that I am   35   years of age and a citizen by blood   , of the   Chickasaw   Nation; that I am the lawful wife of   Bill Jones   , who is a citizen, ~~by~~ .... of the   United States   Nation; that a   male   child was born to me on   1st   day of   October   , 1902; that said child has been named   Elmer E. Jones   , and was living March 4, 1905.

Died July 16 1903

Applications for Enrollment of Chickasaw Newborn
Act of 1905   Volume I

Witnesses To Mark:
{

Subscribed and sworn to before me this .... day of ...., 190....

....
Notary Public.

AFFIDAVIT OF ATTENDING PHYSICIAN OR MID-WIFE.

UNITED STATES OF AMERICA, Indian Territory, }
....DISTRICT. }

I, ..., a ...., on oath state that I attended on Mrs. Susan Jones, wife of ~~This child Died~~ 1st day of October, 1902; that there was born to her on said date, a *July 16, 1903* male child; that said child was living March 4, 1905, and is said to have ~~been named~~ Elmer E Jones

Died July 16 = 1903   *(illegible...)*

Bill Jones

Witnesses To Mark:
{

Subscribed and sworn to before me this .... day of ...., 190....

....
Notary Public.

It appearing from the within affidavits that Elmer E. Jones, born October 1, 1902, for whose enrollment as a citizen by blood of the Chickasaw Nation blood of the Chickasaw Nation, application was made under the Act of Congress approved March 3, 1905, (33 Stats., 1048), 1071), died July 16, 1903, it is hereby ordered that the application for the enrollment of said Elmer E. Jones as a citizen by blood of the Chickasaw Nation be dismissed.

        Tams Bixby
         Commissioner.
      Muskogee, Indian Territory.
        AUG 23 1905

Applications for Enrollment of Chickasaw Newborn
Act of 1905   Volume I

Department of the Interior,
COMMISSION TO THE FIVE CIVILIZED TRIBES.

In the matter of the death of   Elmer E Jones   a citizen of the Chickasaw Nation, who formerly resided at or near   Owl   , Ind. Ter., and died on the 16 day of July , 1903

AFFIDAVIT OF RELATIVE.

UNITED STATES OF AMERICA,
   INDIAN TERRITORY,
Central District.

I, TW Jones , on oath state that I am 21 years of age and a citizen by Entermarriage[sic] , of the Chocktaw[sic] Nation; that my postoffice address is Owl, Ind. Ter.; that I am Uncle of Elmer E Jones who was a citizen, by Blood , of the Chocktaw Nation and that said Elmer E Jones died on the 16 day of July , 190 3

TW Jones

Witnesses To Mark:
  { Luis Jones
    WE Jones

Subscribed and sworn to before me this 24 day of July , 1905.

D A Spears
Notary Public.

AFFIDAVIT OF ACQUAINTANCE.

UNITED STATES OF AMERICA,
   INDIAN TERRITORY,
Central District.

I, May Acker , on oath state that I am 21 years of age, and a citizen by Entermarriage of the Chocktaw Nation; that my postoffice address is Owl , Ind. Ter.; that I was personally acquainted with Elmer E Jones who was a citizen, by Blood , of the Chickasaw Nation; and that said Elmer E Jones died on the 16 day of July , 1903

May Acker

Witnesses To Mark:
  { Luis Jones
    WE Jones

Applications for Enrollment of Chickasaw Newborn
Act of 1905   Volume I

Subscribed and sworn to before me this   24   *day of*   July   , 1905.

>D A Spears
>*Notary Public.*

>?-??,

>Muskogee, Indian Territory, November 24, 1902.

Bill Jones,
    Owl, Indian Territory.

Dear Sir:

    Receipt is hereby acknowledged of the application for enrollment as a citizen of the Chickasaw Nation of Elmer E. Jones, infant son of Bill and Susan Jones, born October 1, 1902.

    You are advised that the Commission is without authority to consider the application for enrollment of this child as a citizen of the Chickasaw Nation, it appearing that said child was born October 1, 1902, subsequent to the ratification by the citizens of the Choctaw and Chickasaw Nations on September 25, 1902, of an act of Congress approved July 1, 1902 (32 Stats., 641).

    Section twenty-eight thereof provides as follows:

    "The names of all persons living on the date of the final ratification of this agreement entitled to be enrolled as provided in section 27 hereof shall be placed upon the rolls made by said Commission; and no child born thereafter to a citizen or freedman and no person intermarried thereafter to a citizen shall be entitled to enrollment or to participate in the distribution of the tribal property of the Choctaws and Chickasaws."

>Respectfully,

>Acting Chairman.

Applications for Enrollment of Chickasaw Newborn
Act of 1905   Volume I

9 N. B. 12

Muskogee, Indian Territory, April 12, 1905.

Bill Jones,
    Owl, Indian Territory.

Dear Sir:

    There is inclosed you herewith for execution application for the enrollment of your infant child, Elmer E. Jones, born October 1, 1902.

    The affidavits heretofore filed with the Commission show the child was living on November 19, 1902. It is necessary, for the child to be enrolled, that he was living on March 4, 1905. Please insert mother's age in space provided for the purpose.

    In having these affidavits executed care should be exercised to see that all names are written in full, as they appear in the body of the affidavit, and in the event that either of the persons signing the affidavit are unable to write, signatures by mark must be attested by two witnesses. Each affidavit must be executed before a Notary Public and the notarial seal and signature of the officer must be attached to each separate affidavit.

    Respectfully,

LM 12-15.

Commissioner in Charge.

---

9 N. B. 12

Muskogee, Indian Territory, May 9, 1905.

Bill Jones,
    Owl, Indian Territory.

Dear Sir:

    There is enclosed you herewith for execution application for the enrollment of your infant child, Elmer E. Jones, born October 1, 1902.

    The affidavits heretofore filed with the Commission show the child was living on November 19, 1902. It is necessary, for the child to be enrolled, that he was living on March 4, 1905. You will please insert the age of the mother in the place left blank for that purpose.

    In having these affidavits executed care should be exercised to see that all names are written in full, as they appear in the body of the affidavit, and in the event that either of the persons signing the affidavit are unable to write, signatures by mark must be

Applications for Enrollment of Chickasaw Newborn
Act of 1905 Volume I

attested by two witnesses. Each affidavit must be executed before a Notary Public and the notarial seal and signature of the officer must be attached to each separate affidavit.

Respectfully,

V 9/1.

Commissioner in Charge.

Muskogee, Indian Territory, July 3, 1905.

Bill Jones,
    Owl, Indian Territory.

Dear Sir:

    There is enclosed herewith for execution application the enrollment of your infant child, Elmer E. Jones, born October 1, 1902. In the affidavits heretofore filed in this office it appears that the child was living on November 19, 1902. It is necessary for him to be enrolled that he was living on March 4, 1905.

    In having these affidavits executed care should be exercised to see that all names are written in full as they appear in the body of the affidavit, and if either of the persons signing the affidavits is unable to write, signature by mark must be attested by two witnesses. Each affidavit must be executed before a Notary Public and the notarial seal and signature of the officer must be attached to each separate affidavit.

Respectfully,

DeB--1/3

Commissioner.

9-NB-12

Muskogee, Indian Territory, July 12, 1905.

Bill Jones,
    Owl, Indian Territory.

Dear Sir:

    Receipt is hereby acknowledged of your letter without date stating that your child Elmer E. Jones died July 16, 1903, and for the purpose of making his death a matter of record there is inclosed herewith blank form for proof of death which please have executed and returned to this office as early as practicable.

Applications for Enrollment of Chickasaw Newborn
Act of 1905   Volume I

Respectfully,

Commissioner.

9-NB-12

Muskogee, Indian Territory, July 21, 1905.

T. W. Jones,
    Owl, Indian Territory.

Dear Sir:

    Receipt is hereby acknowledged of the partially executed proof of death of your child, Elmer E. Jones, and the same is returned you herewith for the reason that the affidavit of May Underwood has not been signed by her, and that neither of the affidavits appear to have been acknowledged before a Notary Public, as the signature and seal of such officer have not been attached.

    Kindly have May Underwood sign the affidavit prepared for her and have both affidavits executed before a Notary Public, have him sign the same and affix his jurat and seal to each affidavit.

Respectfully,

LM 5-20.

Commissioner.

9-NB-12

COPY

Muskogee, Indian Territory, August 23, 1905.

Bill Jones,
    Owl, Indian Territory.

Dear Sir:

    You are hereby advised that it appearing from the records of this office that your child Elmer E. Jones, dies prior to March 4, 1905, the Commissioner to the Five Civilized Tribes on August 23, 1905, dismissed the application for the enrollment of said child as a citizen by blood of the Chickasaw Nation.

Respectfully,
SIGNED

Tams Bixby
Commissioner.

Applications for Enrollment of Chickasaw Newborn
Act of 1905 Volume I

7-NB-12

Muskogee, Indian Territory, July 28, 1905.

T. W. Jones,
    Owl, Indian Territory.

Dear Sir:

    Receipt is hereby acknowledged of the affidavits of T. W. Jones and May Acker to the death of Elmer E. Jones a citizen of the Chickasaw Nation which occurred July 16, 1903, and the same have been filed as evidence of the death of the above named citizen.

        Respectfully,

            Commissioner.

9-NB-12

COPY

Muskogee, Indian Territory, August 23, 1905.

Mansfield, McMurray & Cornish,
    Attorneys for Choctaw and Chickasaw Nations,
        South McAlester, Indian Territory.

Gentlemen:

    You are hereby advised that it appearing from the records of this office that Elmer E. Jones died prior to March 4, 1905, the Commissioner to the Five Civilized Tribes on August 23, 1905, dismissing the application for the enrollment of said child as a citizen by blood of the Chickasaw Nation.

        Respectfully,
        SIGNED

            Tams Bixby
            Commissioner.

Applications for Enrollment of Chickasaw Newborn
Act of 1905 Volume I

Chic. N.B - 13
    (Charles Claud Stewart
    Born July 6, 1904)

BIRTH AFFIDAVIT.

DEPARTMENT OF THE INTERIOR.
COMMISSION TO THE FIVE CIVILIZED TRIBES.

    IN RE APPLICATION FOR ENROLLMENT, as a citizen of the   Chickasaw   Nation, of   Charles Claud Stewart   , born on the   6"   day of   July   , 1904

Name of Father: Revie Stewart   a citizen of the   U. S.   ~~Nation~~.
Name of Mother: Minnie Stewart   a citizen of the   Chickasaw   Nation.

                 Postoffice   Davis, Ind. Ter.

AFFIDAVIT OF MOTHER.

UNITED STATES OF AMERICA, Indian Territory, }
       Southern   DISTRICT.

    I,   Minnie Stewart   , on oath state that I am 26   years of age and a citizen by Blood   , of the   Chickasaw   Nation; that I am the lawful wife of   Revie Stewart, who is a citizen, by .... of the   U. S.   Nation; that a   male child was born to me on   6"   day of   July   , 1904, that said child has been named Charles Claud Stewart   , and is now living.

                             Minnie Stewart
Witnesses To Mark:
{

    Subscribed and sworn to before me this   3rd day of   September   , 1904

                          H. W. Fielding
                              Notary Public.

AFFIDAVIT OF ATTENDING PHYSICIAN OR MID-WIFE.

UNITED STATES OF AMERICA, Indian Territory, }
       Southern   DISTRICT.

    I,   A. P. Brown   , a   Physician   , on oath state that I attended on Mrs. Minnie Stewart   , wife of   Revie Stewart   on the   6"   day of   July   , 1904;

Applications for Enrollment of Chickasaw Newborn
Act of 1905 Volume I

that there was born to her on said date a   male   child; that said child is now living and is said to have been named Charles Claud Stewart

A.P. Brown M.D.

Witnesses To Mark:
{

Subscribed and sworn to before me this 3rd day of September , 1904

H. W. Fielding
Notary Public.

BIRTH AFFIDAVIT.

DEPARTMENT OF THE INTERIOR.
COMMISSION TO THE FIVE CIVILIZED TRIBES.

IN RE APPLICATION FOR ENROLLMENT, as a citizen of the   Chickasaw   Nation, of   Charlie Claud Stewart   , born on the 6th day of July , 1904

Name of Father: Revie Stewart   a citizen of the .... Nation.
Name of Mother: Minnie Stewart   a citizen of the Chickasaw Nation.

Postoffice   Davis, Ind. Ty.

AFFIDAVIT OF MOTHER.

UNITED STATES OF AMERICA, Indian Territory, }
    Southern   DISTRICT.

I,   Minnie Stewart   , on oath state that I am   26   years of age and a citizen by   blood   , of the   Chickasaw   Nation; that I am the lawful wife of   Revie Stewart   , who is a citizen, by .... of the .... Nation; that a male   child was born to me on 6th day of July   , 1904; that said child has been named   Charlie Claud Stewart   , and was living March 4, 1905.

Minnie Stewart

Witnesses To Mark:
{

Subscribed and sworn to before me this 18th day of March   , 1905

W.F. Parker
Notary Public.

Applications for Enrollment of Chickasaw Newborn
Act of 1905   Volume I

AFFIDAVIT OF ATTENDING PHYSICIAN OR MID-WIFE.

UNITED STATES OF AMERICA, Indian Territory, }
   Southern   DISTRICT. }

      I, A.P. Brown , a Physician , on oath state that I attended on Mrs. Minnie Stewart , wife of Revie Stewart on the 6" day of July , 1904; that there was born to her on said date a male child; that said child was living March 4, 1905, and is said to have been named Charlie Claud Stewart

                                                A.P. Brown M.D.
Witnesses To Mark:
{

      Subscribed and sworn to before me this 18 day of Mch , 1905

                                      W.F. Parker
                                                Notary Public.

(The letter below typed as given.)

                                    (C O P Y)

                                  Davis, Ind. Ter., Sept., 30th., 1904.

Commission to the Five Civilized Tribes,
            Muskogee, I.T.,

Gentlemen:

      Replying to your favor of the 16th., inst., concerning the application for enrollment of Charles Claud Stewart born July 6th., 1904, I beg to advise that the maiden name of applicant's mother was Minnie Thomas. The names of her parents were William Thomas and Zila Wilnati (as near as I can make it).

      This I beleive, covers the grounds inquired about in your laetter.

                                    Yours Respectfully,

                                            (signed) H. W. Fielding.

Applications for Enrollment of Chickasaw Newborn
Act of 1905   Volume I

Muskogee, Indian Territory, March 28, 1905.

Revie Stewart,
    Davis, Indian Territory.

Dear Sir:

    There have been received at this office affidavits of Minnie Stewart and A. P. Brown to the birth of Charlie Claud Stewart, son of Revie and Minnie Stewart, July 6, 1904. It is stated in the affidavit of the mother that she is a citizen by blood of the Chickasaw Nation. If this is correct you are requested to state when, where and under what name she made application for enrollment, the names of her parents and such other information as will enable us to identify her upon our records. The matter of the affidavits above referred to will then receive consideration.

                      Respectfully,

                               Chairman.

9-879

Muskogee, Indian Territory, April 6, 1905.

Revie Stewart,
    Davis, Indian Territory.

Dear Sir:

    Receipt is hereby acknowledged of your letter of April 1, 1905, giving information relative to Minnie Stewart and the information contained therein has enabled the Commission to identify her upon our records as an enrolled citizen by blood of the Chickasaw Nation. Her affidavit and the affidavit of A. T[sic]. Brown to the birth of Charley Claud Stewart, son of Revie and Minnie Stewart July 6, 1904, have therefore been filed with our records as an application for the enrollment of said child.

                      Respectfully,

                               Commissioner in Charge.

Applications for Enrollment of Chickasaw Newborn
Act of 1905 Volume I

Chic. N.B - 14
    (Burruss Andrew Horton
    Born January 11, 1905)

BIRTH AFFIDAVIT.

    IN RE-APPLICATION FOR ENROLLMENT, as a citizen of the   Chickasaw   Nation, of   Burruss Andrew Horton , born on the   11   day of   Jan , 1905

Name of Father: Herbert Horton   a citizen of the   U. S.   ~~Nation~~.
Name of Mother: Mintie Horton   a citizen of the   Chickasaw   Nation.

              Postoffice   Center, I. N.

AFFIDAVIT OF MOTHER.

UNITED STATES OF AMERICA, INDIAN TERRITORY, ⎱
     Southern   District. ⎰

     I,   Mintie Horton , on oath state that I am   25   years of age and a citizen by blood , of the   Chickasaw   Nation; that I am the lawful wife of   Herbert Horton , who is a citizen, ~~by~~ .... of the   U S   Nation; that a   male   child was born to me on   11   day of   Jan   , 1905, that said child has been named   Burruss Andrew Horton , and is now living.

                                            Mintie Horton
Witnesses To Mark:

     Subscribed and sworn to before me this   8   day of   Feb , 1905.

                                        J J Copeland
                                              Notary Public.

AFFIDAVIT OF ATTENDING PHYSICIAN OR MID-WIFE.

UNITED STATES OF AMERICA, INDIAN TERRITORY, ⎱
     Southern   District. ⎰

     I,   J R Craig , a   Physician , on oath state that I attended on Mrs.   Herbert Horton , wife of   Herbert Horton   on the   11   day of   Jan , 190 5; that there was born to her on said date a   male   child; that said child is now living and is said to have been named   Burruss Andrew Horton

                                        J R Craig M.D.
Witnesses To Mark:

Applications for Enrollment of Chickasaw Newborn
Act of 1905 Volume I

Subscribed and sworn to before me this   8   day of   Feb   , 1905.

J J Copeland
Notary Public.

BIRTH AFFIDAVIT.

DEPARTMENT OF THE INTERIOR.
COMMISSION TO THE FIVE CIVILIZED TRIBES.

IN RE APPLICATION FOR ENROLLMENT, as a citizen of the   Chickasaw   Nation, of   Burruss Andrew Horton   , born on the   11th day of   January   , 1905

Name of Father: Herbert Horton   a citizen of the   U S   Nation.
Name of Mother: Mintie Horton (Lewis)   a citizen of the Chickasaw   Nation.

Postoffice   Center I.T.

AFFIDAVIT OF MOTHER.

UNITED STATES OF AMERICA, Indian Territory, }
   Southern   DISTRICT.

I,   Mintie Horton (Lewis)   , on oath state that I am   25   years of age and a citizen by   blood   , of the   Chickasaw   Nation; that I am the lawful wife of Herbert Horton   , who is a citizen, ~~by~~ .... of the   United States   ~~Nation~~; that a   male   child was born to me on   11th day of   January   , 1905; that said child has been named   Burruss Andrew Horton   , and was living March 4, 1905.

Mintie Horton (Lewis)

Witnesses To Mark:
{

Subscribed and sworn to before me this   17   day of   Apr   , 1905.

J J Copeland
Notary Public.

Applications for Enrollment of Chickasaw Newborn
Act of 1905   Volume I

AFFIDAVIT OF ATTENDING PHYSICIAN OR MID-WIFE.

UNITED STATES OF AMERICA, Indian Territory,
Southern DISTRICT.

I, J R Craig , a Physician , on oath state that I attended on Mrs. Mintie Horton (Lewis) , wife of Herbert Horton on the 11th day of January , 1905; that there was born to her on said date a male child; that said child was living March 4, 1905, and is said to have been named Burruss Andrew Horton

J. R. Craig M.D.

Witnesses To Mark:

Subscribed and sworn to before me this 17 day of Apr , 1905

J J Copeland
Notary Public.

Muskogee, Indian Territory, March 27, 1905.

Mintie Horton,
Center, Indian Territory.

Madam:

Receipt is hereby acknowledged of your affidavit and the affidavit of J. R. Craig to the birth of Burruss Andrew Horton, January 11, 1905.

It is stated in the affidavit that you are a citizen by blood of the Chickasaw Nation, but the Commission is unable to identify you as such upon its records.

You are requested, therefore, to state under what name you were listed for enrollment, the name of your parents and the other members of your family who have been enrolled, and the name under which you received an allotment of lands in the Chickasaw Nation.

Respectfully,

Chairman.

Applications for Enrollment of Chickasaw Newborn
Act of 1905 Volume I

9 N.B. 14.

Muskogee, Indian Territory, April 12, 1905.

Herbert Horton,
    Center, Indian Territory.

Dear Sir:

There is inclosed you herewith for execution application for the enrollment of your infant child, Burruss Andrew Horton, born January 11, 1905.

The affidavits heretofore filed with the Commission show the child was living on February 8, 1905. It is necessary, for the child to be enrolled, that he was living on March 4, 1905.

In having these affidavits executed care should be exercised to see that all names are written in full, as they appear in the body of the affidavit, and in the event that either of the persons signing the affidavit are unable to write, signatures by mark must be attested by two witnesses. Each affidavit must be executed before a Notary Public and the notarial seal and signature of the officer must be attached to each separate affidavit.

Respectfully,

LM 12-12

Commissioner in Charge.

Chic. N.B - 15
    (Mary Mickie Ashton
    Born September 17, 1904)

BIRTH AFFIDAVIT.

DEPARTMENT OF THE INTERIOR.
COMMISSION TO THE FIVE CIVILIZED TRIBES.

IN RE APPLICATION FOR ENROLLMENT, as a citizen of the Chickasaw Nation, of Mary Mickie Ashton , born on the 17th day of September , 1904

Name of Father: Bird I. Ashton   a citizen of the Chickasaw Nation.
Name of Mother: Julia V. Ashton   a citizen of the Chickasaw Nation.

Applications for Enrollment of Chickasaw Newborn
Act of 1905   Volume I

Postoffice   Davis, Ind. Ter.

AFFIDAVIT OF MOTHER.

UNITED STATES OF AMERICA, Indian Territory,
Southern   DISTRICT.

I, Julia V. Ashton, on oath state that I am 26 years of age and a citizen by blood, of the Chickasaw Nation; that I am the lawful wife of Bird I. Ashton, who is a citizen, by marriage of the Chickasaw Nation; that a female child was born to me on 17th day of September, 1904, that said child has been named Mary Mickie Ashton, and is now living.

Julia V. Ashton

Witnesses To Mark:
{

Subscribed and sworn to before me this 16th day of January, 1905.

Eugene E. White
Notary Public.

AFFIDAVIT OF ATTENDING PHYSICIAN OR MID-WIFE.

UNITED STATES OF AMERICA, Indian Territory,
Southern   DISTRICT.

I, George W Slover, a Physician, on oath state that I attended on Mrs. Julia V. Ashton, wife of Bird I. Ashton on the 17th day of September, 1904; that there was born to her on said date a female child; that said child is now living and is said to have been named Mary Mickie Ashton

Geo. W. Slover M.D.

Witnesses To Mark:
{

Subscribed and sworn to before me this 16th day of January, 1905.

Eugene E. White
Notary Public.

Applications for Enrollment of Chickasaw Newborn
Act of 1905 Volume I

BIRTH AFFIDAVIT.

DEPARTMENT OF THE INTERIOR.
COMMISSION TO THE FIVE CIVILIZED TRIBES.

IN RE APPLICATION FOR ENROLLMENT, as a citizen of the Chickasaw Nation, of Mary Mickie Ashton, born on the 17 day of Sept, 1904

Name of Father: Bird I Ashton   a citizen of the Chickasaw Nation.
Name of Mother: Julia V Ashton   a citizen of the Chickasaw Nation.

Postoffice   Davis, I.T.

AFFIDAVIT OF MOTHER.

UNITED STATES OF AMERICA, Indian Territory, }
    Southern   DISTRICT.

    I, Julia V Ashton, on oath state that I am 26 years of age and a citizen by blood, of the Chickasaw Nation; that I am the lawful wife of Bird I Ashton, who is a citizen, by marriage of the Chickasaw Nation; that a Female child was born to me on 17 day of Sept, 1904; that said child has been named Mary Mickie Ashton, and was living March 4, 1905.

                                     Julia V. Ashton

Witnesses To Mark:
{

    Subscribed and sworn to before me this 14th day of April, 1905

                                     J M Webster
                                     Notary Public.

AFFIDAVIT OF ATTENDING PHYSICIAN OR MID-WIFE.

UNITED STATES OF AMERICA, Indian Territory, }
    Southern   DISTRICT.

    I, G.W. Slover, a Physician, on oath state that I attended on Mrs. Julia V Ashton, wife of Bird I Ashton on the 17 day of September, 1904; that there was born to her on said date a Female child; that said child was living March 4, 1905, and is said to have been named Mary Mickie Ashton

                                   G.W. Slover M.D.

Witnesses To Mark:
{

Applications for Enrollment of Chickasaw Newborn
Act of 1905 Volume I

Subscribed and sworn to before me this 14th day of April , 1905

J M Webster
Notary Public.

My comm expires Jan. 22, 1906-

9-106

Muskogee, Indian Territory, January 19, 1905.

Julia V. Ashton,
    Davis, Indian Territory.

Dear Madam:

    Receipt is hereby acknowledged of your affidavit and the affidavit of George W. Stover[sic] to the birth of Mary Mickie Ashton, infant daughter of Julia V. and Bird I. Ashton September 17, 1904, which it is presumed has been forwarded as an application for enrollment of said child.

    You are advised that under the provisions of the act of Congress approved July 1, 1902, no children born subsequent to September 25, 1902, the date of the ratification of said act, are entitled to enrollment and allotment.

Respectfully,

Chairman.

Chickasaw N.B.
15.

Muskogee, Indian Territory, April 27, 1905.

Bird I. Ashton,
    Davis, Indian Territory.

Dear Sir:

    Receipt is hereby acknowledged of the affidavits of Julia V. Ashton and G.W. Slover to the birth of Mary Mickie Ashton, daughter of Bird I. and Julia V. Ashton, September 17, 1904, and the same have been filed with our records in the matter of the enrollment of said child.

Respectfully,

Chairman.

Applications for Enrollment of Chickasaw Newborn
Act of 1905 Volume I

9 N. B. 15

Muskogee, Indian Territory, April 12, 1905.

Bird I. Ashton,
    Davis, Indian Territory.

Dear Sir:

    There is inclosed you herewith for execution application for the enrollment of your infant child, Mary Mickie Ashton, born September 17, 1904.

    The affidavits heretofore filed with the Commission show the child was living on January 16, 1905. It is necessary, for the child to be enrolled, that she was living on March 4, 1905.

    In having these affidavits executed care should be exercised to see that all names are written in full, as they appear in the body of the affidavit, and in the event that either of the persons signing the affidavit are unable to write, signatures by mark must be attested by two witnesses. Each affidavit must be executed before a Notary Public and the notarial seal and signature of the officer must be attached to each separate affidavit.

    Respectfully,

LM 12-20.   Commissioner in Charge.

Chic. N.B - 16
    (Lucrecia Exa Perry
    Born February 9, 1904)

Applications for Enrollment of Chickasaw Newborn
Act of 1905 Volume I

123

BIRTH AFFIDAVIT.

IN RE-APPLICATION FOR ENROLLMENT, as a citizen of the Chickasaw Nation, of Lucrecia Exa Perry , born on the 9th day of Feb , 1904

Name of Father: Eli Perry   a citizen of the Chickasaw Nation.
Name of Mother: Emma B. Perry   a citizen of the ——— Nation.

Postoffice Yuba I.T.

AFFIDAVIT OF MOTHER.

UNITED STATES OF AMERICA, INDIAN TERRITORY, }
Central   District.

I, Emma B. Perry , on oath state that I am 22 years of age and a citizen by ——— , of the .... Nation; that I am the lawful wife of Eli Perry , who is a citizen, by Blood of the Chickasaw Nation; that a Female child was born to me on 9th day of Feb. , 1904 , that said child has been named Lucrecia Exa Perry , and is now living.

Emma B Perry
Witnesses To Mark:

Subscribed and sworn to before me this 24th day of Feb , 1905.

W.J. O'Donley
Notary Public.

AFFIDAVIT OF ATTENDING PHYSICIAN OR MID-WIFE.

UNITED STATES OF AMERICA, INDIAN TERRITORY, }
Central   District.

I, M. M. Pantsky , a Mid-wife , on oath state that I attended on Mrs. Emma B. Perry , wife of Eli Perry on the 9th day of Feb , 190 4; that there was born to her on said date a Female child; that said child is now living and is said to have been named Lucrecia Exa Perry her

M. M. x Pantsky
Witnesses To Mark: mark
 P.A. Landeth
 L M. Landeth

Applications for Enrollment of Chickasaw Newborn
Act of 1905   Volume I

Subscribed and sworn to before me this   24th   day of   Feb   , 1905.

>W.J. O'Donley
>Notary Public.

BIRTH AFFIDAVIT.

DEPARTMENT OF THE INTERIOR.
COMMISSION TO THE FIVE CIVILIZED TRIBES.

IN RE APPLICATION FOR ENROLLMENT, as a citizen of the   Chickasaw   Nation, of   Lucrecia Exa Perry   , born on the 9th   day of   Feb   , 1904

Name of Father: Eli Perry   a citizen of the Chickasaw Nation.
Name of Mother: Emma B. Perry   a citizen of the ———   Nation.

Postoffice   Yuba I.T.

AFFIDAVIT OF MOTHER.

UNITED STATES OF AMERICA, Indian Territory, }
   Central   DISTRICT.

I, Emma B. Perry   , on oath state that I am   22   years of age and a citizen by — — —, of the — — — — Nation; that I am the lawful wife of   Eli Perry   , who is a citizen, by Blood   of the   Chickasaw   Nation; that a   Female   child was born to me on   9th   day of   Feb   , 1904; that said child has been named   Lucrecia Exa Perry   , and was living March 4, 1905.

>Emma B Perry

Witnesses To Mark:
{

Subscribed and sworn to before me this   25th   day of   March   , 1905.

>W.J. O'Donley
>Notary Public.

69

Applications for Enrollment of Chickasaw Newborn
Act of 1905 Volume I

AFFIDAVIT OF ATTENDING PHYSICIAN OR MID-WIFE.

UNITED STATES OF AMERICA, Indian Territory, }
Central   DISTRICT.

I, M. M. Pantskey, a Midwife, on oath state that I attended on Mrs. Emma B Perry, wife of Eli Perry on the 9th day of Feb, 1904; that there was born to her on said date a Female child; that said child was living March 4, 1905, and is said to have been named Lucrecia Exa Perry

                                                          her
                                            Mary M x Pantsky

Witnesses To Mark: mark
  { A.J. Wells
    (Name Illegible)

Subscribed and sworn to before me this 25th day of March, 1905

                                        W.J. O'Donley
                                        Notary Public.

                                                        Chickasaw 108

                          Muskogee, Indian Territory, March 31, 1905.

Eli Perry,
    Yuba, Indian Territory.

Dear Sir:

    Receipt is hereby acknowledged of the affidavits of Emma B. Perry and Mary M. Pantsky to the birth of Lucrecia Exa Perry, daughter of Eli and Emma B. Perry, February 9, 1904, and the same have been filed with our records as an application for the enrollment of said child.

                                Respectfully,

                                                Chairman.

Applications for Enrollment of Chickasaw Newborn
Act of 1905   Volume I

9 N.B. 18

Muskogee, Indian Territory, April 12, 1905.

Eli Perry,
    Yuba, Indian Territory.

Dear Sir:

    You are hereby advised that before the application for the enrollment of your infant child, Lucrecia Exa Perry, can be finally disposed of, it will be necessary for you to furnish the Commission with either the original or a certified copy of the license and certificate of marriage of yourself and Emma B. Perry.

    Please give this matter your immediate attention.

Respectfully,

Commissioner in Charge.

Chic. N.B - 17
    (Ruby Colley
    Born October 12, 1904)
    (Myrtle Colley
    Born February 6, 1903)

BIRTH AFFIDAVIT.

DEPARTMENT OF THE INTERIOR.
COMMISSION TO THE FIVE CIVILIZED TRIBES.

    IN RE APPLICATION FOR ENROLLMENT, as a citizen of the Chickasaw Nation, of Ruby Colley, born on the 12th day of October, 1904

Name of Father: William E. Colley   a citizen of the Chickasaw Nation.
Name of Mother: Ella Colley   a citizen of the Chickasaw Nation.

Postoffice   Pontotoc I.T.

Applications for Enrollment of Chickasaw Newborn
Act of 1905   Volume I

AFFIDAVIT OF MOTHER.

UNITED STATES OF AMERICA, Indian Territory, }
   Southern   DISTRICT.

   I,   Ella Colley   , on oath state that I am   26   years of age and a citizen by Blood   , of the   Chickasaw   Nation; that I am the lawful wife of   William E. Colley   , who is a citizen, by marriage   of the   Chickasaw   Nation; that a   female   child was born to me on 12th day of   October   , 1904; that said child has been named   Ruby   , and was living March 4, 1905.

Ella Colley

Witnesses To Mark:
{

   Subscribed and sworn to before me this   30th day of   March   , 1905

M.S. Bradford
Notary Public.

AFFIDAVIT OF ATTENDING PHYSICIAN OR MID-WIFE.

UNITED STATES OF AMERICA, Indian Territory, }
   Southern   DISTRICT.

   I,   William H. Norman   , a   Physician   , on oath state that I attended on Mrs.   Ella Colley   , wife of   William E. Colley   on the 12th day of October, 1904; that there was born to her on said date a   female   child; that said child was living March 4, 1905, and is said to have been named   Ruby

William H. Norman M.D.

Witnesses To Mark:
{

   Subscribed and sworn to before me this   30th day of   March   , 1905

M.S. Bradford
Notary Public.

Applications for Enrollment of Chickasaw Newborn
Act of 1905   Volume I

BIRTH AFFIDAVIT.

DEPARTMENT OF THE INTERIOR.
COMMISSION TO THE FIVE CIVILIZED TRIBES.

IN RE APPLICATION FOR ENROLLMENT, as a citizen of the   Chickasaw   Nation, of   Myrtle Colley   , born on the 6th day of   February   , 1903

Name of Father: William E. Colley   a citizen of the Chickasaw   Nation.
Name of Mother: Ella Colley   a citizen of the Chickasaw   Nation.

Postoffice   Pontotoc I.T.

AFFIDAVIT OF MOTHER.

UNITED STATES OF AMERICA, Indian Territory, }
Southern   DISTRICT.

I,   Ella Colley   , on oath state that I am   26   years of age and a citizen by Blood   , of the   Chickasaw   Nation; that I am the lawful wife of   William E. Colley   , who is a citizen, by Marriage   of the   Chickasaw   Nation; that a female   child was born to me on   6th day of   February   , 1903; that said child has been named   Myrtle   , and was living March 4, 1905.

Ella Colley

Witnesses To Mark:
{

Subscribed and sworn to before me this   30th day of   March   , 1905

M.S. Bradford
Notary Public.

AFFIDAVIT OF ATTENDING PHYSICIAN OR MID-WIFE.

UNITED STATES OF AMERICA, Indian Territory, }
Southern   DISTRICT.

I,   William H. Norman   , a   Physician   , on oath state that I attended on Mrs.   Ella Colley   , wife of   William E. Colley   on the   6th day of   Feb   , 1903; that there was born to her on said date a   female   child; that said child was living March 4, 1905, and is said to have been named Myrtle

William H. Norman M.D.

Witnesses To Mark:
{

Applications for Enrollment of Chickasaw Newborn
Act of 1905 Volume I

Subscribed and sworn to before me this 30th day of March , 1905

M.S. Bradford
Notary Public.

Chickasaw 116.

Muskogee, Indian Territory, April 7, 1905.

William E. Colley,
    Pontotoc, Indian Territory.

Dear Sir:

    Receipt is hereby acknowledged of the affidavits of Ella Colley and William H. Norman to the birth of Myrtle Colley and Ruby Colley, children of William E. and Ella Colley, born February 6, 1903 and October 12, 1904, respectively, and the same have been filed with our records as an application for the enrollment of said children.

Respectfully,

Commissioner in Charge.

Chic. N.B - 18
    (Fleda Dickerson
    Born September 7, 1903)

BIRTH AFFIDAVIT.
DEPARTMENT OF THE INTERIOR.
COMMISSION TO THE FIVE CIVILIZED TRIBES.

    IN RE APPLICATION FOR ENROLLMENT, as a citizen of the Chickasaw Nation, of Fleda Dickerson , born on the 7" day of September , 1903

Name of Father: L. D. Dickerson   a citizen of the Chickasaw Nation.
Name of Mother: Lillie Dickerson   a citizen of the Chickasaw Nation.

Postoffice   Purcell, Ind. Terr.

Applications for Enrollment of Chickasaw Newborn
Act of 1905   Volume I

AFFIDAVIT OF MOTHER.

UNITED STATES OF AMERICA, Indian Territory, }
Southern   DISTRICT.

I,   Lillie Dickerson   , on oath state that I am   Thirty   years of age and a citizen by   blood   , of the   Chickasaw   Nation; that I am the lawful wife of L.D. Dickerson   , who is a citizen, by   intermarriage   of the   Chickasaw Nation; that a   female   child was born to me on   7" day of   September   , 1903; that said child has been named   Fleda Dickerson   , and was living March 4, 1905.

Lillie Dickerson

Witnesses To Mark:
{

Subscribed and sworn to before me this 22" day of May   , 1905

Joseph P. Smith
Notary Public.

AFFIDAVIT OF ATTENDING PHYSICIAN OR MID-WIFE.

UNITED STATES OF AMERICA, Indian Territory, }
Southern   DISTRICT.

I,   G.M. Tralle   , a   Physician   , on oath state that I attended on Mrs.   Lillie Dickerson   , wife of   L.D. Dickerson   on the   7" day of September   , 1903; that there was born to her on said date a   female   child; that said child was living March 4, 1905, and is said to have been named Fleda Dickerson

G.M. Tralle, M.D.

Witnesses To Mark:
{

Subscribed and sworn to before me this 22 day of May   , 1905

Joseph P. Smith
Notary Public.

Applications for Enrollment of Chickasaw Newborn
Act of 1905 Volume I

#93

DEPARTMENT OF THE INTERIOR,
COMMISSION TO THE FIVE CIVILIZED TRIBES.

IN RE *Application for Enrollment,* as a citizen of the Chickasaw Nation, of Fleda Dickerson , born on the 7th day of September , 1903

Name of Father: Lorenzo D. Dickerson   a citizen of the Chickasaw Nation.
Name of Mother: Lillie Dickerson   a citizen of the Chickasaw Nation.

Post-Office: Purcell, Ind. Terr.

AFFIDAVIT OF MOTHER.

UNITED STATES OF AMERICA, }
   INDIAN TERRITORY.
   Southern   District.

    I, Lillie Dickerson , on oath state that I am 28 years of age and a citizen by Blood , of the Chickasaw Nation; that I am the lawful wife of Lorenzo D. Dickerson , who is a citizen, by Intermarriage of the Chickasaw Nation; that a female child was born to me on 7th day of September , 1903 , that said child has been named Fleda Dickerson , and is now living.

                            Lillie Dickerson

WITNESSES TO MARK:

    Subscribed and sworn to before me this 5" day of May , 1904

                            Joseph P Smith
                                 NOTARY PUBLIC.

AFFIDAVIT OF ATTENDING PHYSICIAN OR MID-WIFE.

UNITED STATES OF AMERICA, }
   INDIAN TERRITORY.
   Southern   District.

    I, G. M. Tralle , a Physician , on oath state that I attended on Mrs. Lillie Dickerson , wife of Lorenzo D Dickerson on the 7th day of September , 1903 ; that there was born to her on said date a female child; that said child is now living and is said to have been named Fleda Dickerson

Applications for Enrollment of Chickasaw Newborn
Act of 1905   Volume I

G.M. Tralle

WITNESSES TO MARK:
{

Subscribed and sworn to before me this 5" day of May, 1904

Joseph P Smith
NOTARY PUBLIC.

BIRTH AFFIDAVIT.

IN RE-APPLICATION FOR ENROLLMENT, as a citizen of the Chickasaw Nation, of Fleda Dickerson, born on the 27[sic] day of September, 190 3

Name of Father: Lorenzo D Dickerson   a citizen of the Chickasaw Nation.
Name of Mother: Lillie Dickerson   a citizen of the Chickasaw Nation.

Postoffice   Purcell, Ind. Ter.

AFFIDAVIT OF MOTHER.

UNITED STATES OF AMERICA, INDIAN TERRITORY, }
Southern   District.

I, Lillie Dickerson, on oath state that I am Thirty years of age and a citizen by Blood, of the Chickasaw Nation; that I am the lawful wife of Lorenzo D Dickerson, who is a citizen, by Intermarriage of the Chickasaw Nation; that a Female child was born to me on 27th day of September, 1903, that said child has been named Fleda Dickerson, and is now living.

Lillie Dickerson

Witnesses To Mark:
{

Subscribed and sworn to before me this 22 day of Feby, 1905.

Joseph P Smith
Notary Public.

AFFIDAVIT OF ATTENDING PHYSICIAN OR MID-WIFE.

UNITED STATES OF AMERICA, INDIAN TERRITORY, }
Southern   District.

I, Geo M Tralle, a Physician, on oath state that I attended on Mrs. Lilly Dickerson, wife of Lorenzo D Dickerson on the 27 day of Sept,

Applications for Enrollment of Chickasaw Newborn
Act of 1905   Volume I

190 3; that there was born to her on said date a   Female   child; that said child is now living and is said to have been named   Fleda Dickerson

                                                G.M. Tralle M.D.

Witnesses To Mark:

    Subscribed and sworn to before me this   22   day of   Feby   , 1905.

                                                Joseph P Smith
                                                    Notary Public.

(The letter below typed as given.)

                                  (COPY)

                              Purcell, Ind. Ter.   5/24.

Hon Dawes Commission,
    Muskogee, I.T.

                        Dear Sirs:

                                            Enclosed you will find application for my infant daughter, Fleda Dickerson. I see in the application you sent me the date of birth read Sept 27/ 1903 It should have been Sept 7th 1903. If the application I sent you before read Sept. 27th it was an error as my wife said it was Sept 7th, and then I saw the doctor and he turned to his journal and saw where he had charge me on that date with the visit. Will this error have any bearing on the case. I changed the date to the proper time and had my wife and the physician to swear to the application as corrected. hoping it is all o/k/ as changed and hoping to hear from you on the subject as soon as practicable, I am
                Yours truly
                      L. D. Dickerson.

Applications for Enrollment of Chickasaw Newborn
Act of 1905   Volume I

9 N.B. 18.

Muskogee, Indian Territory, June 1, 1905.

L. D. Dickerson,
 Purcell, Indian Territory.

Dear Sir:

    Receipt is hereby acknowledged of your letter of May 24, enclosing the affidavits of Lillie Dickerson and G. M. Tralle, M.D., to the birth of Fleda Dickerson, daughter of L. D. and Lillie Dickerson, September 7, 1903, and stating that the correct date of the birth of your child, Fleda Dickerson, is September 7, 1903, instead of September 27, and this information has been made a matter of record.

    In the event further evidence is necessary to enable us to determine the right of this child to enrollment, you will be duly notified.

Respectfully,

(End of letter)

9-148

Muskogee, Indian Territory, March 18, 1905.

L. D. Dickerson,
 Purcell, Indian Territory.

Dear Sir:

    Receipt is hereby acknowledged of your letter of March 9, 1905, enclosing the affidavits of Lillie Dickerson and J. M. Trawle[sic] to the birth of Fleda Dickerson, infant daughter of Lorenzo Dickerson and Lillie Dickerson, September 27, 1903, and the same have been filed with our records as an application for the enrollment of said child.

Respectfully,

Chairman.

Applications for Enrollment of Chickasaw Newborn
Act of 1905   Volume I

9-N.B. 18.

Muskogee, Indian Territory, May 9, 1905.

L. D. Dickerson,
    Purcell, Indian Territory.

Dear Sir:

    There is enclosed you herewith for execution application for the enrollment of your infant child, Fleda Dickerson, born September 27, 1903.

    The affidavits heretofore filed with the Commission show the child was living on February 22, 1905. It is necessary, for the child to be enrolled, that she was living on March 4, 1905. You will please insert the age of the mother in place left blank for that purpose.

    In having these affidavits executed care should be exercised to see that all names are written in full, as they appear in the body of the affidavit, and in the event that either of the persons signing the affidavit are unable to write, signatures by mark must be attested by two witnesses. Each affidavit must be executed before a Notary Public and the notarial seal and signature of the officer must be attached to each separate affidavit.

                                Respectfully,

                                                Commissioner in Charge.

V. 9/4.

Chic. N.B - 19
    (William Willington Spence
    September 5, 1903)

Applications for Enrollment of Chickasaw Newborn
Act of 1905 Volume I

BIRTH AFFIDAVIT. *No 74*

DEPARTMENT OF THE INTERIOR.
COMMISSION TO THE FIVE CIVILIZED TRIBES.

IN RE APPLICATION FOR ENROLLMENT, as a citizen of the Chickasaw Nation, of William Willington Spence, born on the 5 day of September, 1903

Name of Father: W.A. Spence   a citizen of the U.S. Nation.

was

Name of Mother: Alice L Spence nee Brown   a citizen of the Chickasaw Nation.

Postoffice Stonewall I.T.

AFFIDAVIT OF MOTHER.

UNITED STATES OF AMERICA, Indian Territory,
.... DISTRICT.

Deceased

I, ..., on oath state that I am .... years of age and a citizen by ...., of the .... Nation; that I am the lawful wife of ...., who is a citizen, by .... of the .... Nation; that a .... child was born to me on .... day of ...., 1......., that said child has been named ...., and is now living.

Witnesses To Mark:
{ ....
{ ....

Subscribed and sworn to before me this .... day of ...., 1905.

Notary Public.

AFFIDAVIT OF ATTENDING PHYSICIAN OR MID-WIFE.

UNITED STATES OF AMERICA, Indian Territory,
    Southern   DISTRICT.

I, Emma House, a Mid-wife, on oath state that I attended on Mrs. Allice[sic] L Spence nee Brown, wife of W.A. Spence on the 5th day of September, 1902[sic]; that there was born to her on said date a male child; that said child is now living and is said to have been named William Willington Spence

Applications for Enrollment of Chickasaw Newborn
Act of 1905   Volume I

Emma House

Witnesses To Mark:
{

Subscribed and sworn to before me this 31 day of Jan , 1905.

Minnie Lillard
Notary Public.

BIRTH AFFIDAVIT.

DEPARTMENT OF THE INTERIOR.
COMMISSION TO THE FIVE CIVILIZED TRIBES.

IN RE APPLICATION FOR ENROLLMENT, as a citizen of the Chickasaw Nation, of William Willington , born on the 5 day of Sep , 1903

Name of Father: W.A. Spence   a citizen of the U.S. Nation.
                      N.E. Brown
Name of Mother: Alice L Spence   a citizen of the Chickasaw Nation.

Postoffice Stonewall I.T.

AFFIDAVIT OF MOTHER.

UNITED STATES OF AMERICA, Indian Territory, }   *Mother Deceased*
Southern   DISTRICT.

I, ..., on oath state that I am .... years of age and a citizen by ...., of the .... Nation; that I am the lawful wife of ...., who is a citizen, by .... of the .... Nation; that a .... child was born to me on .... day of ...., 1......, that said child has been named ...., and is now living.

Witnesses To Mark:
{

Subscribed and sworn to before me this .... day of ...., 1905.

Notary Public.

82

Applications for Enrollment of Chickasaw Newborn
Act of 1905 Volume I

AFFIDAVIT OF ATTENDING PHYSICIAN OR MID-WIFE.

UNITED STATES OF AMERICA, Indian Territory, }
   Southern   DISTRICT. }

    I,   Emma House , a   Mid Wife , on oath state that I attended on Mrs. Alice L Spence ne[sic] Brown , wife of W.A. Spence on the 5 day of Sep , 1903; that there was born to her on said date a   male child; that said child is now living and is said to have been named William Willington Spence

                                    Emma House

Witnesses To Mark:
{

    Subscribed and sworn to before me this 4 day of   Jan , 1905.

                                Minnie B. Lillard
                                     Notary Public.
                Com expires 2/26/06

BIRTH AFFIDAVIT.

DEPARTMENT OF THE INTERIOR.
COMMISSION TO THE FIVE CIVILIZED TRIBES.

    IN RE APPLICATION FOR ENROLLMENT, as a citizen of the   Chickasaw Nation, of William W. Spence , born on the 5 day of Sep , 1903

Name of Father: W.A. Spence   a citizen of the U. S. Nation.
Name of Mother: Alice L Spence Ne Brown   a citizen of the Chickasaw Nation.

                       Postoffice   Stonewall Ind Ter

AFFIDAVIT OF MOTHER.

UNITED STATES OF AMERICA, Indian Territory, }
....DISTRICT. }

    I, ..., on oath state that I am *Deceased* years of age and a citizen by ...., of the .... Nation; that I am the lawful wife of ...., who is a citizen, by .... of the .... Nation; that a .... child was born to me on ..... day of ...., 1 ...., that said child has been named ...., and was living March 4, 1905.

                                     ....

Applications for Enrollment of Chickasaw Newborn
Act of 1905   Volume I

Witnesses To Mark:

{ ....
.... }

Subscribed and sworn to before me this .... day of ...., 1905.

....
Notary Public.

AFFIDAVIT OF ATTENDING PHYSICIAN OR MID-WIFE.

UNITED STATES OF AMERICA, Indian Territory, }
116th DISTRICT.   }

I,   Emma House   , a   Mid-Wife   , on oath state that I attended on Mrs.   Allice L Spence ne Brown   , wife of W A Spence   on the 5 day of Sept   , 1903; that there was born to her on said date a   male   child; that said child was living March 4, 1905, and is said to have been named William W. Spence

Emma House

Witnesses To Mark:

{

Subscribed and sworn to before me this 21 day of   April   , 1905

Minnie Lillard
Notary Public.

To Whom it may concern,

I, Geo H Truax, certify that William W. Spence is the child of Alice L Spence wife of W. A. Spence and the child is now living, and was on March 4th 1905.

Dr Geo H Truax

Personally appeared before me this   MAY 4-1905   Dr Geo H. Truax and certified to the forgoing instrument.

Minnie Lillard
Notary Public
STONEWALL, I.T.

Applications for Enrollment of Chickasaw Newborn
Act of 1905   Volume I

To Whom it may concern,

I, L. W. Spence, certify that William W. Spence is the child of Alice L. Spence wife of W. A. Spence and that the child is now living -

                        L. W. Spence

Personally appeared before me this MAY 4-1905   L. W. Spence and certified to the foregoing instrument

                        Minnie Lillard
                        Notary Public
                        STONEWALL, I.T.

                    Muskogee, Indian Territory, January 12, 1905.

W. A. Spence,
    Stonewall, Indian Territory.

Dear Sir:

    Receipt is hereby acknowledged of the affidavit of Emma House to the birth of William Wellington Spence, son of Alice L. Spence, formerly Brown, and W. A. Spence, September 5, 1903.

    It is stated that Alice L. Spence, now deceased was formerly Alice L. Brown, and you are advised that there are several Alice Browns upon our records and it is impracticable to identify your wife from the information therein.

    If you will state her age, the name under which she was listed for enrollment, the names of her parents and other members of her family for whom application was made at the same time, and any other information in your possession which would enable us to identify Alice L. Spence formerly Brown, as a citizen of the Choctaw Nation; as claimed, the matter will receive further consideration.

                        Respectfully,

                                  Chairman.

Applications for Enrollment of Chickasaw Newborn
Act of 1905   Volume I

Chickasaw 147

Reply to letter DC 12332.1905

Muskogee, Indian Territory, January 20, 1905.

W. A. Spence,
    Stonewall, Indian Territory.

Dear Sir:

    Receipt is hereby acknowledged of your letter of January 16, relative to the enrollment of Alice L. Spence, formerly Brown, as a citizen of the Chickasaw Nation.

    You are advised that the information therein contained has enabled the Commission to identify her as having been enrolled as a citizen by blood of the Chickasaw Nation, her name appearing opposite Number 470 upon the approved roll of the citizens by blood of said nation.

    Referring, however, to the affidavit of Emma House to the birth of William Wellington Spence, infant son of W. A. and Alice L. Spence, on September 5, 1903, you are advised that under the provisions of the act of Congress approved July 1, 1902, no children born to citizens of the Choctaw and Chickasaw Nations subsequent to September 25, 1902, the date of the ratification of said act, are entitled to enrollment and allotment as citizens of the Choctaw and Chickasaw Nations.

                      Respectfully,

                        Chairman.

Chickasaw
N. B. 19.

Muskogee, Indian Territory, April 28, 1905.

W. A. Spence,
    Stonewall, Indian Territory.

Dear Sir:

    Receipt is hereby acknowledged of the affidavit of Emma House to the birth of William W. Spence, son of W. A. and Alice L. Spence, and the same has been filed with the records in the matter of the enrollment of said child.

    It appears that the mother is dead, and you are advised that it will be necessary for you to forward the affidavit of two persons who know of the birth of said child, that it is the child of your wife, Alice L. Spence and that it was living on March 4, 1905.

Applications for Enrollment of Chickasaw Newborn
Act of 1905   Volume I

This matter should receive your immediate attention in order that proper disposition may be made of the application for the enrollment of the above named child.

Respectfully,

Chairman.

9-N.B. 19.

Muskogee, Indian Territory, May 9, 1905.

W. A. Spence,
Stonewall, Indian Territory.

Dear Sir:

Receipt is hereby acknowledged of the affidavits of George H. Truax and L. W. Spence to the birth of your child, William Wellington Spence, and the same have been filed with our records in the matter of the enrollment of said child.

Respectfully,

Commissioner in Charge.

$W^m O.B.$

| COMMISSIONERS:
TAMS BIXBY,
THOMAS B. NEEDLES,
C.R. BRECKINBRIDGE.
WM. O. BEALL
Secretary | **DEPARTMENT OF THE INTERIOR,**
COMMISSIONER TO THE FIVE CIVILIZED TRIBES. | REFER IN REPLY TO THE FOLLOWING:
9-NB-19. |

ADDRESS ONLY THE
COMMISSION TO THE FIVE CIVILIZED TRIBES.

Muskogee, Indian Territory, June 9, 1905.

W. A. Spence,
Stonewall, Indian Territory.

Dear Sir:

Referring to the application for the enrollment of your infant child, William W. Spence, it is noted that the affidavits of George H. Truax and L. W. Spence, heretofore filed in this office in place of the affidavit of the mother who is dead, fail to give the date of the applicant's birth.

Applications for Enrollment of Chickasaw Newborn
Act of 1905 Volume I

Before this matter can be finally determined, it will be necessary for you to file in this office the affidavits of two persons who are disinterested and not related to the applicant, who have actual knowledge of the facts: that the child was born, the date of his birth, that he was living on March 4, 1905, and that Alice L. Spence was his mother.

Respectfully,
T.B. Needles
Commissioner in Charge.

---

9 NB 19

Muskogee, Indian Territory, June 21, 1905.

W. A. Spence,
Stonewall, Indian Territory.

Dear Sir:

Receipt is hereby acknowledged of the affidavits of George H. Truax and Zeno M. McCurtain to the birth of William W. Spence, son of Alice L. and W. A. Spence, September 5, 1903, and the same have been filed with our records in the matter of the enrollment of said child.

Respectfully,

Chairman.

TOM HOPE, PRESIDENT.   R.E. CHAMBERS, VICE PRESIDENT   W.N. Mooney, CASHIER.
7654

FIRST NATIONAL BANK
OF STONEWALL, I.T.
CAPITAL $25,000.00

Stonewall, I.T.   6/17   190 5

Ind. Ter. Southern Dist.

Be it remembered that on this 17th June 1905 before me Jno W. Fuller a Notary Public in and for the Southern Dist. of the Ind. Ter. personally appeared Dr. Geo. H. Truax one of the subscribing witnesses to the fact, that a male child named William W. Spence was borned[sic] to Alice L. Spence (Brown) wife of W. A. Spence, on Sept. 5/1903, that he was living on March 4, 1905

In testimony whereof I have here unto set my hand and seal as Notary Public within and for the Southern Judicial Dist. of the Ind. Ter. the day and year above written.

Applications for Enrollment of Chickasaw Newborn
Act of 1905   Volume I

(Sig. Witness)   Dr Geo. H. Truax

Jno. W. Fuller N.P.
For the Southern Dist. Ind Ter.

Chic. N.B - 20
(Mary Ellen Hatcher
Born January 24, 1904)

BIRTH AFFIDAVIT.

DEPARTMENT OF THE INTERIOR.
COMMISSION TO THE FIVE CIVILIZED TRIBES.

IN RE APPLICATION FOR ENROLLMENT, as a citizen of the   Chickasaw   Nation, of   Mary Ellen Hatcher , born on the 24"   day of Jan. , 1904

Name of Father: Robert E Hatcher   a citizen of the United States Nation.
Name of Mother: Lillie May Hatcher   a citizen of the   Chickasaw   Nation.

Postoffice   Bebee

AFFIDAVIT OF MOTHER.

UNITED STATES OF AMERICA, Indian Territory, ⎫
         Southern   DISTRICT.   ⎭

I,   Lillie May Hatcher , on oath state that I am 19 years of age and a citizen by blood , of the   Chickasaw   Nation; that I am the lawful wife of   Robert E Hatcher , who is a citizen, by   blood[sic]   of the   Chickasaw [sic]   Nation; that a   female   child was born to me on 24 day of Jan , 1904, that said child has been named Mary Ellen Hatcher , and is now living.

Lillie May Hatcher

Witnesses To Mark:
{

Subscribed and sworn to before me this 22 day of Dec , 1905.4

Jno P Crawford
Notary Public.

Applications for Enrollment of Chickasaw Newborn
Act of 1905 Volume I

AFFIDAVIT OF ATTENDING PHYSICIAN OR MID-WIFE.

UNITED STATES OF AMERICA, Indian Territory, }
   Southern   DISTRICT.

    I, Thenie C Borring, a midwife, on oath state that I attended on Mrs. Lillie May Hatcher, wife of Robert E Hatcher on the 24 day of January, 1904; that there was born to her on said date a female child; that said child is now living and is said to have been named Mary Ellen Hatcher

                                          her
                              Thenie C x Borring
Witnesses To Mark: mark
{ Jno P Crawford
{ G.L. Thompson

    Subscribed and sworn to before me this 22 day of Dec, 1905.4

                              Jno P Crawford
                              Notary Public.

BIRTH AFFIDAVIT.

DEPARTMENT OF THE INTERIOR.
COMMISSION TO THE FIVE CIVILIZED TRIBES.

    IN RE APPLICATION FOR ENROLLMENT, as a citizen of the Chickasaw Nation, of Mary Ellen Hatcher, born on the 24 day of Jan, 1904

                              non citizen
Name of Father: Robert Lee Hatcher   a citizen of the .... Nation.
Name of Mother: Lillie May Hatcher   a citizen of the Chickasaw Nation.

                      Postoffice   Bebee Ind Ter

AFFIDAVIT OF MOTHER.

UNITED STATES OF AMERICA, Indian Territory, }
   Southern   DISTRICT.

    I, Lillie May Hatcher, on oath state that I am Twenty years of age and a citizen by Blood, of the Chickasaw Nation; that I am the lawful wife of Robert Lee Hatcher, who is a ~~citizen~~ *non*, by citizen of the .... Nation; that a female child was born to me on 24 day of Jan, 1904; that said child has been named Mary Ellen Hather, and was living March 4, 1905.

Applications for Enrollment of Chickasaw Newborn
Act of 1905 Volume I

Lillie May Hatcher

Witnesses To Mark:
{ Lizzie Haley
{ Mattie Taplin

Subscribed and sworn to before me this 27 day of March , 1905

G.N. Waldby
Notary Public.

AFFIDAVIT OF ATTENDING PHYSICIAN OR MID-WIFE.

UNITED STATES OF AMERICA, Indian Territory, }
Southern   DISTRICT.

I, Thenie Caraline Boring , a ...., on oath state that I attended on Mrs. Lillie May Hatcher , wife of Robert Lee Hatcher on the 24 day of Jan , 1904; that there was born to her on said date a female child; that said child was living March 4, 1905, and is said to have been named Mary Ellen Hatcher

her
Thenie Caraline x Boring
mark

Witnesses To Mark:
{ Robert Lee Hatcher
{ Jane Boring

Subscribed and sworn to before me this 27 day of March , 1905

George N. Waldby
Notary Public.

9-159

Muskogee, Indian Territory, March 25, 1905.

Mrs. Lillie M. Hatcher,
    Bebee, Indian Territory.

Dear Madam:

Receipt is hereby acknowledged of your letter of March 17, 1905, stating that you made application for the enrollment of your daughter Mary Ellen Hatcher born January 34[sic], 1904, and you wish to know if the application has been received.

In reply to your letter you are informed that it does not appear from our records that application has been made to this Commission for the enrollment of your daughter

Applications for Enrollment of Chickasaw Newborn
Act of 1905   Volume I

Mary Ellen Hatcher born January 24, 1904, and for your convenience there is inclosed herewith a blank for the enrollment of an infant child which you should have executed and returned to this office within sixty days from March 3, 1905.

                        Respectfully,

                                            Chairman.

B. C.

                        9-159

                  Muskogee, Indian Territory, April 4, 1905.

Mrs. Lillian[sic] Hatcher,
    Bebee, Indian Territory.

Dear Madam:

    Receipt is hereby acknowledged of your letter of March 29, 1905, enclosing affidavits of Lillie May Hatcher and Thenie Caraline Boring to the birth of Mary Ellen Hatcher, daughter of Robert Lee and Lillie May Hatcher, January 24, 1904, and the same have been filed with our records as an application for the enrollment of said child.

                        Respectfully,

                                            Chairman.

Chic. N.B - 21
    (Mary Luella Nolatubbee
    Born April 13, 1903)

BIRTH AFFIDAVIT.

DEPARTMENT OF THE INTERIOR,
COMMISSION TO THE FIVE CIVILIZED TRIBES.

    ***IN RE** Application for Enrollment,* as a citizen of the   Chickasaw   Nation, of   Mary Luella Nolatubbee , born on the   13th day of   Apr , 1903

Name of Father: James Nolatubbee   a citizen of the   Chickasaw Nation.
Name of Mother: Bessie Nolatubbee   a citizen of the   Chickasaw Nation.

Applications for Enrollment of Chickasaw Newborn
Act of 1905 Volume I

Post-Office: Ardmore I.T.

AFFIDAVIT OF MOTHER.

UNITED STATES OF AMERICA,
   INDIAN TERRITORY.
Southern   District.

I,   Bessie Nolatubbee   , on oath state that I am   20   years of age and a citizen by   marriage   , of the Chickasaw   Nation; that I am the lawful wife of   James Nolatubbee   , who is a citizen, by   Blood   of the Chickasaw   Nation; that a Female   child was born to me on   13th day of   Apr   1903   ; that said child has been named   Mary Luella Nolatubbee   , and is now living.

Bessie Nolatubbee

WITNESSES TO MARK:

Subscribed and sworn to before me this   8th day of   Apr   , 1904

O. Gregory
NOTARY PUBLIC.

AFFIDAVIT OF ATTENDING PHYSICIAN OR MID-WIFE.

UNITED STATES OF AMERICA,
   INDIAN TERRITORY.
Southern   District.

I,   Dr. F.P. Von Keller   , a   Physician   , on oath state that I attended on Mrs. Bessie Nolatubbee   , wife of   James Nolatubbee   on the   13th day of   Apr , 1903 ; that there was born to her on said date a   Female   child; that said child is now living and is said to have been named   Mary Luella Nolatubbee

F.P. Von Keller an M.D.

WITNESSES TO MARK:

Subscribed and sworn to before me this   20   day of   Mch   , 1905.

O.Gregory
NOTARY PUBLIC.

Applications for Enrollment of Chickasaw Newborn
Act of 1905 Volume I

BIRTH AFFIDAVIT.

DEPARTMENT OF THE INTERIOR.
COMMISSION TO THE FIVE CIVILIZED TRIBES.

IN RE APPLICATION FOR ENROLLMENT, as a citizen of the Chickasaw Nation, of Mary Luella Nolatubbee, born on the 13' day of April, 1903

Name of Father: James Nolatubbee   a citizen of the Chickasaw Nation.
Name of Mother: Bessie Nolatubbee   a citizen of the Chickasaw Nation.

Postoffice   Ardmore I.T.

AFFIDAVIT OF MOTHER.

UNITED STATES OF AMERICA, Indian Territory, }
Southern   DISTRICT.

I, Bessie Nolatubbee, on oath state that I am 21 years of age and a citizen by intermarriage, of the Chickasaw Nation; that I am the lawful wife of James Nolatubbee, who is a citizen, by blood of the Chickasaw Nation; that a female child was born to me on 13th day of April, 1903; that said child has been named Mary Luella Nolatubbee, and was living March 4, 1905.

                                        Bessie Nolatubbee

Witnesses To Mark:
   { Ed Byrd
     Kinzy Dillard

Subscribed and sworn to before me this 18 day of April, 1905

                                        U.T. Rexroat
                                        Notary Public.

AFFIDAVIT OF ATTENDING PHYSICIAN OR MID-WIFE.

UNITED STATES OF AMERICA, Indian Territory, }
Southern   DISTRICT.

I, Frederick P. von Keller MD, a Physician, on oath state that I attended on Mrs. Bessie Nolatubbee, wife of James Nolatubbee on the 13" day of April, 1903; that there was born to her on said date a female child; that said child was living March 4, 1905, and is said to have been named Mary Luella Nolatubbee

                                        Frederick P von Keller M.D.

Applications for Enrollment of Chickasaw Newborn
Act of 1905   Volume I

Witnesses To Mark:
{

Subscribed and sworn to before me this 20 day of   May   , 1905

U.T. Rexroat
Notary Public.

$W^m O.B.$

COMMISSIONERS:
TAMS BIXBY,
THOMAS B. NEEDLES,
C.R. BRECKINRIDGE.

DEPARTMENT OF THE INTERIOR,
COMMISSIONER TO THE FIVE CIVILIZED TRIBES.

REFER IN REPLY TO THE FOLLOWING:

9-N.B. 21.

WM. O. BEALL
Secretary

ADDRESS ONLY THE
COMMISSION TO THE FIVE CIVILIZED TRIBES.

Muskogee, Indian Territory, May 11, 1905.

James Nolatubbee,
   Ardmore, Indian Territory.

Dear Sir:

    There is enclosed you herewith for execution application for the enrollment of your infant child, Mary Luella Nolatubbee, born April 13, 1903.

    Your wife's affidavit, heretofore filed with the Commission shows the child living on April 8, 1904. It is necessary, for the child to be enrolled, that she was living on March 4, 1905. You will please have the enclosed affidavit of the applicant's mother executed.

    In having these affidavits executed care should be exercised to see that all names are written in full, as they appear in the body of the affidavit, and in the event that either of the persons signing the affidavit are unable to write, signatures by mark must be attested by two witnesses. Each affidavit must be executed before a Notary Public and the notarial seal and signature of the officer must be attached to each separate affidavit.

Respectfully,
Tams Bixby
Chairman.

V. 10/8.

Applications for Enrollment of Chickasaw Newborn
Act of 1905   Volume I

Chic. N.B - 22
*(Zora Hamilton
Born November 3, 1903)*

BIRTH AFFIDAVIT.

DEPARTMENT OF THE INTERIOR.
COMMISSION TO THE FIVE CIVILIZED TRIBES.

IN RE APPLICATION FOR ENROLLMENT, as a citizen of the Chickasaw Nation, of Zora Hamilton, born on the 3" day of November, 1903

Name of Father: Simeon Hamilton   a citizen of the Chickasaw Nation.
Name of Mother: Caroline Wisdom   a citizen of the Chickasaw Nation.

Postoffice   Reagan, I.T.

AFFIDAVIT OF MOTHER.

UNITED STATES OF AMERICA, Indian Territory,
.... DISTRICT.

I, Caroline Wisdom, on oath state that I am about 36 years of age and a citizen by blood, of the Chickasaw Nation; that I am *not* the lawful wife of Simeon Hamilton, who is a citizen, by blood of the Chickasaw Nation; that a female child was born to me on 3" day of November, 1903; that said child has been named Zora Hamilton, and was living March 4, 1905.

                                                 her
                                  Caroline x Wisdom
Witnesses To Mark: mark
{ A.A. Chapman
{ D.F. Underwood

Subscribed and sworn to before me this 22nd day of May, 1905

                                      A A Chapman
                                      Notary Public.

Applications for Enrollment of Chickasaw Newborn
Act of 1905   Volume I

AFFIDAVIT OF ATTENDING PHYSICIAN OR MID-WIFE.

UNITED STATES OF AMERICA, Indian Territory,
.... DISTRICT.

   I,..................................., a..................................., on oath state that I attended on Mrs.   Caroline Wisdom   , wife of .... on the   3^d day of November   , 1903; that there was born to her on said date a   female   child; that said child was living March 4, 1905, and is said to have been named Zora Hamilton

Mary Lewis

Witnesses To Mark:
 { A.A. Chapman
   D.F. Underwood

   Subscribed and sworn to before me this   22nd   day of   May   , 1905

A A Chapman
Notary Public.

BIRTH AFFIDAVIT.

DEPARTMENT OF THE INTERIOR,
COMMISSION TO THE FIVE CIVILIZED TRIBES.

   IN RE Application for Enrollment, as a citizen of the   Chickasaw   Nation, of   Zora Hamilton   , born on the   3rd day of   November   , 1903

Name of Father: Simeon Hamilton   a citizen of the   Chickasaw   Nation.
Name of Mother: Caroline Wisdom   a citizen of the   Chickasaw   Nation.

Post-Office: Reagan I.T.

AFFIDAVIT OF MOTHER.

UNITED STATES OF AMERICA,
      INDIAN TERRITORY.
Southern   District.

   I,   Caroline Wisdom   , on oath state that I am about 36   years of age and a citizen by   Blood   , of the   Chickasaw   Nation; that I am the ~~lawful~~ *Cohort* wife of Simeon Hamilton   , who is a citizen, by   Blood   of the   Chickasaw   Nation; that a female   child was born to me on   3rd   day of   November   , 1903 , that said child has been named   Zora Hamilton   , and is now living.

97

Applications for Enrollment of Chickasaw Newborn
Act of 1905   Volume I

                                                    her
                                        Caroline x Wisdom

WITNESSES TO MARK: mark
    { Martin Brown
      DF Underwood

Subscribed and sworn to before me this   1st   day of   March   , 1905.

                                              A. A. Chapman
                                                  NOTARY PUBLIC.

AFFIDAVIT OF ATTENDING PHYSICIAN OR MID-WIFE.

UNITED STATES OF AMERICA, }
    INDIAN TERRITORY.
  Southern   District.

    I,   Mary Lewis   , a   midwife   , on oath state that I attended on Mrs. Caroline Wisdom , ~~wife of~~ *Cohort of* Simeon Hamilton on the 3rd day of November , 1903 ; that there was born to her on said date a female child; that said child is now living and is said to have been named Zora Hamilton

                                               her
                                     Mary x Lewis
WITNESSES TO MARK: mark
    { Martin Brown
      DF Underwood

Subscribed and sworn to before me this   1st   day of   March   , 1905.

                                              A. A. Chapman
                                                  NOTARY PUBLIC.

Applications for Enrollment of Chickasaw Newborn
Act of 1905 Volume I

9-185

Muskogee, Indian Territory, March 9, 1905.

A. A. Chapman,
    Ravia, Indian Territory.

Dear Sir:

    Receipt is hereby acknowledged of your letter of March 6, 1905, enclosing the affidavits of Caroline Wisdom and Mary Lewis to the birth of Zora Hamilton, daughter of Simeon Hamilton and Caroline Wisdom, November 3, 1903, and the same have been filed with our records as an application for the enrollment of said child.

                  Respectfully,

                              Chairman.

---

9 N B 22.

Muskogee, Indian Territory, April 15, 1905.

Simeon Hamilton,
    Reagan, Indian Territory.

Dear Sir:

    Referring to the affidavits heretofore forwarded relative to the enrollment of your infant child, Zora Hamilton, it appears that you are a citizen by blood of the Chickasaw Nation.

    If this is correct you are requested to state when, where and under what name you were listed for enrollment, the names of your parents and other members of your family for whom application was made at the same time, and if you have selected an allotment, give your roll number as the same appears upon your allotment certificate.

                  Respectfully,

                              Chairman.

Applications for Enrollment of Chickasaw Newborn
Act of 1905 Volume I

9-NB-22.

Muskogee, Indian Territory, May 13, 1905.

Caroline Wisdom,
    Reagan, Indian Territory.

Dear Madam:

    There is enclosed you herewith for execution application for the enrollment of your infant child, Zora Hamilton, born November 3, 1903.

    The affidavits heretofore filed with the Commission show the child was living on March 1, 1905. It is necessary, for the child to be enrolled, that she was living on March 4, 1905.

    In having these affidavits executed care should be exercised to see that all names are written in full, as they appear in the body of the affidavit, and in the event that either of the persons signing the affidavit are unable to write, signatures by mark must be attested by two witnesses. Each affidavit must be executed before a Notary Public and the notarial seal and signature of the officer must be attached to each separate affidavit.

    Respectfully,

    Chairman.

V. 10/5.

---

9 NB 22

Muskogee, Indian Territory, June 8, 1905.

Simeon Hamilton,
    Reagan, Indian Territory.

Dear Sir:

    Receipt is hereby acknowledged of the affidavits of Caroline Wisdom and Mary Lewis to the birth of Zora Hamilton, daughter of Simeon Hamilton and Caroline Wisdom, November 3, 1903, and the same have been filed in the matter of the enrollment of said child.

    Respectfully,

    Chairman.

Applications for Enrollment of Chickasaw Newborn
Act of 1905 Volume I

Chic. N.B - 23
(Samuel C. Davis, Jr.
Born June 12, 1904)

BIRTH AFFIDAVIT.

DEPARTMENT OF THE INTERIOR.
COMMISSION TO THE FIVE CIVILIZED TRIBES.

IN RE APPLICATION FOR ENROLLMENT, as a citizen of the Chickasaw Nation, of Samuel C Davis Jr , born on the 12 day of June , 1904

Name of Father: Samuel C Davis   a citizen of the Chickasaw Nation.
Name of Mother: Linnie K Davis   a citizen of the Chickasaw Nation.

Postoffice Hart, Ind. Terr.

AFFIDAVIT OF MOTHER.

UNITED STATES OF AMERICA, Indian Territory, }
Southern DISTRICT. }

I, Linnie K Davis , on oath state that I am 28 years of age and a citizen by Intermarriage , of the Chickasaw Nation; that I am the lawful wife of Samuel C Davis , who is a citizen, by Blood of the Chickasaw Nation; that a male child was born to me on 12 day of June , 1904, that said child has been named Samuel C Davis Jr , and is now living.

Linnie K Davis

Witnesses To Mark:
{ Kittie Pirth
{ H.C. Filmore

Subscribed and sworn to before me this 16 day of March , 1905.

J. J. Hart
Notary Public.

Applications for Enrollment of Chickasaw Newborn
Act of 1905 Volume I

AFFIDAVIT OF ATTENDING PHYSICIAN OR MID-WIFE.

UNITED STATES OF AMERICA, Indian Territory, }
   Southern   DISTRICT.

      I,   S. C. Davis   , a Physician , on oath state that I attended on Mrs. Linnie K. Davis , wife of Samuel C Davis on the 12 day of June , 1904; that there was born to her on said date a male child; that said child is now living and is said to have been named Samuel C Davis Jr

                                            S.C. Davis

Witnesses To Mark:
  { J L Davis
    J.N. Gilliland

      Subscribed and sworn to before me this 16 day of March , 1905.

                                    J. J. Hart
                                              Notary Public.

                                          9-213

                  Muskogee, Indian Territory, March 21, 1905.

Samuel C. Davis,
    Hart, Indian Territory.

Dear Sir:

      Receipt is hereby acknowledged of the affidavits of Linnie K. Davis and Samuel C. Davis to the birth of Samuel C. Davis, Jr., child of Samuel C. and Minnie[sic] K. Davis, June 12, 1904, and the same have been filed with our records as an application for the enrollment of said child.

                                Respectfully,

                                                      Chairman.

Applications for Enrollment of Chickasaw Newborn
Act of 1905 Volume I

Chic. N.B - 24
(Odneal Rice
Born December 24, 1902)

BIRTH AFFIDAVIT.

Department of the Interior,
COMMISSION TO THE FIVE CIVILIZED TRIBES.

IN RE APPLICATION FOR ENROLLMENT, as a citizen of the Chickasaw Nation, of Odneal Rice , born on the 24" day of December , 190 2

Name of Father: O.E. Rice   a citizen of the Chickasaw Nation.
Name of Mother: Surena M Rice   a citizen of the Chickasaw Nation.

Post-Office: Norman, Okla Terr

AFFIDAVIT OF MOTHER.

UNITED STATES OF AMERICA,
~~INDIAN TERRITORY,~~
Territory of Oklahoma ~~District~~.
County of Cleveland

I, Surena M. Rice , on oath state that I am 26 years of age and a citizen by Blood , of the Chickasaw Nation; that I am the lawful wife of O.E. Rice , who is a citizen, by Intermarriage of the Chickasaw Nation; that a male child was born to me on 24" day of December , 190 2, that said child has been named Odneal Rice , and is now living.

Surena M Rice

WITNESSES TO MARK:
{ Laura *(Illegible)*
{ A McDaniel

Subscribed and sworn to before me this 24" day of September , 1903

H.P. Doughty
Notary Public.

My commission expires July 16" 1906.

Applications for Enrollment of Chickasaw Newborn
Act of 1905   Volume I

AFFIDAVIT OF ATTENDING PHYSICIAN OR MID-WIFE.

UNITED STATES OF AMERICA,
~~INDIAN TERRITORY,~~
Territory of Oklahoma ~~District~~.
County of Cleveland

I, Mary A Williams , a midwife , on oath state that I attended on Mrs. Surena M Rice , wife of O.E. Rice on the 24" day of December , 1902; that there was born to her on said date a male child; that said child is now living and is said to have been named Odneal Rice

Mary A Williams

WITNESSES TO MARK:
{ Laura *(Illegible)*
{ A McDaniel

Subscribed and sworn to before me this 24" day of September , 1903

H.P. Doughty
Notary Public.

My commission expires July 16" 1906.

BIRTH AFFIDAVIT.

DEPARTMENT OF THE INTERIOR.
COMMISSION TO THE FIVE CIVILIZED TRIBES.

IN RE APPLICATION FOR ENROLLMENT, as a citizen of the Chickasaw Nation, of Odneal Rice , born on the 24 day of December , 1902

Name of Father: O. E. Rice   a citizen of the Chickasaw Nation.
Name of Mother: Surena M Rice   a citizen of the Chickasaw Nation.

Postoffice   Norman Okla Ter

AFFIDAVIT OF MOTHER.

UNITED STATES OF AMERICA, Indian Territory,
.... DISTRICT.

I, Surena M Rice , on oath state that I am............. years of age and a citizen by Blood , of the Chickasaw Nation; that I am the lawful wife of O. E. Rice , who is a citizen, by Intermarriage of the Chickasaw Nation; that a male child was born to me on 24 day of December , 1902; that said child has been named Odneal Rice , and was living March 4, 1905.

Surena Rice

104

Applications for Enrollment of Chickasaw Newborn
Act of 1905 Volume I

Witnesses To Mark:
{ James Potoch

    Subscribed and sworn to before me this 30th day of May , 1905

                          Dorant Carter
                          Notary Public.

AFFIDAVIT OF ATTENDING PHYSICIAN OR MID-WIFE.

UNITED STATES OF AMERICA, Indian Territory,
Hickory County Missouri DISTRICT.

    I, Mary A Williams , a ...., on oath state that I attended on Mrs. Surena M Rice , wife of O. E. Rice on the 24" day of December , 1902; that there was born to her on said date a male child; that said child was living March 4, 1905, and is said to have been named Odneal Rice

                          Mary A Williams
Witnesses To Mark:
{

    Subscribed and sworn to before me this 17 day of June , 1905

                          Henry P Leggett
My Com Expires Feby 12-1908   Notary Public.

                              9-N.B. 24.

            Muskogee, Indian Territory, May 10, 1905.

O.F[sic]. Rice,
    Norman, Oklahoma Territory.

Dear Sir:

    There is enclosed you herewith for execution application for the enrollment of your infant child, Odneal Rice, born December 24, 1902.

    The affidavits heretofore filed with the Commission show the child was living on September 24, 1903. It is necessary, for the child to be enrolled, that he was living on March 4, 1905.

Applications for Enrollment of Chickasaw Newborn
Act of 1905   Volume I

In having these affidavits executed care should be exercised to see that all names are written in full, as they appear in the body of the affidavit, and in the event that either of the persons signing the affidavit are unable to write, signatures by mark must be attested by two witnesses. Each affidavit must be executed before a Notary Public and the notarial seal and signature of the officer must be attached to each separate affidavit.

Respectfully,

Chairman.

V. 10/3.

9-NB-24.

Muskogee, Indian Territory, June 6, 1905.

O. E. Rice,
    Norman, Oklahoma Territory.

Dear Sir:

    Receipt is hereby acknowledged of the affidavit of Surena Rice to the birth of your infant child, Odneal Rice, born December 24, 1902, which is returned herewith for the reason that the affidavit of the attending physician or midwife, attached thereto, was returned unexecuted.

    The affidavit of Mary A. Williams, the midwife, heretofore filed in this office shows that the applicant was living on September 24, 1903. It is necessary, for the child to be enrolled, that he was living on March 4, 1905. You will, therefore, please secure the midwife's affidavit to this effect by using the enclosed blank; but if she is dead or you are unable to secure her affidavit it will be necessary that you secure the affidavits of two persons, who are disinterested and not related to the applicant, who have actual knowledge of the facts that the child was born, the date of his birth, that he was living on March 4, 1905, and that Surena Rice is his mother.

    In having this affidavit executed care should be exercised to see that all the names are written in full, as they appear in the body of the affidavit, and in the event that the person signing the affidavit is unable to write, signatures by mark must be attested by two witnesses. The affidavit must be executed before a Notary Public and the notarial seal and signature of the officer must be attached thereto.

Respectfully,

VR. 6-1.

Applications for Enrollment of Chickasaw Newborn
Act of 1905   Volume I

Chickasaw N B 24

Muskogee, Indian Territory, June 26, 1905.

O. E. Rice,
    Norman, Oklahoma.

Dear Sir:

    Receipt is hereby acknowledged of the affidavits of Surena Rice and Mary A. Williams to the birth of Odneal Rice, son of O. E. and Surena Rice, December 24, 1902, and the same have been filed with our records in the matter of the enrollment of said child.

        Respectfully,

            Chairman.

Chic. N.B - 25
    (Ella Greenwood
    Born May 14, 1904)

BIRTH AFFIDAVIT.

    IN RE-APPLICATION FOR ENROLLMENT, as a citizen of the   Chickasaw   Nation, of Ella Greenwood , born on the 14 day of May , 190 4

Name of Father: Hogan Greenwood   a citizen of the Chickasaw Nation.
Name of Mother: Mahala Greenwood   a citizen of the Chickasaw Nation.

        Postoffice   Connerville I.T.

        AFFIDAVIT OF MOTHER.

UNITED STATES OF AMERICA, INDIAN TERRITORY,
    Southern   District.

    I, Mahala Greenwood , on oath state that I am 37 years of age and a citizen by Blood , of the Chickasaw Nation; that I am the lawful wife of Hogan Greenwood , who is a citizen, by Blood of the Chickasaw Nation; that a Female child was born to me on 14 day of May , 1904 , that said child has been named Ella Greenwood , and is now living.

Applications for Enrollment of Chickasaw Newborn
Act of 1905 Volume I

                                      her
                              Mahala x Greenwood
Witnesses To Mark: mark
{ Jim Frazier
{ R.L. Bradford

    Subscribed and sworn to before me this 24 day of Feb , 1905.

                                  M.S. Bradford
                                  Notary Public.

AFFIDAVIT OF ATTENDING PHYSICIAN OR MID-WIFE.

UNITED STATES OF AMERICA, INDIAN TERRITORY, }
Southern   District. }

    I, Seely Owens , a Midwife , on oath state that I attended on Mrs. Mahala Greenwood , wife of Hogan Greenwood on the 14 day of May , 190 4; that there was born to her on said date a Female child; that said child is now living and is said to have been named Ella Greenwood

                                    her
                              Seely x Owens
Witnesses To Mark: mark
{ Jim Frazier
{ R.L. Bradford

    Subscribed and sworn to before me this 24 day of Feb , 1905.

                                  M.S. Bradford
                                  Notary Public.

BIRTH AFFIDAVIT.

DEPARTMENT OF THE INTERIOR.
COMMISSION TO THE FIVE CIVILIZED TRIBES.

    IN RE APPLICATION FOR ENROLLMENT, as a citizen of the Chickasaw Nation, of Eller[sic] Greenwood , born on the 14 day of May , 1904

Name of Father: Hogan Greenwood   a citizen of the Chickasaw Nation.
Name of Mother: Mahaly[sic] Greenwood   a citizen of the Chickasaw Nation.

                       Postoffice Connerville, Ind. Ter.

Applications for Enrollment of Chickasaw Newborn
Act of 1905 Volume I

AFFIDAVIT OF MOTHER.

UNITED STATES OF AMERICA, Indian Territory, }
Southern   DISTRICT.

I, Mahaly Greenwood , on oath state that I am 37 years of age and a citizen by Blood , of the Chickasaw Nation; that I am the lawful wife of Hogan Greenwood , who is a citizen, by Blood of the Chickasaw Nation; that a female child was born to me on 14 day of May , 1904; that said child has been named Eller Greenwood , and was living March 4, 1905.

            her
        Mahaly x Greenwood
Witnesses To Mark: mark
{ J.W. Webb
 H.M. Stamper

Subscribed and sworn to before me this 21st day of April , 1905

        M.S. Bradford
         Notary Public.

AFFIDAVIT OF ATTENDING PHYSICIAN OR MID-WIFE.

UNITED STATES OF AMERICA, Indian Territory, }
Southern   DISTRICT.

I, Sarah Owens , a Mid Wife , on oath state that I attended on Mrs. Mahaly Greenwood , wife of Hogan Greenwood on the 14 day of May , 1904; that there was born to her on said date a female child; that said child was living March 4, 1905, and is said to have been named Eller Greenwood

          her
       Sarah x Owens
Witnesses To Mark: mark
{ J.W. Webb
 H.M. Stamper

Subscribed and sworn to before me this 21st day of April , 1905

        M.S. Bradford
         Notary Public.

Applications for Enrollment of Chickasaw Newborn
Act of 1905   Volume I

BIRTH AFFIDAVIT.

DEPARTMENT OF THE INTERIOR.
COMMISSION TO THE FIVE CIVILIZED TRIBES.

IN RE APPLICATION FOR ENROLLMENT, as a citizen of the Chickasaw Nation, of Ella Greenwood, born on the 14th day of May, 1904

Name of Father: Hogan Greenwood   a citizen of the Chickasaw Nation.
Name of Mother: Mahali[sic] Greenwood   a citizen of the Chickasaw Nation.

Postoffice   Connerville, Ind. Ter.

AFFIDAVIT OF MOTHER.

UNITED STATES OF AMERICA, Indian Territory,
Southern   DISTRICT.

I, Mahali Greenwood, on oath state that I am 37 years of age and a citizen by blood, of the Chickasaw Nation; that I am the lawful wife of Hogan Greenwood, who is a citizen, by blood of the Chickasaw Nation; that a female child was born to me on 14th day of May, 1904; that said child has been named Eller Greenwood, and was living March 4, 1905.

         her
      Mahali x Greenwood
Witnesses To Mark: mark
 { W.T. Ferris
 { C J Bradford

Subscribed and sworn to before me this 18 day of July, 1905

      M.S. Bradford
      Notary Public.

AFFIDAVIT OF ATTENDING PHYSICIAN OR MID-WIFE.

UNITED STATES OF AMERICA, Indian Territory,
Southern   DISTRICT.

I, Sarah Owens, a Mid Wife, on oath state that I attended on Mrs. Mahali Greenwood, wife of Hogan Greenwood on the 14th day of May, 1904; that there was born to her on said date a female child; that said child was living March 4, 1905, and is said to have been named Ella Greenwood

       her
     Sarah x Owens
      mark

Applications for Enrollment of Chickasaw Newborn
Act of 1905 Volume I

Witnesses To Mark:
{ W.T. Ferris
C J Bradford

    Subscribed and sworn to before me this 18 day of July , 1905

                            M.S. Bradford
                            Notary Public.

                            7-5
                            9-235

         Muskogee, Indian Territory, March 27, 1905.

T. L. Wright,
    Attorney at Law,
        Tishomingo, Indian Territory.

Dear Sir:

    Receipt is hereby acknowledged of your letter of March 21, 1905, enclosing affidavits of Mahala Greenwood and Seely Owens to the birth of Ellen[sic] Greenwood daughter of Hogan and Mahaly Greenwood May 14, 1904; also the affidavits of Malinda Wolfe and Cicen Carney to the birth of Reuben Wright son of Esau S. and Malinda Wright, March 18, 1904, and the same have been filed with our records as an application for the enrollment of said children.

    Replying to that portion of your letter in which you ask to be advised if these applications are sufficient proof for the enrollment of thes[sic] two children and invite attention particularly to the application of Reuben Wright whose father through a full blood Indian has never been enrolled, you are advised that the affidavits above f

(End of letter.)

                          9-N.B. 25.

         Muskogee, Indian Territory, May Lo[sic], 1905.

Homan[sic] Greenwood,
    Connerville, Indian Territory.

Dear Sir:

    There is enclosed you herewith for execution application for the enrollment of your infant child, Ella Greenwood, born May 14, 1904.

Applications for Enrollment of Chickasaw Newborn
Act of 1905   Volume I

The affidavits heretofore filed with the Commission show the child was living on February 24, 1905. It is necessary, for the child to be enrolled, that she was living on March 4, 1905.

In having these affidavits executed care should be exercised to see that all names are written in full, as they appear in the body of the affidavit, and in the event that either of the persons signing the affidavit are unable to write, signatures by mark must be attested by two witnesses. Each affidavit must be executed before a Notary Public and the notarial seal and signature of the officer must be attached to each separate affidavit.

Respectfully,

Chairman.

V. 10/2.

9-N.B. 25.

Muskogee, Indian Territory, May 29, 1905.

Hogan Greenwood,
   Connerville, Indian Territory.

Dear Sir:

Receipt is hereby acknowledged of the affidavits of Mahaley[sic] Greenwood and Sarah Owens to the birth of Eller Greenwood, daughter of Hogan and Mahaley Greenwood, May 14, 1904, and the same have been filed with our records in the matter of the enrollment of said child.

Respectfully,

Chairman.

9-NB-25.

Muskogee, Indian Territory, July 3, 1905.

Hogen[sic] Greenwood,
   Connerville, Indian Territory.

Dear Sir:

There is enclosed herewith for execution application the enrollment of your infant child, born May 14, 1904. In the affidavits of February 24, 1905, heretofore filed in this office the name of your child is given as Ella Greenwood, while in the affidavits of April 21, 1905 it appears as Eller Greenwood.

Applications for Enrollment of Chickasaw Newborn
Act of 1905 Volume I

In the enclosed application the name of the applicant is left blank. You will please insert the correct name, and when the affidavits are properly executed return them to this office. In having these affidavits executed care should be exercised to see that all names are written in full, as they appear in the body of the affidavit, and in the event either person signing the affidavits is unable to write, signature by mark must be attested by two witnesses. Each affidavit must be executed before a Notary Public and the notarial seal and signature must be attached to each separate affidavit.

You are requested to give this matter your immediate attention as no further action can be taken until these affidavits are filed in this office.

Respectfully,

Chairman.

DeB--2/3

9-NB-25

Muskogee, Indian Territory, July 25, 1905.

Hogan Greenwood,
    Connersville, Indian Territory.

Dear Sir:

Receipt is hereby acknowledged of the affidavits of Maliah[sic] Greenwood and Sarah Owens to the birth of Ella Greenwood, daughter of Hogan and Mahali Greenwood, May 14, 1904, and the same have been filed with the records of this office in the matter of the enrollment of said child.

Respectfully,

Commissioner.

Chic. N.B - 26
    (Allice Victoria Filmore
    Born October 19, 1903)

Applications for Enrollment of Chickasaw Newborn
Act of 1905   Volume I

Certificate of Record of Marriage

United States of America, ⎫
    Indian Territory, ⎬ sct.
    Southern District. ⎭

DEPARTMENT OF THE INTERIOR,
COMMISSION TO THE FIVE CIVILIZED TRIBES.
F I L E D
MAY 24 1905

I, C. M. CAMPBELL, Clerk of the United States Court, in the Territory and District aforesaid DO HEREBY CERTIFY, that the License for and Certificate of Marriage of

MR   H.C. Filmore   and
M   Minnie D. Gooden

F I L E D
JAN 3 1903 8 AM
C. M. CAMPBELL, Clerk.
Southern Dist. Ind. Ter.

were filed in my office in said Territory and District the   3"   day of   January A.D., 190 3 and duly recorded in Book   G of Marriage Record, Page   70

WITNESS my hand and Seal of said Court, at Ardmore, this   3"   day of January   A.D. 190 3

C. M. Campbell
CLERK.

Return this License to the United States Clerk at Ardmore, that it may be recorded, when it will be mailed to the proper address.

Ardmoreite Steam Print.

 MARRIAGE LICENSE

N°.

UNITED STATES OF AMERICA, ⎫
  INDIAN TERRITORY, ⎬ ss:
  SOUTHERN DISTRICT. ⎭

To Any Person Authorized by Law to Solemnize Marriage, Greeting:

𝔜ou are hereby commanded to solemnize the Rite and publish the Banns of Matrimony between Mr.   H.C. Filmore   of   Roff   in the Indian Territory, aged   22   years, and

Applications for Enrollment of Chickasaw Newborn
Act of 1905   Volume I

Miss   Minnie D Gooden   of   Hart   in the Indian Territory, aged   17   years, according to law; and do you officially sign and return this License to the parties therein named.

Witness my hand and official Seal, this   18   day of   Dec   A. D. 1902

C.M. Campbell
Clerk of the United States Court.
By: John S. Hammond

| Certificate of Marriage. |

UNITED STATES OF AMERICA,
INDIAN TERRITORY,   } ss:
SOUTHERN DISTRICT.

I, T.O. Leece a minister of the gospel do hereby certify that on the   21   day of   Dec   , A. D. 190 2 , I did duly according to law, as commanded in the foregoing License, solemnize the Rite and publish the Banns of Matrimony between the parties therein named.

Witness my hand this   21   day of   December   A. D. 190 2

My credentials are recorded in the office of the Clerk of the United States Court, Indian Territory, Southern District, at Ardmore, Book A, Page 2526

(NOTE-The person officiating should fill in the spaces for book and page and sign here.)

T.O. Leece
a   musster[sic] of the gospel

NOTE (a)-The License and Certificate of Marriage must be returned to the office of the Clerk of the United States Court in the Indian Territory, at Ardmore, within sixty days from the date thereof, or the party to whom the License was issued will be liable in the amount of One Hundred Dollars ($100).

NOTE (b)-No person is authorized to perform the Marriage Ceremony in the Southern District unless the proper credentials have first been recorded in the Clerk's office.

BIRTH AFFIDAVIT.

DEPARTMENT OF THE INTERIOR.

Applications for Enrollment of Chickasaw Newborn
Act of 1905   Volume I

COMMISSION TO THE FIVE CIVILIZED TRIBES.

IN RE APPLICATION FOR ENROLLMENT, as a citizen of the   Chickasaw   Nation, of   Allice Victora[sic] Filmore   , born on the   19   day of   Oct   , 1903

Name of Father: H. C. Filmore   a citizen of the   Chickasaw Nation.
Name of Mother: Minnie L. Filmore   a citizen of the United States Nation.

Postoffice   Hart Ind Terr

AFFIDAVIT OF MOTHER.

UNITED STATES OF AMERICA, Indian Territory, ⎱
   Southern   DISTRICT. ⎰

I,   Minnie L. Filmore   , on oath state that I am   Nineteen   years of age and a citizen by   United States   , ~~of the~~ .... Nation; that I am the lawful wife of   Henry C. Filmore   , who is a citizen, by   Blood   of the   Chickasaw   Nation; that a   Female   child was born to me on   19   day of   Oct   , 1903, that said child has been named   Allice Victoria Filmore   , and is now living.

                                        Minnie L. Filmore
Witnesses To Mark:
 ⎰ Kittie Pirtle
 ⎱ Alice Lindsay

Subscribed and sworn to before me this 16 day of March , 1905.

                                        J. J. Hart
                                        Notary Public.

AFFIDAVIT OF ATTENDING PHYSICIAN OR MID-WIFE.

UNITED STATES OF AMERICA, Indian Territory, ⎱
   Southern   DISTRICT. ⎰

I,   C. E. Logan   , a   Physician   , on oath state that I attended on Mrs. Minnie L. Filmore , wife of Henry C Filmore   on the 19 day of Oct. , 1903; that there was born to her on said date a   Female   child; that said child is now living and is said to have been named Allice Victoria Filmore

                                        C.E. Logan
Witnesses To Mark:
 ⎰

Applications for Enrollment of Chickasaw Newborn
Act of 1905 Volume I

Subscribed and sworn to before me this 21 day of Mch , 1905.

(Name Illegible)
Notary Public.

Chickasaw 242.

Muskogee, Indian Territory, April 7, 1905.

H. C. Fillmore,
    Hart, Indian Territory.

Dear Sir:

    Receipt is hereby acknowledged of your letter of March 30, enclosing affidavits of Minnie L. Fillmore and C. E. Logan to the birth of Allice Victoria Fillmore, daughter of H. C. and Minnie L. Fillmore, October 19, 1903.

    You are requested to furnish this office your full given name and the names of your parents in order that you may be definitely identified upon the records of the Commission.

Respectfully,

Commissioner in Charge.

9-242.

Muskogee, Indian Territory, April 26, 1905.

Henry Filmore,
    Hart, Indian Territory.

Dear Sir:

    Receipt is hereby acknowledged of your letter of April 11, 1905, giving the names of your father and mother, and this information has enabled the Commission to identify you upon its records as a citizen by blood of the Chickasaw Nation.

    The affidavits heretofore forwarded to the birth of your child, Alice Victoria Gilmore, have been filed with our records as an application for the enrollment of said child.

Respectfully,

Chairman.

Applications for Enrollment of Chickasaw Newborn
Act of 1905   Volume I

9-N.B. 26.

Muskogee, Indian Territory, May 10, 1905.

H. C. Filmore,
    Hart, Indian Territory.

Dear Sir:

    In the matter of the application for the enrollment of your infant child, Allice Victora[sic] Filmore, born October 19, 1903, it is noted from the affidavits heretofore filed in this office that the applicant claims through you. In this event it will be neccessary[sic] for you to file with the Commission either the original or a certified copy of the license and certificate of your marriage to the applicant's mother, Minnie L. Filmore.

    Please give this matter your immediate attention.

Respectfully,

Chairman.

9-N.B. 26.

Muskogee, Indian Territory, May 25, 1905.

H. C. Filmore,
    Hart, Indian Territory.

Dear Sir:

    Receipt is hereby acknowledged of your letter of May 18, transmitting marriage license and certificate between H. C. Filmore and Minnie D. Gooden, which you offer in support of the application for the enrollment of your child, Allice Victoria Filmore, and the same have been filed with the record in this case.

Respectfully,

Chairman.

Applications for Enrollment of Chickasaw Newborn
Act of 1905   Volume I

9-NB-26.

Muskogee, Indian Territory, July 3, 1905.

Henry Filmore,
    Hart, Indian Territory.

Dear Sir:

    Referring to the application for the enrollment of your infant child, Allice Victoria Filmore, born October 19, 1903, in the affidavits and marriage license heretofore filed in this office, your name appears as Henry C. Filmore and H. C. Filmore, while it appears upon the records of this office as Henry Filmore.

    Before this case can be finally determined it will be necessary for you to file in this office an affidavit to the fact that these three names are of one and the same person and that you are that person.

                    Respectfully,

                                   Commissioner.

Hart, Ind. Ter. July 6, 1905.

Commission to the Five Civilized Tribes,

Gentlemen:

    I do hereby state that I am Henry Filmore and that to be my correct name, not knowing that it made any change before the Commission. I have signed it H.C. Filmore but as there are no Notary Public near I make this my volantary[sic] statement. Also I was before the Notary Public for the birth of my child Allice Victoria Filmore. I came to go before a Notary but he being absent from town I make this my statement. Let me hear at once.

                    Yours respectfully,

                          Henry Filmore.

Applications for Enrollment of Chickasaw Newborn
Act of 1905 Volume I

9-NB-26

Muskogee, Indian Territory, July 12, 1905.

Henry Filmore,
    Hart, Indian Territory.

Dear Sir:

    Receipt is hereby acknowledged of your letter of July 6, 1905, stating that your correct name is Henry Filmore but that sometimes you sign it H. C. Filmore; receipt is also acknowledged of your letter of July 8, enclosing affidavit to the effect that you are the Henry Filmore who is the father of Alice Victoria Filmore and the same has been filed with the record in this case.

    Respectfully,

Commissioner.

9-NB-26

Muskogee, Indian Territory, August 1, 1905.

Harry[sic] Filmore,
    Hart, Indian Territory.

Dear Sir:

    Receipt is hereby acknowledged of your letter of July 25, 1905, asking relative to the enrollment of your daughter Alice Victoria Filmore.

    In reply to your letter you are advised that the name of your child Alice Victoria Filmore has not yet been placed upon a schedule of citizens by blood of the Chickasaw Nation prepared for forwarding to the Secretary of the Interior but in event further evidence is necessary to enable this office to determine her right you will be duly advised.

    Respectfully,

Commissioner.

Applications for Enrollment of Chickasaw Newborn
Act of 1905 Volume I

9-NB 26

Muskogee, Indian Territory, September 7, 1905.

Henry Filmore,
    Hart, Indian Territory.

Dear Sir:

Receipt is hereby acknowledged of your letter of August 31st in reference to the enrollment of your minor child as a citizen of the Chickasaw Nation.

You are advised that on August 26, 1905, the Commissioner to the Five Civilized Tribes transmitted to the Secretary of the Interior for his approval, the schedule of newborn citizens by blood of the Chickasaw Nation, the name of your child, Allice Victoria Filmore appearing upon said schedule opposite number 520. When her enrollment has been approved by the Secretary of the Interior you will be advised thereof.

                Respectfully,

                            Acting Commissioner.

        Hart Ind Ter 7/7 - 05
        To the Commission to the Five Civilized Tribes
    This is to certify that I the under signed am the Henry Filmore that you have on Roll Father of the applicant child Allice Victoria Filmore
    Witness my hand at Hart State of I.T. this the 7 day of July 1905
                            Henry Filmore

Subscribed and sworn to before me this the 7 day of July 1905

                        J.J. Hart

Chic. N.B - 27
    (Floy Nelson
    Born January 23, 1905)
    (Doss Nelson
    Born December 15, 1902)

Applications for Enrollment of Chickasaw Newborn
Act of 1905 Volume I

BIRTH AFFIDAVIT.

DEPARTMENT OF THE INTERIOR.
COMMISSION TO THE FIVE CIVILIZED TRIBES.

IN RE APPLICATION FOR ENROLLMENT, as a citizen of the Chickasaw Nation, of Floy Nelson, born on the 23rd day of Jan, 1905

Name of Father: Columbus Nelson   a citizen of the Chickasaw Nation.
Name of Mother: Sudie Nelson   a citizen of the Chickasaw Nation.

Postoffice Chigley, I.T.

AFFIDAVIT OF MOTHER.

UNITED STATES OF AMERICA, Indian Territory, }
Southern   DISTRICT. }

I, Sudie Nelson, on oath state that I am 31 years of age and a citizen by Intermarriage, of the Chickasaw Nation; that I am the lawful wife of Columbus Nelson, who is a citizen, by blood of the Chickasaw Nation; that a male child was born to me on 23rd day of January, 1905; that said child has been named Floy Nelson, and was living March 4, 1905.

Sudie x Nelson

Witnesses To Mark:
{ J R Clemmons
{ CB McClusky

Subscribed and sworn to before me this 23rd day of March, 1905

W.N. Lewis
Notary Public.

AFFIDAVIT OF ATTENDING PHYSICIAN OR MID-WIFE.

UNITED STATES OF AMERICA, Indian Territory, }
Southern   DISTRICT. }

I, Annie Kelly, a midwife, on oath state that I attended on Mrs. Sudie Nelson, wife of Columbus Nelson on the 23rd day of Jan, 1905; that there was born to her on said date a male child; that said child was living March 4, 1905, and is said to have been named Floy Nelson

Annie x Kelly

Applications for Enrollment of Chickasaw Newborn
Act of 1905 Volume I

Witnesses To Mark:
- J R Clemmons
- CB McClusky

Subscribed and sworn to before me this 23rd day of March, 1905

W.N. Lewis
Notary Public.

BIRTH AFFIDAVIT.

DEPARTMENT OF THE INTERIOR.
COMMISSION TO THE FIVE CIVILIZED TRIBES.

IN RE APPLICATION FOR ENROLLMENT, as a citizen of the Chickasaw Nation, of Doss Nelson, born on the 15th day of Dec, 1902

Name of Father: Columbus Nelson   a citizen of the Chickasaw Nation.
Name of Mother: Sudie Nelson   a citizen of the Chickasaw Nation.

Postoffice   Chigley, I.T.

AFFIDAVIT OF MOTHER.

UNITED STATES OF AMERICA, Indian Territory,
Southern DISTRICT.

I, Sudie Nelson, on oath state that I am 31 years of age and a citizen by Intermarriage, of the Chickasaw Nation; that I am the lawful wife of Columbus Nelson, who is a citizen, by blood of the Chickasaw Nation; that a male child was born to me on 15th day of December, 1902; that said child has been named Doss Nelson, and was living March 4, 1905.

                 her
             Sudie x Nelson
Witnesses To Mark: mark
- J R Clemmons
- CB McClusky

Subscribed and sworn to before me this 23rd day of March, 1905

W.N. Lewis
Notary Public.

Applications for Enrollment of Chickasaw Newborn
Act of 1905 Volume I

AFFIDAVIT OF ATTENDING PHYSICIAN OR MID-WIFE.

UNITED STATES OF AMERICA, Indian Territory, }
Southern DISTRICT. }

I, Annie Kelly, a midwife, on oath state that I attended on Mrs. Sudie Nelson, wife of Columbus Nelson on the 15th day of Dec, 1902; that there was born to her on said date a male child; that said child was living March 4, 1905, and is said to have been named Doss Nelson

                                        her
                                  Annie x Kelly
Witnesses To Mark: mark
  { J R Clemmons
    CB McClasky

Subscribed and sworn to before me this 23rd day of March, 1905

                                W.N. Lewis
                                Notary Public.

Southern District,
Indian Territory.

On this the 17th, day of May, 1905, before me the undersigned authority within and for the Southern District of the Indian Territory, appeared in person Sudie Nelson who being by me first duly sworn deposes and says:-

That Sudie Nelson and Susie Nelson are one and the same person but that the correct name of affiant is Sudie Nelson and that she the said affiant is the wife of Columbus Nelson and the mother of Doss Nelson and Floy Nelson.

Also appeared Columbus Nelson and being by me duly sworn says that Sudie Nelson and Susie Nelson are one and the same person and that her correct name is Sudie Nelson and that the said Susie Nelson is his wife.

                                  her
Witnesses to mark   Sudie x Nelson
                                  mark
W.N. Lewis   his
                            Columbus x Nelson
Zach Cooper   mark

Subscribed and sworn to before me this the 17th day of May, 1905

                              W. N. Lewis
                              Notary Public.

Applications for Enrollment of Chickasaw Newborn
Act of 1905   Volume I

9-255

Muskogee, Indian Territory, March 30, 1905.

W. M[sic]. Lewis,
    Attorney at Law,
        Davis, Indian Territory.

Dear Sir:

    Receipt is hereby acknowledged of your letter of March 23, 1905, transmitting affidavits of Sudie Nelson and Annie Kelly to the birth of Doss Nelson and Floy Nelson, infant children of Columbus and Sudie Nelson, December 15, 1902 and January 23, 1905, and the same have been filed with our records as an application for the enrollment of said child.

        Respectfully,

                Chairman.

Chickasaw N B 27

Muskogee, Indian Territory, May 20, 1905.

Columbus Nelson,
    Chigley, Indian Territory.

Dear Sir:

    Receipt is hereby acknowledged of joint affidavit of Sudie and Columbus Nelson to the effect that Sudie and Susie Nelson are identical and the same has been filed with the record in the matter of the enrollment of your children, Doss and Floy Nelson as citizens by blood of the Chickasaw Nation.

        Respectfully,

                Chairman.

Applications for Enrollment of Chickasaw Newborn
Act of 1905   Volume I

9-N.B. 27.

Muskogee, Indian Territory, May 11, 1905.

Columbus Nelson,
    Chigley, Indian Territory.

Dear Sir:

Referring to the application for the enrollment of your infant children, Doss Nelson and Floy Nelson, born December 15, 1902, and January 23, 1905, respectively, it appears from the affidavits heretofore filed with the Commission that Sudie Nelson is your wife, while the records of this office show your wife to be Susie Nelson.

If Sudie Nelson and Susie Nelson is the same person you will please submit an affidavit to the effect. If they are not, it will be necessary for you to file in this office either the original or a certified copy of the license and certificate of your marriage to Sudie Nelson.

Respectfully,

Chairman.

Chic. N.B - 28
    (Earl Eugene Harrison
    Born March 5, 1904)

BIRTH AFFIDAVIT.

DEPARTMENT OF THE INTERIOR.
COMMISSION TO THE FIVE CIVILIZED TRIBES.

IN RE APPLICATION FOR ENROLLMENT, as a citizen of the Chickasaw Nation, of ~~Erle~~ Earl Eugene Harrison, born on the 5th day of March, 1904

Name of Father: D. P. Harrison   a citizen of the Chickasaw Nation.
Name of Mother: Mary Harrison   a citizen of the United States Nation.

Postoffice   Stonewall

Applications for Enrollment of Chickasaw Newborn
Act of 1905   Volume I

AFFIDAVIT OF MOTHER.

UNITED STATES OF AMERICA, Indian Territory, }
  Southern   DISTRICT.

    I, Mary Harrison, on oath state that I am 35 years of age and a citizen by Marriage, of the Chickasaw Nation; that I am the lawful wife of D.P. Harrison, who is a citizen, by blood of the Chickasaw Nation; that a male child was born to me on the 5th day of March, 1904, that said child has been named Earl Eugene Harrison, and is now living.

                                Mary Harrison

Witnesses To Mark:
{

    Subscribed and sworn to before me this 23rd day of Feb, 1904

                              W.F. Harrison
                              Notary Public.

AFFIDAVIT OF ATTENDING PHYSICIAN OR MID-WIFE.

UNITED STATES OF AMERICA, Indian Territory, }
  Southern   DISTRICT.

    I, Berthena Bradshaw, a midwife, on oath state that I attended on Mrs. Mary Harrison, wife of D P Harrison on the 5th day of March, 1904; that there was born to her on said date a .... child; that said child is now living and is said to have been named Earl Eugene Harrison

                            Berthena Bradshaw

Witnesses To Mark:
{

    Subscribed and sworn to before me this 23rd day of Feb, 1904

                              W.F. Harrison
                              Notary Public.

Applications for Enrollment of Chickasaw Newborn
Act of 1905 Volume I

BIRTH AFFIDAVIT.

DEPARTMENT OF THE INTERIOR.
COMMISSION TO THE FIVE CIVILIZED TRIBES.

IN RE APPLICATION FOR ENROLLMENT, as a citizen of the Chickasaw Nation, of Earle Eugene Harrison, born on the 5th day of March, 1904

Name of Father: Daniel Peyton Harrison   a citizen of the Chickasaw Nation.
Name of Mother: Mary Harrison   a citizen of the Intermarried Nation.

Postoffice   Stonewall IT

AFFIDAVIT OF MOTHER.

UNITED STATES OF AMERICA, Indian Territory, }
Southern   DISTRICT.

I, Mary Harrison, on oath state that I am 35 years of age and a citizen by intermarriage, of the Chickasaw Nation; that I am the lawful wife of Daniel Peyton Harrison, who is a citizen, by blood of the Chickasaw Nation; that a male child was born to me on 5th day of March, 1904; that said child has been named Earle Eugene Harrison, and was living March 4, 1905.

           Mary Harrison

Witnesses To Mark:
{

Subscribed and sworn to before me this 29th day of March, 1905

          A. B. Rogers
          Notary Public.

AFFIDAVIT OF ATTENDING PHYSICIAN OR MID-WIFE.

UNITED STATES OF AMERICA, Indian Territory, }
Southern   DISTRICT.

I, Berthena Bradshaw, a midwife, on oath state that I attended on Mrs. Mary Harrison, wife of Daniel Peyton Harrison on the 5th day of March, 1904; that there was born to her on said date a male child; that said child was living March 4, 1905, and is said to have been named Earle Eugene Harrison

          Berthena Bradshaw

Witnesses To Mark:
{

Applications for Enrollment of Chickasaw Newborn
Act of 1905   Volume I

Subscribed and sworn to before me this 29th day of March, 1905

A. B. Rogers
Notary Public.

Chickasaw 257.

Muskogee, Indian Territory, April 4, 1905.

Daniel Peyton Harrison,
Stonewall, Indian Territory.

Dear Sir:

Receipt is hereby acknowledged of the affidavits of Mary Harrison and Bertha[sic] Bradshaw to the birth of Earle Eugene Harrison, son of Daniel Peyton and Mary Harrison, March 5, 1904, and the same have been filed with our records as an application for the enrollment of said child.

Respectfully,

Commissioner in Charge.

Chic. N.B - 29
   (Lillian Lucile Saxon
   Born September 11, 1904)

BIRTH AFFIDAVIT.

DEPARTMENT OF THE INTERIOR.
COMMISSION TO THE FIVE CIVILIZED TRIBES.

IN RE APPLICATION FOR ENROLLMENT, as a citizen of the Chickasaw Nation, of Lillian Lucile Saxon, born on the 11 day of Sept, 1904

Name of Father: .... a citizen of the .... Nation.
Name of Mother: Laura Josephine Harrison   a citizen of the Chickasaw Nation.

Postoffice   Stonewall, I.T.

Applications for Enrollment of Chickasaw Newborn
Act of 1905   Volume I

AFFIDAVIT OF MOTHER.

UNITED STATES OF AMERICA, Indian Territory, }
.... DISTRICT.

  I, Laura Josephine Harrison , on oath state that I am 21 years of age and a citizen by Blood , of the Chickasaw Nation; that I am the lawful wife of ...., who is a citizen, by .... of the .... Nation; that a Female child was born to me on the 11th day of Sept , 1904, that said child has been named Lillian Lucile Saxon , and is now living.

                Laura Harrison

Witnesses To Mark:
{

  Subscribed and sworn to before me this 23 day of Feb , 1905.

                W.F. Harrison
                   Notary Public.

AFFIDAVIT OF ATTENDING PHYSICIAN OR MID-WIFE.

UNITED STATES OF AMERICA, Indian Territory, }
 Southern   DISTRICT.

  I, J. H. Blackburn , a Physician , on oath state that I attended on Mrs. Laura Harrison , wife of .... on the 11th day of Sept , 1904; that there was born to her on said date a Female child; that said child is now living and is said to have been named Lillian Lucile Saxon

                J.H. Blackburn

Witnesses To Mark:
{

  Subscribed and sworn to before me this 23rd day of Feb , 1905.

                W.F. Harrison
                   Notary Public.

Applications for Enrollment of Chickasaw Newborn
Act of 1905 Volume I

BIRTH AFFIDAVIT.

DEPARTMENT OF THE INTERIOR.
COMMISSION TO THE FIVE CIVILIZED TRIBES.

IN RE APPLICATION FOR ENROLLMENT, as a citizen of the Chickasaw Nation, of Lillie Harrison, born on the 11th day of September, 1904

Name of Father: .... a citizen of the .... Nation.
Name of Mother: Laura Harrison   a citizen of the Chickasaw Nation.

Postoffice   Stonewall, IT

AFFIDAVIT OF MOTHER.

UNITED STATES OF AMERICA, Indian Territory, } Southern DISTRICT.

I, Laura Harrison, on oath state that I am 21 years of age and a citizen by blood, of the Chickasaw Nation; that I am the lawful wife of ...., who is a citizen, by .... of the .... Nation; that a female child was born to me on the 11th day of September, 1904, that said child has been named Lillie Harrison, and is now living.

Laura Harrison

Witnesses To Mark:
{

Subscribed and sworn to before me this 29th day of March, 1905.

U. B. Rogers
Notary Public.

AFFIDAVIT OF ATTENDING PHYSICIAN OR MID-WIFE.

UNITED STATES OF AMERICA, Indian Territory, } Southern DISTRICT.

I, J. H. Blackburn, a Physician, on oath state that I attended on Mrs. Laura Harrison, wife of .... on the 11th day of September, 1904; that there was born to her on said date a female child; that said child is now living and is said to have been named Lillie Harrison

J.H. Blackburn

Witnesses To Mark:
{

Applications for Enrollment of Chickasaw Newborn
Act of 1905 Volume I

Subscribed and sworn to before me this 29th day of March , 1905.

                                        U. B. Rogers
                                        Notary Public.

                                                            Chickasaw 257.

                            Muskogee, Indian Territory, April 4, 1905.

Laura Harrison,
    Stonewall, Indian Territory.

Dear Madam:

    Receipt is hereby acknowledged of the affidavits of Laura Harrison and J. H. Blackburn to the birth of your daughter, Lillie Harrison, September 11, 1904, and the same have been filed with our records as an application for the enrollment of said child.

                                        Respectfully,

                                                   Commissioner in Charge.

Chic. N.B - 30
    (Vera Jemison
    Born December 2, 1900)

BIRTH AFFIDAVIT.

DEPARTMENT OF THE INTERIOR,
COMMISSION TO THE FIVE CIVILIZED TRIBES.

    IN RE *Application for Enrollment,* as a citizen of the   Chickasaw   Nation, of   Vera Jemison , born on the 2nd day of December , 1900

Name of Father: WP Jemison   a citizen of the   Chickasaw Nation.
Name of Mother: Eula E Jemison   a citizen of the   Chickasaw Nation.

                          Post-Office: Oconee I.T.

Applications for Enrollment of Chickasaw Newborn
Act of 1905 Volume I

AFFIDAVIT OF MOTHER.

UNITED STATES OF AMERICA, }
INDIAN TERRITORY.
Central   District.

I,   Eula E Jemison   , on oath state that I am   27   years of age and a citizen by   Blood   , of the Chickasaw Nation; that I am the lawful wife of   W P Jemison   , who is a citizen, by   Marriage   of the Chickasaw Nation; that a   female   child was born to me on 2nd day of   December   , 1900 , that said child has been named   Vera Jemison   , and is now living.

Eula E Jemison

WITNESSES TO MARK:
{ E R Harl
{ J Remison

Subscribed and sworn to before me this   11   day of   January   , 1901

W.B. Harl
NOTARY PUBLIC.

AFFIDAVIT OF ATTENDING PHYSICIAN OR MID-WIFE.

UNITED STATES OF AMERICA, }
INDIAN TERRITORY.
Central   District.

I,   T B Dodson   , a   M. D.   , on oath state that I attended on Mrs.   Eula E Jemison   , wife of   W P Jemison   on the 2nd day of   December   , 1900; that there was born to her on said date a   female   child; that said child is now living and is said to have been named   Vera Jemison

T.B. Dodson

WITNESSES TO MARK:
{ W A Patten
{ H.H. Redwine

Subscribed and sworn to before me this   8   day of   January   , 1901

W B Harl
NOTARY PUBLIC.

Applications for Enrollment of Chickasaw Newborn
Act of 1905   Volume I

9-266

Muskogee, Indian Territory, March 23, 1905.

William P. Jemison,
    Ocomee[sic], Indian Territory.

Dear Sir:

    Receipt is hereby acknowledged of the affidavits of Eula E. Jemison and J. D. Enfield[sic] to the birth of May[sic] Jemison, daughter of William P. and Eula E. Jemison, May 9, 1904, and the same have been filed with our records as an application for the enrollment of said child.

    Respectfully,

Chairman.

Chic. N.B - 31
    (James J. Statler
    Born February 2, 1904)

BIRTH AFFIDAVIT.   #127

DEPARTMENT OF THE INTERIOR,
COMMISSION TO THE FIVE CIVILIZED TRIBES.

    IN RE *Application for Enrollment,* as a citizen of the Chickasaw Nation, of James J Statler, born on the 2 day of Feby, 1904

Name of Father: Gale Statler   a citizen of the Chickasaw Nation.
Name of Mother: Dacie Statler   a citizen of the Chickasaw Nation.

    Post-Office: Jesse I.T.

Applications for Enrollment of Chickasaw Newborn
Act of 1905 Volume I

AFFIDAVIT OF MOTHER.

UNITED STATES OF AMERICA,
INDIAN TERRITORY.
Southern District.

I, Dacie Statler, on oath state that I am 25 years of age and a citizen by blood, of the Chickasaw Nation; that I am the lawful wife of Gale Statler, who is a citizen, by intermarriage of the Chickasaw Nation; that a male child was born to me on 2nd day of Feby, 1904, that said child has been named James Johnson Statler, and is now living.

Dacie Statler

WITNESSES TO MARK:

{

Subscribed and sworn to before me this 22nd day of Feby, 1905.

My commission expires
Jany 1st 1906

Price Statler
NOTARY PUBLIC.

AFFIDAVIT OF ATTENDING PHYSICIAN OR MID-WIFE.

UNITED STATES OF AMERICA,
INDIAN TERRITORY.
Southern District.

I, A.H. Hathaway, a Physician, on oath state that I attended on Mrs. Dacie Statler, wife of Gale Statler on the 2nd day of Feby, 1904; that there was born to her on said date a male child; that said child is now living and is said to have been named James J Statler *To the best of my knowledge now living*

A.H. Hathaway

WITNESSES TO MARK:
{ *(Name Illegible)*
  J.W. Stewart

Subscribed and sworn to before me this 17 day of Oct, 1904[sic]

R.K. Hathaway
NOTARY PUBLIC.

Applications for Enrollment of Chickasaw Newborn
Act of 1905 Volume I

BIRTH AFFIDAVIT.

DEPARTMENT OF THE INTERIOR.
COMMISSION TO THE FIVE CIVILIZED TRIBES.

IN RE APPLICATION FOR ENROLLMENT, as a citizen of the Chickasaw Nation, of James J Statler, born on the 2nd day of February, 1904

Name of Father: Gale Statler   a citizen of the Chickasaw Nation.
Name of Mother: Dacie Statler   a citizen of the Chickasaw Nation.

Postoffice   Jesse, I.T.

AFFIDAVIT OF MOTHER.

UNITED STATES OF AMERICA, Indian Territory, }
Southern   DISTRICT.

I, Dacie Statler, on oath state that I am 25 years of age and a citizen by blood, of the Chickasaw Nation; that I am the lawful wife of Gale Statler, who is a citizen, by intermarriage of the Chickasaw Nation; that a male child was born to me on 2" day of February, 1904; that said child has been named James J Statler, and was living March 4, 1905.

                               Dacie Statler

Witnesses To Mark:
{

Subscribed and sworn to before me this 15th day of May, 1905

                               Price Statler
                               Notary Public.

AFFIDAVIT OF ATTENDING PHYSICIAN OR MID-WIFE.

UNITED STATES OF AMERICA, Indian Territory, }
Southern   DISTRICT.

I, A.H. Hathaway, a Physician, on oath state that I attended on Mrs. Dacie Statler, wife of Gale Statler on the 2nd day of February, 1904; that there was born to her on said date a male child; that said child was living March 4, 1905, and is said to have been named James J Statler

                               A.H. Hathaway

Witnesses To Mark:
{

Applications for Enrollment of Chickasaw Newborn
Act of 1905   Volume I

Subscribed and sworn to before me this 17 day of May, 1905

R. K. Hathaway
Notary Public.

9-N.B. 31.

Muskogee, Indian Territory, May 10, 1905.

Gale Statler,
    Jesse, Indian Territory.

Dear Sir:

    There is enclosed you herewith for execution application for the enrollment of your infant child, James J. Statler, born February 2, 1904.

    The affidavits heretofore filed with the Commission show the child was living on February 22, 1905. It is necessary, for the child to be enrolled, that he was living on March 4, 1905.

    In having these affidavits executed care should be exercised to see that all names are written in full, as they appear in the body of the affidavit, and in the event that either of the persons signing the affidavit are unable to write, signatures by mark must be attested by two witnesses. Each affidavit must be executed before a Notary Public and the notarial seal and signature of the officer must be attached to each separate affidavit.

Respectfully,

Chairman.

V. 10/4.

9-N.B. 31

Muskogee, Indian Territory, June 2, 1905.

Gale Statler,
    Jesse, Indian Territory.

Dear Sir:

    Receipt is hereby acknowledged of the affidavits of Davie Statler and A. H. Hathaway to the birth of James J. Statler, son of Gale and Davie Statler, February 2, 1904, and the same have been filed with our records in the matter of the enrollment of said child.

Applications for Enrollment of Chickasaw Newborn
Act of 1905   Volume I

Respectfully,

Commissioner in Charge.

Chic. N.B - 31
    (Sallie Carney
    Born November 10, 1902)
    (Sarah Carney
    Born February 20, 1905)

BIRTH AFFIDAVIT.

Department of the Interior,
COMMISSION TO THE FIVE CIVILIZED TRIBES.

IN RE APPLICATION FOR ENROLLMENT, as a citizen of the Chickasaw Nation, of Sallie Carney, born on the 10 day of November, 190 2

Name of Father: Burney Carney   a citizen of the Chickasaw Nation.
Name of Mother: Josephine Carney   a citizen of the Chickasaw Nation.

Post-Office: Stonewall, I.T.

AFFIDAVIT OF MOTHER.

UNITED STATES OF AMERICA,
   INDIAN TERRITORY,
  Southern   District.

I, Josephine Carney, on oath state that I am 22 years of age and a citizen by blood, of the Chickasaw Nation; that I am the lawful wife of Burney Carney, who is a citizen, by blood of the Chickasaw Nation; that a female child was born to me on 10 day of November, 190 2, that said child has been named Sallie Carney, and is now living.

                                          her
                             Josephine x Carney
WITNESSES TO MARK: mark
  { Zeno McCurtain
    A.H. Hayes

Applications for Enrollment of Chickasaw Newborn
Act of 1905 Volume I

Subscribed and sworn to before me this 17th day of December , 1902

Zeno McCurtain
Notary Public.

AFFIDAVIT OF ATTENDING PHYSICIAN OR MID-WIFE.

UNITED STATES OF AMERICA, ⎫
   INDIAN TERRITORY,   ⎬
 Southern   District. ⎭

   I, Lizzie Panacha , a Physician , on oath state that I attended on Mrs. Josephine Carney , wife of Burney Carney on the 10 day of November , 190 2; that there was born to her on said date a female child; that said child is now living and is said to have been named Sallie Carney

                                      her
                            Lizzie x Panacha
WITNESSES TO MARK: mark
 ⎰ A.H. Hayes
 ⎱ Zeno McCurtain

Subscribed and sworn to before me this 17th day of December , 1902

Zeno McCurtain
Notary Public.

BIRTH AFFIDAVIT.

DEPARTMENT OF THE INTERIOR.
COMMISSION TO THE FIVE CIVILIZED TRIBES.

                                                      Chicosow[sic]
   IN RE APPLICATION FOR ENROLLMENT, as a citizen of the   ~~Sallie Carney~~ Nation, of Sallie Carney , born on the 10 day of Sept[sic] , 1902

Name of Father: Burney Carney   a citizen of the Chicosow Nation.
Name of Mother: Josephine   a citizen of the Chicosow Nation.

                          Postoffice   Connerville I.T.

Applications for Enrollment of Chickasaw Newborn
Act of 1905   Volume I

AFFIDAVIT OF MOTHER.

UNITED STATES OF AMERICA, Indian Territory, ⎫
   Sou   DISTRICT. ⎭

    I, Josephine Carney , on oath state that I am Twenty five years of age and a citizen by blood , of the Chicosow Nation; that I am the lawful wife of Burney Carney , who is a citizen, by blood of the Chicosow Nation; that a Female child was born to me on 10th day of ~~Sept~~ *November* , 1902, that said child has been named Sallie , and is now living.

                                                    her
                                     Josephine x Carney
Witnesses To Mark: mark
  ⎰ B.F. Byrd
  ⎱ W H Clark

    Subscribed and sworn to before me this 3rd day of Jan , 1905.

                                       W.H. Burdeshaw
                                          Notary Public.

AFFIDAVIT OF ATTENDING PHYSICIAN OR MID-WIFE.

UNITED STATES OF AMERICA, Indian Territory, ⎫
   Sou   DISTRICT. ⎭

    I, Sonelia[sic] Thom , a midwife , on oath state that I attended on Mrs. Josephine Carney , wife of Burney Carney on the 10 day of ~~Sept~~ *November* 1902 , 1......; that there was born to her on said date a Female child; that said child is now living and is said to have been named Sallie Carney

                                                    her
                                     Salena x Thom
Witnesses To Mark: mark
  ⎰ B.F. Byrd
  ⎱ W H Clark

    Subscribed and sworn to before me this 3rd day of Jan , 1905.

                                       W.H. Burdeshaw
                                          Notary Public.

Applications for Enrollment of Chickasaw Newborn
Act of 1905 Volume I

BIRTH AFFIDAVIT.

DEPARTMENT OF THE INTERIOR.
COMMISSION TO THE FIVE CIVILIZED TRIBES.

IN RE APPLICATION FOR ENROLLMENT, as a citizen of the Chickasaw Nation, of Sallie Carney, born on the 10 day of Nov, 1902

Name of Father: Burney Carney   a citizen of the Chickasaw Nation.
Name of Mother: Josephine Carney   a citizen of the Chickasaw Nation.

Postoffice   Pontotoc I.T.

AFFIDAVIT OF MOTHER.

UNITED STATES OF AMERICA, Indian Territory, }
Southern DISTRICT.

I, Josephine Carney, on oath state that I am 25 years of age and a citizen by Blood, of the Chickasaw Nation; that I am the lawful wife of Burney Carney, who is a citizen, by Blood of the Chickasaw Nation; that a female child was born to me on 10 day of Nov, 1902; that said child has been named Sallie Carney, and was living March 4, 1905.

                her
         Josephine x Carney
Witnesses To Mark: mark
{ G.W. Burris
  Marcum Dulin

Subscribed and sworn to before me this 12 day of April, 1905

         M.S. Bradford
          Notary Public.

AFFIDAVIT OF ATTENDING PHYSICIAN OR MID-WIFE.

UNITED STATES OF AMERICA, Indian Territory, }
Southern DISTRICT.

I, Selina Thom, a Midwife, on oath state that I attended on Mrs. Josephine Carney, wife of Burney Carney on the 10 day of Nov, 1902; that there was born to her on said date a .... child; that said child was living March 4, 1905, and is said to have been named Sallie Carney

              her
       Selina x Thom
          mark

Applications for Enrollment of Chickasaw Newborn
Act of 1905   Volume I

Witnesses To Mark:
{ J.L. Boatright
{ C.M. Bradford

Subscribed and sworn to before me this 12 day of   April   , 1905

M.S. Bradford
Notary Public.

BIRTH AFFIDAVIT.

DEPARTMENT OF THE INTERIOR.
COMMISSION TO THE FIVE CIVILIZED TRIBES.

IN RE APPLICATION FOR ENROLLMENT, as a citizen of the   Chickasaw   Nation, of   Sarah Carney   , born on the   20th day of   Feb   , 1905

Name of Father: Burney Carney   a citizen of the Chickasaw Nation.
Name of Mother: Josephine Carney   a citizen of the Chickasaw Nation.

Postoffice   Connerville I.T.

AFFIDAVIT OF MOTHER.

UNITED STATES OF AMERICA, Indian Territory, }
      Southern   DISTRICT.   }

I, Josephine Carney , on oath state that I am 25 years of age and a citizen by   Blood   , of the   Chickasaw   Nation; that I am the lawful wife of Burney Carney , who is a citizen, by Blood   of the   Chickasaw   Nation; that a Female child was born to me on 20th day of February , 1905; that said child has been named   Sarah Carney , and was living March 4, 1905.

                                       her
                              Josephine x Carney
Witnesses To Mark: mark
{ Edmon McCurtain
{ J.L. Boatright

Subscribed and sworn to before me this 1st day of   April   , 1905

M.S. Bradford
Notary Public.

Applications for Enrollment of Chickasaw Newborn
Act of 1905 Volume I

AFFIDAVIT OF ATTENDING PHYSICIAN OR MID-WIFE.

UNITED STATES OF AMERICA, Indian Territory,
Southern   DISTRICT.

I, Lizia Carney, a Mid Wife, on oath state that I attended on Mrs. Josephine Carney, wife of Burney Carney on the 20th day of February, 1905; that there was born to her on said date a Female child; that said child was living March 4, 1905, and is said to have been named Sarah Carney

her
Lizia x Carney
mark

Witnesses To Mark:
   Edmon McCurtain
   J.L. Boatright

Subscribed and sworn to before me this 1st day of April, 1905

M.S. Bradford
Notary Public.

9-276.

Muskogee, Indian Territory, December 23, 1902.

Burney Carney,
   Stonewall, Indian Territory.

Dear Sir:

   Receipt is hereby acknowledged of the application for enrollment as a citizen of the Chickasaw Nation of Sallie Carney, infant daughter of Burney and Josephine Carney, born November 10, 1902.

   You are advised that the Commission is without authority to enroll this child as a citizen of the Chickasaw Nation, it appearing that said child was born November 10, 1902, subsequent to the ratification by the citizens of the Choctaw and Chickasaw Nations September 25, 1902, of an act of Congress approved July 1, 1902 (32 Stats., 641).

   Section twenty-eight thereof provides as follows:

   "The names of all persons living on the date of the final ratification of this agreement entitled to be enrolled as provided in section 27 hereof shall be placed upon the rolls made by said Commission; and no child born thereafter to a citizen or freedman and no person intermarried thereafter to a citizen shall be

Applications for Enrollment of Chickasaw Newborn
Act of 1905   Volume I

entitled to enrollment or to participate in the distribution of the tribal property of the Choctaws and Chickasaws."

Respectfully,

Acting Chairman.

———

9-278

Muskogee, Indian Territory, April 20, 1905.

Burney Carney,
　　Connerville, Indian Territory.

Dear Sir:

　　Receipt is hereby acknowledged of the affidavits of Josiephine[sic] Carney and Lizia Carney, to the birth of Sarah Carney daughter of Burney and Josiephine carney, February 20, 1905, and the same have been filed with our records as an application for the enrollment of said child.

Respectfully,

Chairman.

Chic. N.B - 33
　　(James Henry Colbert
　　Born June 9, 1904)

BIRTH AFFIDAVIT.
DEPARTMENT OF THE INTERIOR.
COMMISSION TO THE FIVE CIVILIZED TRIBES.

IN RE APPLICATION FOR ENROLLMENT, as a citizen of the Chickasaw Nation, of   James Henry Colbert   , born on the 9   day of June , 1904

Name of Father: Emil F Colbert　　　　a citizen of the Chickasaw Nation.
Name of Mother: Annie E Colbert　　　a citizen of the Chickasaw Nation.

Postoffice　　Kiowa Ind Ter

Applications for Enrollment of Chickasaw Newborn
Act of 1905   Volume I

AFFIDAVIT OF MOTHER.

UNITED STATES OF AMERICA, Indian Territory, }
Central   DISTRICT.

I, Annie E Colbert , on oath state that I am 25 years of age and a citizen by marriage , of the Chickasaw Nation; that I am the lawful wife of Emil F Colbert , who is a citizen, by Blood of the Chickasaw Nation; that a male child was born to me on 9 day of June , 1904, that said child has been named James Henry Colbert , and is now living.

Annie E. Colbert

Witnesses To Mark:
{

Subscribed and sworn to before me this 13 day of Aug , 1904

H B Rowley
Notary Public.

AFFIDAVIT OF ATTENDING PHYSICIAN OR MID-WIFE.

UNITED STATES OF AMERICA, Indian Territory, }
Central   DISTRICT.

I, S W Jackson , a Physician , on oath state that I attended on Mrs. Annie E Colbert , wife of Emil F Colbert on the 9 day of June , 1904; that there was born to her on said date a male child; that said child is now living and is said to have been named James Henry Colbert

SW Jackson MD

Witnesses To Mark:
{

Subscribed and sworn to before me this 13 day of Aug , 1904

H B Rowley
Notary Public.

Applications for Enrollment of Chickasaw Newborn
Act of 1905 Volume I

BIRTH AFFIDAVIT.

DEPARTMENT OF THE INTERIOR.
COMMISSION TO THE FIVE CIVILIZED TRIBES.

IN RE APPLICATION FOR ENROLLMENT, as a citizen of the Chickasaw Nation, of James Henry Colbert , born on the 9 day of June , 1904

Name of Father: Emil F Colbert a citizen of the Chickasaw Nation.
Name of Mother: Annie E Colbert a citizen of the Chickasaw Nation.

Postoffice Kiowa IT

AFFIDAVIT OF MOTHER.

UNITED STATES OF AMERICA, Indian Territory, }
Central DISTRICT.

I, Annie E Colbert , on oath state that I am 26 years of age and a citizen by marriage , of the Chickasaw Nation; that I am the lawful wife of Emil F Colbert , who is a citizen, by Blood of the Chickasaw Nation; that a male child was born to me on 9 day of June , 1904; that said child has been named James Henry Colbert , and was living March 4, 1905.

Annie E Colbert

Witnesses To Mark:
{

Subscribed and sworn to before me this 8 day of April , 1905

H B Rowley
Notary Public.

AFFIDAVIT OF ATTENDING PHYSICIAN OR MID-WIFE.

UNITED STATES OF AMERICA, Indian Territory, }
Central DISTRICT.

I, S W Jackson , a Physician , on oath state that I attended on Mrs. Annie E Colbert , wife of Emil F Colbert on the 9 day of June , 1904; that there was born to her on said date a male child; that said child was living March 4, 1905, and is said to have been named James Henry Colbert

SW Jackson MD

Witnesses To Mark:
{

Applications for Enrollment of Chickasaw Newborn
Act of 1905   Volume I

Subscribed and sworn to before me this 10   day of   April   , 1905

>H B Rowley
>Notary Public.

9-282

Muskogee, Indian Territory, August 17, 1904.

E. F. Colbert,
   Kiowa, Indian Territory.

Dear Sir :-

Receipt is hereby acknowledged of the affidavits of Annie E. Colbert and S. W. Jackson, relative to the birth of James Henry Colbert, son of Annie E. Colbert and Emil F. Colbert, citizens by blood of the Chickasaw Nation, June 9, 1904, which it is presumed has been forwarded as an application for enrollment of said child as a citizen by blood of the Chickasaw Nation.

You are advised that the Act of Congress approved July 1, 1904, which was ~~approved~~ *ratified* by the citizens of the Choctaw and Chickasaw Nations, September 25, 1902, among other things provides that no child born to a citizen of either of said Nations subsequent to the date of said ratification shall be entitled to enrollment or to participate in the distribution of the tribal property of the Choctaw and Chickasaws.

>Respectfully,

>Commissioner in Charge.

9-282

Muskogee, Indian Territory, April 16, 1905.

Emil F. Colbert,
   Kiowa, Indian Territory.

Dear Sir:

Receipt is hereby acknowledged of the affidavits of Annie E. Colbert and S. W. Jackson, to the birth of James Henry Colbert, son of Emil F. Colbert and Annie E. Colbert, June 9, 1904, and the same have been filed with our records as an application for the enrollment of said child.

Applications for Enrollment of Chickasaw Newborn
Act of 1905   Volume I

Respectfully,

Commissioner in Charge.

Chic. N.B - 34
(Oscar Colbert, Jr.
Born December 17, 1903)

BIRTH AFFIDAVIT.

DEPARTMENT OF THE INTERIOR.
COMMISSION TO THE FIVE CIVILIZED TRIBES.

IN RE APPLICATION FOR ENROLLMENT, as a citizen of the Chickasaw Nation, of Oscar Colbert, Jr., born on the 17th day of December, 1903

Name of Father: Oscar Colbert, Sr.   a citizen of the Chickasaw Nation.
Name of Mother: Orva L. Colbert   a citizen of the   "   Nation.

Postoffice   Kiowa, Ind. Ty

AFFIDAVIT OF MOTHER.

UNITED STATES OF AMERICA, Indian Territory, }
Central   DISTRICT.

I, Orva L Colbert, on oath state that I am 21 years of age and a citizen by Intermarriage, of the Chickasaw Nation; that I am the lawful wife of Oscar Colbert Sr, who is a citizen, by Blood of the Chickasaw Nation; that a male child was born to me on 17th day of December, 1903; that said child has been named Oscar Colbert Jr, and was living March 4, 1905.

Orva L Colbert

Witnesses To Mark:
{

Subscribed and sworn to before me this 29th day of March, 1905

My commission expires   W.A. Foyil
   Feby 28th 1907   Notary Public.

Applications for Enrollment of Chickasaw Newborn
Act of 1905 Volume I

AFFIDAVIT OF ATTENDING PHYSICIAN OR MID-WIFE.

UNITED STATES OF AMERICA, Indian Territory,
Central DISTRICT.

I, Mrs Katinka Colbert , a Mid-wife , on oath state that I attended on Mrs. Orva L Colbert , wife of Oscar Colbert Sr on the 17th day of December , 1903; that there was born to her on said date a male child; that said child was living March 4, 1905, and is said to have been named Oscar Colbert, Jr

Katinka Colbert

Witnesses To Mark:
{

Subscribed and sworn to before me this 29th day of March , 1905

My commission expires
Feby 28th 1907

W.A. Foyil
Notary Public.

9-282

Muskogee, Indian Territory, April 3, 1905.

Oscar Colbert,
    Kiowa, Indian Territory.

Dear Sir:

Receipt is hereby acknowledged of the affidavits of Orva L. Colbert and Katinka Colbert to the birth of Oscar Colbert, Jr., son of Oscar and Orva L. Colbert, December 17, 1903, and the same have been filed with our records as an application for the enrollment of said child.

Respectfully,

Chairman.

Applications for Enrollment of Chickasaw Newborn
Act of 1905 Volume I

Chic. N.B - 35
(Holman Colbert
Born April 16, 1903)

BIRTH AFFIDAVIT.

DEPARTMENT OF THE INTERIOR,
COMMISSION TO THE FIVE CIVILIZED TRIBES.

In Re Application for Enrollment, as a citizen of the Chickasaw Nation, of Holman Colbert, born on the 16th day of April, 1903

Name of Father: Edmon Colbert   a citizen of the Chickasaw Nation.
Name of Mother: Martha Colbert   a citizen of the Chickasaw Nation.

Post-office   Guertie

AFFIDAVIT OF MOTHER.

UNITED STATES OF AMERICA, }
   INDIAN TERRITORY,
Central   District.

   I, Martha Colbert, on oath state that I am 33 years of age and a citizen by Blood, of the Chickasaw Nation; that I am the lawful wife of Edmon Colbert, who is a citizen, by Blood of the Chickasaw Nation; that a male child was born to me on 16th day of April, 1903, that said child has been named Holman, and is now living.

                                                     her
                                      Martha x Colbert
WITNESSES TO MARK: mark
{ A.J. Childers
{ Enoch Homer

Subscribed and sworn to before me this 12th day of April, 1904

                                          Ben F. Gillum
                                          NOTARY PUBLIC.

Applications for Enrollment of Chickasaw Newborn
Act of 1905 Volume I

AFFIDAVIT OF ATTENDING PHYSICIAN OR MID-WIFE.

UNITED STATES OF AMERICA, }
INDIAN TERRITORY,
Central   District.

I, Susan Pusley, a Midwife, on oath state that I attended on Mrs. Martha Colbert, wife of Edmon Colbert on the 16th day of April, 1903; that there was born to her on said date a male child; that said child is now living and is said to have been named Holman

                                her
                          Susan x Pusley

WITNESSES TO MARK: mark
{ Nannie B. Pusley
{ Ira Randolph

Subscribed and sworn to before me this 14th day of April, 1904

                        Ben F. Gillum
                        NOTARY PUBLIC.

BIRTH AFFIDAVIT.   *No 8*

DEPARTMENT OF THE INTERIOR.
COMMISSION TO THE FIVE CIVILIZED TRIBES.

IN RE APPLICATION FOR ENROLLMENT, as a citizen of the Chickasaw Nation, of Holman Colbert, born on the 16 day of April, 1903

Name of Father: Edmon Colbert   a citizen of the Chickasaw Nation.
Name of Mother: Marty Colbert   a citizen of the Chickasaw Nation.

                    Postoffice   Gurtie, I.T.

AFFIDAVIT OF MOTHER.

UNITED STATES OF AMERICA, Indian Territory, }
Southern   DISTRICT.

I, Martha Colbert, on oath state that I am about Thirty years of age and a citizen by Blood, of the Chickasaw Nation; that I am the lawful wife of Edmon Colbert, who is a citizen, by Blood of the Chickasaw Nation; that a male child was born to me on 16th day of April, 1903, that said child has been named Holman Colbert, and is now living.

Applications for Enrollment of Chickasaw Newborn
Act of 1905   Volume I

                                      her
                                Martha x Colbert
Witnesses To Mark: mark
 { J.C. Chapman
   J.C. Walker

      Subscribed and sworn to before me this 18th day of January , 1905.

                                  W. F. Harrison
                                    Notary Public.

AFFIDAVIT OF ATTENDING PHYSICIAN OR MID-WIFE.

UNITED STATES OF AMERICA, Indian Territory,
   Southern   **DISTRICT.**

     I,   Ihcha Lewis   , a   midwife   , on oath state that I attended on Mrs. Martha Colbert , wife of Edmond[sic] Colbert on the 16th day of April ,1903; that there was born to her on said date a   male   child; that said child is now living and is said to have been named Holman Colbert

                                      her
                              Ihcha x Lewis
Witnesses To Mark: mark
 { J.C. Chapman
   J.C. Walker

      Subscribed and sworn to before me this 18th day of January , 1905.

                                  W. F. Harrison
                                    Notary Public.

BIRTH AFFIDAVIT.
                    DEPARTMENT OF THE INTERIOR.
               COMMISSION TO THE FIVE CIVILIZED TRIBES.

     IN RE APPLICATION FOR ENROLLMENT, as a citizen of the   Chickasaw   Nation, of Holman Colbert   , born on the 16 day of April , 1903

Name of Father: Edmon Colbert   a citizen of the Chictow[sic] Nation.
Name of Mother: Marthy Colbert   a citizen of the   Chictow   Nation.

                         Postoffice   Guertie, I.T.

Applications for Enrollment of Chickasaw Newborn
Act of 1905 Volume I

AFFIDAVIT OF MOTHER.

UNITED STATES OF AMERICA, Indian Territory,
Cent DISTRICT.

    I, Marthy Colbert, on oath state that I am 30 years of age and a citizen by Blood, of the Chictow Nation; that I am the lawful wife of Edmon Colbert, who is a citizen, by Blood of the Chictow Nation; that a male child was born to me on 16 day of April, 1903; that said child has been named Holman Colbert, and was living March 4, 1905.

                                                          her
                                         Marthy x Colbert
Witnesses To Mark: mark
{ F.C. Colwell
  W J McCary

    Subscribed and sworn to before me this 8 day of April, 1905

                                      G.W. McCary
                                      Notary Public.

AFFIDAVIT OF ATTENDING PHYSICIAN OR MID-WIFE.

UNITED STATES OF AMERICA, Indian Territory,
Cent DISTRICT.

    I, Highleatha Louis, a midwife, on oath state that I attended on Mrs. Marthy Colbert, wife of Edmon Colbert on the 16 day of April, 1903; that there was born to her on said date a male child; that said child was living March 4, 1905, and is said to have been named Holman Colbert

                                          her
                                  Highleatha x Louis
Witnesses To Mark: mark
{ F.C. Colwell
  W J McCary

    Subscribed and sworn to before me this 8 day of April, 1905

                                      G.W. McCary
                                      Notary Public.

Applications for Enrollment of Chickasaw Newborn
Act of 1905   Volume I

9-287

Muskogee, Indian Territory, April 20, 1905.

Edward Colbert,
   Guertie, Indian Territory.

Dear Sir:

   Receipt is hereby acknowledged of the affidavits of Marthy Colbert and Hightealha[sic] Louis to the birth of Holman Colbert, son of Edmon and Marthy Colbert, April 16, 1903, and the same have been filed with our records as an application for the enrollment of said child.

Respectfully,

Chairman.

9-NB-35

Muskogee, Indian Territory, May 15, 1906.

J. E. Whitehead,
   Attorney at Law,
      South McAlester, Indian Territory.

Dear Sir:

   Receipt is hereby acknowledged of your letter of May 10, 1906, asking if Holman Colbert, son of Edmond[sic] and Martha Colbert, has been enrolled as a new born citizen of the Chickasaw Nation and his enrollment as such was approved by the Secretary of the Interior, June 21, 1905.

Respectfully,

Acting Commissioner.

Applications for Enrollment of Chickasaw Newborn
Act of 1905   Volume I

Chic. N.B - 36
(Albert Nokomis Aldrich
Born September 1, 1903)

BIRTH AFFIDAVIT.

DEPARTMENT OF THE INTERIOR.
COMMISSION TO THE FIVE CIVILIZED TRIBES.

IN RE APPLICATION FOR ENROLLMENT, as a citizen of the   Chickasaw   Nation, of   Albert Nokomis Aldrich   , born on the 1st day of   Sept   , 1903

Name of Father: Albert Alonzo Aldrich   a citizen of the Chickasaw   Nation.
Name of Mother: Susan N. Aldrich   a citizen of the Chickasaw   Nation.

Postoffice   Mill Creek, Ind. Terr.

AFFIDAVIT OF MOTHER.

UNITED STATES OF AMERICA, Indian Territory,
Southern   DISTRICT.

I, Susan N. Aldrich   , on oath state that I am   35   years of age and a citizen by   blood   , of the   Chickasaw   Nation; that I am the lawful wife of   Albert Alonzo Aldrich   , who is a citizen, by Intermarriage   of the   Chickasaw Nation; that a   male   child was born to me on   The First   day of   September   , 1903; that said child has been named   Albert Nokomis Aldrich   , and was living March 4, 1905.

Susan N. Aldrich

Witnesses To Mark:
   Albert Alonzo Aldrich

Subscribed and sworn to before me this 20   day of   March   , 1905.

James T Walter
Notary Public.

Applications for Enrollment of Chickasaw Newborn
Act of 1905 Volume I

AFFIDAVIT OF ATTENDING PHYSICIAN OR MID-WIFE.

UNITED STATES OF AMERICA, Indian Territory, ⎫
Southern   DISTRICT.   ⎬

I,   G.W. Slover   , a Physician   , on oath state that I attended on Mrs.   Susan N. Aldrich   , wife of   Albert Alonzo Aldrich   on the 1st day of Sept   , 1903; that there was born to her on said date a   male   child; that said child was living March 4, 1905, and is said to have been named Albert Nokomis Aldrich

G.W. Slover M.D.

Witnesses To Mark:
{

Subscribed and sworn to before me this   21st day of   March   , 1905

T.F. Gafford
Notary Public.

9-293

Muskogee, Indian Territory, March 28, 1905.

Albert Alonzo Aldrich,
    Millcreek, Indian Territory.

Dear Sir:

Receipt is hereby acknowledged of the affidavits of Susan Ann Aldrich and G. W. Slover to the birth of Albert Nokomis Aldrich son of Albert Alonzo and Susan Ann Aldrich, September 1, 1903, and the same have been filed with our records as an application for the enrollment of said child.

Respectfully,

Chairman.

Applications for Enrollment of Chickasaw Newborn
Act of 1905   Volume I

Chic. N.B - 37
(Affason Brown
Born February 24, 1903)

BIRTH AFFIDAVIT.

DEPARTMENT OF THE INTERIOR.
COMMISSION TO THE FIVE CIVILIZED TRIBES.

IN RE APPLICATION FOR ENROLLMENT, as a citizen of the   Chickasaw   Nation, of   Affason Brown   , born on the 24   day of   February   , 1903

Name of Father: Tecumseh Brown   a citizen of the Chickasaw   Nation.
Name of Mother: Melinda Celia Brown   a citizen of the Chickasaw   Nation.

Postoffice   Viola I.T

AFFIDAVIT OF MOTHER.

UNITED STATES OF AMERICA, Indian Territory,
  Central   DISTRICT.

I, Melinda Celia Brown   , on oath state that I am 25   years of age and a citizen by   blood   , of the   Chickasaw   Nation; that I am the lawful wife of Tecumseh Brown   , who is a citizen, by blood   of the   Chickasaw   Nation; that a   male   child was born to me on 24th   day of   February   , 1903; that said child has been named   Affason Brown   , and was living March 4, 1905. *that there was no physician, midwife or other person present at the birth of said child except my husband*

                    Malinda Sealy Brown
Witnesses To Mark:

Subscribed and sworn to before me this 29th   day of   March   , 1905

                    WL Richards
                    Notary Public.

Applications for Enrollment of Chickasaw Newborn
Act of 1905   Volume I

AFFIDAVIT OF ATTENDING PHYSICIAN OR MID-WIFE.

UNITED STATES OF AMERICA, Indian Territory,
Central   DISTRICT.

I, *Tecumseh Brown husband of Melinda Celia Brown*, on oath state that I *was present with my wife when she gave birth to a male child* on the 24th day of February, 1903; that there was *no physician, midwife, or other person present at the time* that said child was living March 4, 1905, and is ~~said to have been~~ named Affason Brown

                                          his
                             Tecumseh x Brown
Witnesses To Mark: mark
   { B. Statler
      W.F. Kelly

Subscribed and sworn to before me this 29th day of March, 1905

                                       WL Richards
                                       Notary Public.

(The affidavit below typed as given.)

Before the Commission to the Five Tribes.

United States,   In re enrollment of Afferson Brown
Indian Territory,   ss.   Affidavit.
Central District.

     I Sam Hotubby state on oath that I am a brother to Melinda Caely Brown the wife of Tecumseh Brown, and that my age is 23 years that I reside near Viola, I.T.,

     In the latter part of the year 1902, my sister afore said was in an encient condition, and was confined in childbirth on the twenty fourth day of February, 1903;

     I was at her house a day or two afterward and saw the child which she was nursing and which is yet living, a male child named Afferson Brown.

                                         Sam Hotubby

Subscribed and sworn to before me this 15th day of May, 1905.

                                       WL Richards
                                       Notary Public.

Applications for Enrollment of Chickasaw Newborn
Act of 1905 Volume I

(The affidavit below typed as given.)

United States,   Before the Commission to the
Indian Territory,   Five Tribes.
Central District.
In re enrollment of Affason Brown, Chickasaw by blood.
                            Affidavit.

I, Lyman Worcester being first duly sworn on oath state that I am over twenty one years of age, that I reside near Wapamicka, I.. that I am not related to either of said persons or interested in the matters set forth in this affidavit.

      That on the 24th day of February 1903., the said Malinda Sealey Brown gave birth to a male child, that said child was living on the 4th day of March, 1905., and is yet living and has been named Affason Brown;

      That at the time of the birth of said child and for several years next before the said Malinda Sealey Brown was living in lawful wedlock with her said husband Tecumseh Brown.

                            Lyman D. Worcester

Subscribed and sworn to before me this the 16th day of June, 1905.
My Commission expires Feby 7th 1909.
                            WL Richards

(The affidavit below typed as given.)

United States,
Indian Territory,
Central District.   Before the Commission to the Five Tribes.

      In re enrollment of Affason Brown, Chickasaw blood.
                            Affidavit.

I, Soloman Owens being first duly sworn on oath state that I am over twenty one years old, that I reside near Wapamicka, I.T.

      That I am acquainted with Tecumseh Brown and his wife Malinda Sealey Brown, who reside near Viola, I.T.,

      that I am not related to either of said persons or interested in the matters set forth in this affidavit;

      that on the 24th day of February, 1903, the said Malinda Sealey Brown while living in lawful web lock with her said husband gave birth to a male child, that said child was living on the fourth day of March, 1905., and is yet living and has been named Affason Brown.

                            Soloman Owens

Subscribed and sworn to before me this the 16th day of June 1905.

                            WL Richards
My commission expires Feby 7th 1909   Notary Public.

Applications for Enrollment of Chickasaw Newborn
Act of 1905   Volume I

(The affidavit below typed as given.)

United States,)
Indian Territory,) SS.
Central District.)

Before the Commission to the Five Tribes.

    In matter of the enrollment of Afferson[sic] Brown, as a citizen of the Chickasaw Nation.

AFFIDAVIT.

    I Julia Hotubby state on oath that I am over twenty one years of age, and reside near Viola, in the Chickasaw Nation Indian Territory and am a citizen of the Chickasaw Nation by blood;

    I am the mother of Malinda Caely Brown, the wife of Tecumseh Brown, who live near Viola, I.T.,

    That my said daughter was in an encient condition during the latter part of 1902 and the first part of 1903, and was confined on the 24th day of February 1903, on the day following I heard of it and went over to her house, and found she had given birth to a male child the day preceeding, and was nursing the child, the said child is now living and has been named Afferson Brown, its father and mother are both citizens of the Chickasaw Nation by blood.

                                             her
Witnesses to mark   Julia x Hotubby
A. B. Davis   mark
W Richard

Subscribed and sworn to before me this the 15th day of May, 1905.

                                         WL Richards
                                         Notary Public.

Applications for Enrollment of Chickasaw Newborn
Act of 1905   Volume I

Chickasaw-296.

Muskogee, Indian Territory, April 1, 1905.

Tecumseh Brown,
    Viola, Indian Territory.

Dear Sir:

    Receipt is hereby acknowledged of the affidavits of Malinda Sealy Brown and Tecumseh Brown to the birth of Affason Brown, son of Tecumseh and Malinda Sealy Brown; February 24, 1903; and the same have been filed with our records as an application for the enrollment of said child.

    You are requested to state the name under which your wife was listed for enrollment and the names of her parents. Please furnish this information at once.

Respectfully,

Chairman.

9-NB-37.

Muskogee, Indian Territory, April 19, 1905.

Tecumseh Brown,
    Viola, Indian Territory.

Dear Madam[sic]:

    Receipt is hereby acknowledged of your letter without date in which you give the name under which your wife was enrolled as Malinda Sealy and the information has enabled the Commission to identify her as having been enrolled as a citizen by blood of the Chickasaw Nation and the affidavits heretofore forwarded to the birth of your son Affason Brown have been filed with our records as an application for the enrollment of said child.

Respectfully,

Chairman.

Applications for Enrollment of Chickasaw Newborn
Act of 1905   Volume I

Chickasaw N.B. 37.

Muskogee, Indian Territory, May 1, 1905.

W. L. Richards,
    Attorney at Law,
        Wapanucka, Indian Territory.

Dear Sir:

    Receipt is hereby acknowledged of your letter of April 22, saying that sometime ago you forwarded for Malinda and Tecumseh Brown their application for the enrollment of their child lately born, and that the same came back for further information of some kind, but they were unable to explain the character of the information desired, but that the mother was enrolled as Malinda Sealey, having since married Tecumseh Brown.

    In reply to your letter you are advised that on April 19, 1905, a letter was addressed to Tecumseh Brown, requesting him to advise the name under which his wife was enrolled and this information has been received and the affidavits heretofore forwarded to the birth of Affason Brown, child of Tecumseh and Malinda Brown, have been filed with our records as an application for the enrollment of said child.

    You are advised, however, that it appears from the affidavits forwarded that no person was in attendance on Malinda Brown at the time of the birth of this child, and it will be necessary that they forward the affidavits of two disinterested persons who know of the birth of said child, that it is the child of Malinda Brown, and that it was living on March 4, 1905.

                    Respectfully,

                                    Chairman.

Chickasaw NB 37

Muskogee, Indian Territory, May 19, 1905.

W. L. Richards,
    Attorney at Law,
        Wapanucka, Indian Territory.

Dear Sir:

    Receipt is hereby acknowledged of your letter of May 15, inclosing affidavits of Somie Hotubby and Julia Hotubby to the birth of Afferson Brown, February 24, 1903, and the same have been filed with the record in the matter of the enrollment of said child.

                    Respectfully,

                                    Chairman.

Applications for Enrollment of Chickasaw Newborn
Act of 1905   Volume I

9-NB-37.

Muskogee, Indian Territory, June 9, 1905.

Tecumseh Brown,
    Viola, Indian Territory.

Dear Sir:

    Referring to the application for the enrollment of your infant child, Affason Brown, born February 24, 1903, you filed in this office in reply to the Commission's letter of the first ultimo, the affidavits of Julia Hotubby and Some Hotubby, the grandmother and uncle of the applicant, respectively, in the place of the attending physician's or midwife's affidavit, you being the only one in attendance upon your wife at the time of the birth of the applicant.

    These affidavits do not fulfill the requirements in that they are of persons who are related and interested in the applicant.

    Before this matter can be finally disposed of it will be necessary for you to file in this office the affidavits of two persons who are disinterested and not related to the applicant, ho have actual knowledge of the facts; that the child was born, the date of his birth, that he was living on March 4, 1905 and that Malinda Sealy Brown is his mother.

    Respectfully,

    Chairman.

---

9 NB 37

Muskogee, Indian Territory, June 21, 1905.

Tecumseh Brown,
    Wapanucka, Indian Territory.

Dear Sir:

    Receipt is hereby acknowledged of your letter of June 16, 1905, enclosing affidavits of Lymon[sic] D. Worcester and Solomon Owens to the birth of Affason Brown, daughter[sic] of Tecumseh and Malinda Sealey Brown, February 24, 1903, and the same have been filed with our records in the matter of the enrollment of said child.

    Respectfully,

    Chairman.

Applications for Enrollment of Chickasaw Newborn
Act of 1905 Volume I

Chic. N.B - 38
(Josephine Olive Johnson
Born August 17, 1904)

BIRTH AFFIDAVIT.

DEPARTMENT OF THE INTERIOR.
COMMISSION TO THE FIVE CIVILIZED TRIBES.

IN RE APPLICATION FOR ENROLLMENT, as a citizen of the Chickasaw Nation, of Josephine Olive Johnson , born on the 17" day of August , 1904

Name of Father: Benjamin Franklin Johnson a citizen of the Chickasaw Nation.
Name of Mother: Mamie Olive Johnson a citizen of the United States Nation.

Postoffice Chickasha, Ind. Terr

AFFIDAVIT OF MOTHER.

UNITED STATES OF AMERICA, Indian Territory, }
Southern DISTRICT.

I, Mamie Olive Johnson , on oath state that I am twenty five years of age and a citizen by blood , of the United States ~~Nation~~; that I am the lawful wife of Benjamin Franklin Johnson , who is a citizen, by blood of the Chickasaw Nation; that a Female child was born to me on 17th day of August , 1904; that said child has been named Josephine Olive Johnson , and was living March 4, 1905.

Mamie Olive Johnson
Witnesses To Mark:
{

Subscribed and sworn to before me this 24 day of March , 1905.

(Name Illegible)
Notary Public.

AFFIDAVIT OF ATTENDING PHYSICIAN OR MID-WIFE.

UNITED STATES OF AMERICA, Indian Territory, }
Southern DISTRICT.

I, R.P. Tye , a Physician , on oath state that I attended on Mrs. Mamie Olive Johnson , wife of Benjamin Franklin Johnson on the 17" day of August , 1904; that there was born to her on said date a Female

Applications for Enrollment of Chickasaw Newborn
Act of 1905   Volume I

child; that said child was living March 4, 1905, and is said to have been named Josephine Olive Johnson

R.P. Tye

Witnesses To Mark:
{

Subscribed and sworn to before me this 24 day of   March   , 1905

JE McNeill
Notary Public.

9-305

Muskogee, Indian Territory, March 31, 1905.

Bond & Melton,
    Attorneys at Law,
        Chickasha, Indian Territory.

Gentlemen:

    Receipt is hereby acknowledged of your letter of March 24, 1905, enclosing the affidavits of Mamie Olive Johnson and R. P. Tye to the birth of Josephine Olive Johnson daughter of Benjamin Franklin Johnson and Mamie Olive Johnson, August 17, 1904, and the same have been filed with our records as an application for the enrollment of said child.

Respectfully,

Chairman.

9-N.B. 38.

Muskogee, Indian Territory, May 10, 1905.

Benjamin Franklin Johnson,
    Chickasha, Indian Territory.

Dear Sir:

    In the matter of the application for the enrollment of your infant child, Josephine Olive Johnson, born August 17, 1904, itmis[sic] noted, from the affidavits heretofore filed in this office, that the applicant claims through you. In this event it will be necessary for you to file with the Commission either the original or a certified copy of the license and certificate of your marriage to the applicant's mother, Mamie Olive Johnson.

Applications for Enrollment of Chickasaw Newborn
Act of 1905 Volume I

Please give this matter your immediate attention.

Respectfully,

Chairman.

---

9 NB 38

Muskogee, Indian Territory, June 9, 1905.

United States Indian Agent,
Muskogee, Indian Territory.

Dear Sir:

Receipt is hereby acknowledged of your letter of June 2, 1905, transmitting marriage license and certificate between Benjamin Franklin Johnson and Mamie Olive.

Respectfully,

Chairman.

MARRIAGE CERTIFICATE
The State of Tennessee.
Davidson County
This is to Certify that the
RITES OF MATRIMONY
Between
Ben F. Johnson
and
Mamie Olive
Were Solemnized by G. A. Loftin
Minister of the Gospel
on the 24th day of March 1903
as the same appears of record in the office of the Clerk
of the County Court of the aforesaid County at
Nashville, Tennessee

Witness my hand and the Seal of said Court
at office this the 16 day of May 1905

John Shelton
    Clerk of Davidson County Court

Nashville, Tenn.

Applications for Enrollment of Chickasaw Newborn
Act of 1905 Volume I

Chic. N.B - 39
(Montelee Dilbeck
Born December 28, 1902)

BIRTH AFFIDAVIT.

DEPARTMENT OF THE INTERIOR.
COMMISSION TO THE FIVE CIVILIZED TRIBES.

IN RE APPLICATION FOR ENROLLMENT, as a citizen of the Chickasaw Nation, of Montelee, born on the 28 day of December, 1902

Name of Father: Frank W Dilbeck   a citizen of the United States Nation.
Name of Mother: Luella Dilbeck   a citizen of the Chickasaw Nation.

Postoffice   Dolbert Dist 16 I.T.

AFFIDAVIT OF MOTHER.

UNITED STATES OF AMERICA, Indian Territory,
Southern DISTRICT.

I, Luella Dilbeck, on oath state that I am 26 years of age and a citizen by birth, of the Chickasaw Nation; that I am the lawful wife of Frank W. Dilbeck, who is a citizen, by birth of the United States Nation; that a Female child was born to me on 28th day of December, 1902; that said child has been named Montelee, and was living March 4, 1905.

Luella Dilbeck

Witnesses To Mark:
  E. W. Westhoff
  Willie Cosen

Subscribed and sworn to before me this 25th day of March, 1905

Mrs. E. W. Westhoff
Notary Public.

Applications for Enrollment of Chickasaw Newborn
Act of 1905   Volume I

AFFIDAVIT OF ATTENDING PHYSICIAN OR MID-WIFE.

UNITED STATES OF AMERICA, Indian Territory, }
   Southern   DISTRICT.

     I,   N. D. Meredith , a   Physician , on oath state that I attended on Mrs. Luella Dilbeck , wife of   W. F[sic]. Dilbeck on the 28 day of Dec , 1902; that there was born to her on said date a   Female child; that said child was living March 4, 1905, and is said to have been named Montelee

                                                N. D. Meredith

Witnesses To Mark:
  { F H Dilbeck
    Willie Cosen

    Subscribed and sworn to before me this 25 day of   march , 1905

                                     (Name Illegible)
                                       Notary Public.

                                                      Chickasaw 347

                         Muskogee, Indian Territory, March 17, 1904.

Luella Dilbeck,
    Dolberg, Indian Territory.

Dear Madam:

    Receipt is hereby acknowledged of your letter of March 10, stating that you have an infant child born December 28, 1902, and asking if you will be entitled to hold land for this child.

    In reply to your letter your attention is invited to the following provision of the act of Congress of July 1, 1902, which was ratified by the Choctaw and Chickasaw Nations on September 25, 1902:

    "The names of all persons living on the date of the final ratification of this agreement entitled to be enrolled as provided in section 27 hereof shall be placed upon the rolls made by said Commission; and no child born thereafter to a citizen or freedman and no person intermarried thereafter to a citizen shall be entitled to enrollment or to participate in the distribution of the tribal property of the Choctaws and Chickasaws."

                                      Respectfully,

                                                  Commissioner in Charge.

Applications for Enrollment of Chickasaw Newborn
Act of 1905 Volume I

Chickasaw 347.

Muskogee, Indian Territory, March 31, 1905.

Luella Dilbeck,
    Dolberg, Indian Territory.

Dear Madam:

    Receipt is hereby acknowledged of your affidavit and the affidavit of H[sic]. D. Meredith to the birth of Montelee Dilbeck, child of Frank W. and Luella Dilbeck, December 28, 1902, and the same have been filed with our records as an application for the enrollment of said child.

    Respectfully,

    Chairman.

Chic. N.B - 40
    (William Blanchard Colbert
    Born January 15, 1903)

BIRTH AFFIDAVIT.

DEPARTMENT OF THE INTERIOR,
COMMISSION TO THE FIVE CIVILIZED TRIBES.

    IN RE *Application for Enrollment,* as a citizen of the Chickasaw Nation, of William Blanchard Colbert, born on the 15" day of January, 1903

Name of Father: Joseph E. Colbert   a citizen of the Chickasaw Nation.
Name of Mother: Elizabeth E. Colbert   a citizen of the Chickasaw Nation.

    Post-Office: Wayne, Ind. Ter'y.

Applications for Enrollment of Chickasaw Newborn
Act of 1905   Volume I

AFFIDAVIT OF MOTHER.

UNITED STATES OF AMERICA, }
INDIAN TERRITORY.
Southern   District.

I, Elizabeth E. Colbert , on oath state that I am .... years of age and a citizen by intermarriage , of the Chickasaw Nation; that I am the lawful wife of Joseph E. Colbert , who is a citizen, by blood of the Chickasaw Nation; that a male child was born to me on 15" day of January , 1903, that said child has been named William Blanchard Colbert , and is now living.

                                  Elizabeth E. Colbert

WITNESSES TO MARK:
{ A M Perdue
{ H P Ingram

Subscribed and sworn to before me this 2 *day of* Nov , 190 3

My commission   A. M. Perdue
expires Feb 2-1905   **NOTARY PUBLIC.**

AFFIDAVIT OF ATTENDING PHYSICIAN OR MID-WIFE.

UNITED STATES OF AMERICA, }
INDIAN TERRITORY.
Southern   District.

I, Robert E. Thacker , a physician , on oath state that I attended on Mrs. Elizabeth E. Colbert , wife of Joseph E. Colbert on the 15" day of January , 1903 ; that there was born to her on said date a male child; that said child is now living and is said to have been named William Blanchard Colbert

                                  Robt E Thacker

WITNESSES TO MARK:
{ A M Perdue
{ H P Ingram

Subscribed and sworn to before me this 2 *day of* Nov , 190 3

My commission   A. M. Perdue
expires Feb 2-1905   **NOTARY PUBLIC.**

Applications for Enrollment of Chickasaw Newborn
Act of 1905 Volume I

BIRTH AFFIDAVIT.

DEPARTMENT OF THE INTERIOR.
COMMISSION TO THE FIVE CIVILIZED TRIBES.

IN RE APPLICATION FOR ENROLLMENT, as a citizen of the Chickasaw Nation, of William Blanchard Colbert, born on the 15" day of January, 1903

Name of Father: Joe E. Colbert   a citizen of the Chickasaw Nation.
Name of Mother: Elizabeth Elnora Colbert   a citizen of the Chickasaw Nation.

Postoffice   Lindsay I.T.

AFFIDAVIT OF MOTHER.

UNITED STATES OF AMERICA, Indian Territory,
Southern DISTRICT.

I, Elizabeth Elnora Colbert, on oath state that I am 36 years of age and a citizen by intermarriage, of the Chickasaw Nation; that I am the lawful wife of Joe E. Colbert, who is a citizen, by blood of the Chickasaw Nation; that a male child was born to me on 15" day of January, 1903; that said child has been named William Blanchard Colbert, and was living March 4, 1905.

                                       Elizabeth Elnora Colbert

Witnesses To Mark:
{

Subscribed and sworn to before me this 3rd day of April, 1905

                                 (Illegible) Carter
                                      Notary Public.

AFFIDAVIT OF ATTENDING PHYSICIAN OR MID-WIFE.

Indian Territory
Southern District ~~Oklahoma Territory~~
UNITED STATES OF AMERICA, ~~Indian Territory~~,
~~Cleveland County~~ DISTRICT.

I, Robt E Thacker, a Physician, on oath state that I attended on Mrs. Elizabeth Elnora Colbert, wife of Joe E Colbert on the 15th day of January, 1903; that there was born to her on said date a male child; that said child was living March 4, 1905, and is said to have been named William Blanchard Colbert

                                       Robt E Thacker

Witnesses To Mark:
{

Applications for Enrollment of Chickasaw Newborn
Act of 1905   Volume I

Subscribed and sworn to before me this 3rd day of April , 1905

(Illegible) Carter
Notary Public.

Chic. N.B - 41
   (John M. Yoakum
   Born January 9, 1904)

DEPARTMENT OF THE INTERIOR,
COMMISSION TO THE FIVE CIVILIZED TRIBES.
F I L E D
JUL 13 1905
Tams Bixby CHAIRMAN

F I L E D

MAR 5 1903 8AM

C. M. CAMPBELL, Clerk.
Southern Dist. Ind. Ter.

Certificate of Record of Marriage

United States of America,
   Indian Territory,   } sct.
   Southern District.

I, C. M. CAMPBELL, Clerk of the United States Court, in the Territory and District aforesaid DO HEREBY CERTIFY, that the License for and Certificate of Marriage of

MR   Geo H Yoakum   and

Miss Jewel Marrow

were filed in my office in said Territory and District the   5"   day of   March A.D., 190 3   and duly recorded in Book   G of Marriage Record, Page   194

   WITNESS my hand and Seal of
   said Court, at Ardmore,
   this   5"   day of
      March   A.D. 190 3

   C. M. Campbell
            CLERK.

Return this License to the United States Clerk at Ardmore, that it may be recorded, when it will be mailed to the proper address.

Ardmoreite Steam Print.

Applications for Enrollment of Chickasaw Newborn
Act of 1905   Volume I

 | MARRIAGE LICENSE |

UNITED STATES OF AMERICA,
INDIAN TERRITORY,   ss:
SOUTHERN DISTRICT.

To Any Person Authorized by Law to Solemnize Marriage, Greeting:

You are hereby commanded to solemnize the Rite and publish the Banns of Matrimony between Mr.   George H Yoakum   of   Paole[sic] in the Indian Territory, aged   24   years, and Miss Jewel Marrow of   Paole[sic]   in the Indian Territory, aged   18   years, according to law; and do you officially sign and return this License to the parties therein named.

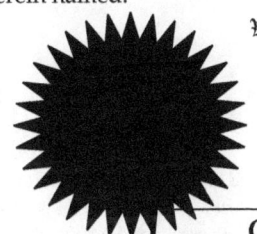

Witness my hand and official Seal, this   3rd   day of   March   A. D. 190 3

C.M. Campbell
Clerk of the United States Court.
By: F.F. Ferrin Deputy

Certificate of Marriage.

UNITED STATES OF AMERICA,
INDIAN TERRITORY,   ss:
SOUTHERN DISTRICT.   I,   J K Florence

a Minister of the gospel   do hereby certify that on the 3rd   day of March, A. D. 190 3, I did duly according to law, as commanded in the foregoing License, solemnize the Rite and publish the Banns of Matrimony between the parties therein named.

Witness my hand this   3rd   day of   March   A. D. 190 3

My credentials are recorded in the office of the Clerk of the United States Court, Indian Territory, Southern District, at Ardmore, Book A , Page 66

Applications for Enrollment of Chickasaw Newborn
Act of 1905   Volume I

(NOTE-The person officiating should fill in the spaces for book and page and sign here.) ☞

J K Florence
a n ordaned[sic] Minister

NOTE (a)-The License and Certificate of Marriage must be returned to the office of the Clerk of the United States Court in the Indian Territory, at Ardmore, within sixty days from the date thereof, or the party to whom the License was issued will be liable in the amount of One Hundred Dollars ($100).

NOTE (b)-No person is authorized to perform the Marriage Ceremony in the Southern District unless the proper credentials have first been recorded in the Clerk's office.

BIRTH AFFIDAVIT.

IN RE-APPLICATION FOR ENROLLMENT, as a citizen of the   Chickasaw   Nation, of   John M Yoakum , born on the   9th day of   Jan , 190 4

Name of Father: George H Yoakum   a citizen of the   Chickasaw   Nation.
Name of Mother: Jewel Yoakum   a citizen of the   Chickasaw   Nation.

Postoffice   Paoli I.T.

AFFIDAVIT OF MOTHER.

UNITED STATES OF AMERICA, INDIAN TERRITORY, }
Southern   District.

I,   Jewel Yoakum , on oath state that I am   17   years of age and a citizen by   Blood , of the   Chickasaw   Nation; that I am the lawful wife of   George H Yoakum , who is a citizen, by   Blood   of the   Chickasaw   Nation; that a   male   child was born to me on   9th day of   January , 1904 , that said child has been named   John M Yoakum , and is now living.

Jewel Yoakum

Witnesses To Mark:
{

Subscribed and sworn to before me this   the 13   day of   March , 1905.

My commission expires Mch 12-1908   A.S. Kelley
                                          Notary Public.

AFFIDAVIT OF ATTENDING PHYSICIAN OR MID-WIFE.

UNITED STATES OF AMERICA, INDIAN TERRITORY, }
Southern   District.

I,   Rebecca Morrow , a   Midwife , on oath state that I attended on Mrs.   Jewel Yoakum , wife of   George H Yoakum   on the   9th day of   Jan ,

Applications for Enrollment of Chickasaw Newborn
Act of 1905 Volume I

1905[sic] ; that there was born to her on said date a male child; that said child is now living and is said to have been named John M. Yoakum

Rebecca Morrow

Witnesses To Mark:
{

Subscribed and sworn to before me this the 13 day of March , 1905.

My commission expires Mch 12-1908   A.S. Kelley
                                          Notary Public.

BIRTH AFFIDAVIT.

DEPARTMENT OF THE INTERIOR.
COMMISSION TO THE FIVE CIVILIZED TRIBES.

IN RE APPLICATION FOR ENROLLMENT, as a citizen of the Chickasaw Nation, of John M Yoakum , born on the 9th day of Jan , 1904

Name of Father: George H Yoakum   a citizen of the Chickasaw Nation.
Name of Mother: Jewel Yoakum   a citizen of the Chickasaw Nation.

Postoffice   Paoli, Ind. Ter.

AFFIDAVIT OF MOTHER.

UNITED STATES OF AMERICA, Indian Territory, }
Southern   DISTRICT.

I, Jewel Yoakum , on oath state that I am 17 years of age and a citizen by blood , of the Choctaw Nation; that I am the lawful wife of George H Yoakum , who is a citizen, by blood of the Chickasaw Nation; that a male child was born to me on 9th day of January , 1904; that said child has been named John M Yoakum , and was living March 4, 1905.

Jewel Yoakum

Witnesses To Mark:
{

Subscribed and sworn to before me this 19th day of May , 1905

A.S. Kelley
Notary Public.

My commission expires Mch 12-1908

Applications for Enrollment of Chickasaw Newborn
Act of 1905 Volume I

AFFIDAVIT OF ATTENDING PHYSICIAN OR MID-WIFE.

UNITED STATES OF AMERICA, Indian Territory,
Southern DISTRICT.

I, Rebecca Morrow, a midwife, on oath state that I attended on Mrs. Jewel Yoakum, wife of George H Yoakum on the 9th day of January, 1904; that there was born to her on said date a male child; that said child was living March 4, 1905, and is said to have been named John M Yoakum

Rebecca Morrow

Witnesses To Mark:
{

Subscribed and sworn to before me this 19th day of May, 1905

A.S. Kelley
Notary Public.

9-371

Muskogee, Indian Territory, March 16, 1905.

George H. Yoakum,
    Paoli, Indian Territory.

Dear Sir:

Receipt is hereby acknowledged of the affidavits of Jewel Yoakum and Rebecca Marrow[sic] to the birth of John M. Yoakum, infant son of George H. and Jewel Yoakum, January 9, 1904, and the same have been filed with our records as an application for the enrollment of said child.

Respectfully,

Chairman.

Applications for Enrollment of Chickasaw Newborn
Act of 1905   Volume I

9-NB-41.

Muskogee, Indian Territory, May 13, 1905.

George H. Yoakum,
    Paoli, Indian Territory.

Dear Sir:

    There is enclosed you herewith for execution application for the enrollment of your infant child, John M. Yoakum, born January 9, 1904.

    In the affidavit of March 13, 1905, the mother gives the date of the applicant's birth as January 9, 1904, while in the affidavit of the mid-wife it is given as January 9, 1905. It will, therefore, be necessary that the enclosed application be executed, giving the correct date of birth.

    In having these affidavits executed care should be exercised to see that all names are written in full, as they appear in the body of the affidavit, and in the event that either of the persons signing the affidavit are unable to write, signatures by mark must be attested by two witnesses. Each affidavit must be executed before a Notary Public and the notarial seal and signature of the officer must be attached to each separate affidavit.

    Respectfully,

(End of letter.)

---

9 N.B. 41.

Muskogee, Indian Territory, May 25, 1905.

George H. Yoakum,
    Paoli, Indian Territory.

Dear Sir:

    Receipt is hereby acknowledged of the affidavits of Jewel Yoakum and Rebecca Morrow to the birth of John M. Yoakum, son of George H. and Jewel Yoakum, January 9, 1904, and the same have been filed with our records in the matter of the enrollment of said child.

    Respectfully,

    Chairman.

Applications for Enrollment of Chickasaw Newborn
Act of 1905 Volume I

Duplicate

9-NB-61,

Muskogee, Indian Territory, June 9, 1905.

George H. Yoakum,
    Paoli, Indian Territory.

Dear Sir:

    Referring to the application for the enrollment of your infant child, John M. Yoakum, born January 9, 1904, it is noted in the affidavits heretofore filed in this office that your wife, Jewel Yoakum, claims to be a citizen by blood of the Chickasaw Nation.

    If this is correct you will please state when, where and under what name she was listed for enrollment, the names of her parents and other members of her family for whom application was made at the same time, and if she has selected her allotment please give her roll number as the same appears upon her allotment certificate.

    If she is not a citizen by blood, it will be necessary for you to file in this office either the original or a certified copy of the license and certificate of your marriage to her.

    This matter should receive your immediate attention.

                      Respectfully,

                                      Commissioner in Charge.

(The letter below typed as given.)

                    Paoli, I. T.

                        6/14/1905

Commission to the five civilized tribes, In reply to your letter of June 9, my wife Jewel Yoakum never claimed to be a citizen by Chickasaw blood. She claimed a citizenship by Choctaw blood she was a court claimant in the C. T. Bottoms case and was turned down by the citizenship court. She is the daughter of J. W. Morrow and Rebecca Morrow and a sister of William F. Morrow, Walter J. Morrow and Johnnie B. Morrow. Please let me know at once what to do I will send you a coppy of our marriage certificate as soon as I hear from you.
Respectfully.

                    G. H. Yoakum.

Applications for Enrollment of Chickasaw Newborn
Act of 1905   Volume I

9 NB 41

Muskogee, Indian Territory, June 17, 1905.

G. H. Yoakum,
   Paoli, Indian Territory.

Dear Sir:

    Receipt is hereby acknowledged of your letter of June 14, 1905, giving information relative to the citizenship case of your wife Jewel Yoakum and the same has enabled us to identify her upon our records as having been denied citizenship in the Choctaw Nation by the Choctaw and Chickasaw Citizenship Court November 28, 1904, in case No. 75 on the Tishomingo docket.

    This information has been made a matter of record.

    Respectfully,

Chairman.

9-NB-41.

Muskogee, Indian Territory, July 1, 1905.

George H. Yoakum,
   Paoli, Indian Territory.

Dear Sir:

    Referring to the application for the enrollment of your infant child, John M. Yoakum, born January 9, 1904, it is noted in the records in this case that the applicant claims through you. It will, therefore, be necessary that you file in this office either the original or a certified copy of the license and certificate of your marriage to the applicants[sic] mother, Jewel Yoakum.

    Please give this matter your immediate attention as no further action can be taken until these affidavits are filed in this office. can be taken until this evidence is filed in this office.

    Respectfully,

Commissioner.

Applications for Enrollment of Chickasaw Newborn
Act of 1905   Volume I

9-NB-41

Muskogee, Indian Territory, July 14, 1905.

George H. Yoakum,
    Paoli, Indian Territory.

Dear Sir:

    Receipt is hereby acknowledged of your letter of July 7, 1905, enclosing marriage license between yourself and Jewel Marrow[sic] which you offer in support of the application for the enrollment of your child John M. Yoakum and the same has been filed with the record in this case.

                  Respectfully,

                                      Commissioner.

9-NB-41

Muskogee, Indian Territory September 16, 1905.

George H. Yoakum,
    Paoli, Indian Territory.

Dear Sir:

    Replying to your letter of the 11th instant, you are advised that on August 26, 1905, the Commissioner to the Five Civilized Tribes transmitted to the Department for approval by the Secretary of the Interior, a schedule of new born citizens by blood of the Chickasaw Nation; the name of your minor child, John M. Yoakum, appearing upon said schedule opposite No. 621.

    When this office is advised of the approval by the Secretary of the Interior of said schedule you will be notified thereof. Until the enrollment of your minor child is so approved, no allotment can be selected for him.

                    Respectfully,

                                  Acting Commissioner.

Applications for Enrollment of Chickasaw Newborn
Act of 1905 Volume I

Chic. N.B - 42
(George W. Yoakum
Born July 12, 1904)

BIRTH AFFIDAVIT.

IN RE-APPLICATION FOR ENROLLMENT, as a citizen of the   Chickasaw   Nation, of   George W Yoakum , born on the 12   day of   July   , 190 4

Name of Father: John T. Yoakum   a citizen of the   Chickasaw   Nation.
Name of Mother: Minnie A Yoakum   a citizen of the   Chickasaw   Nation.

Postoffice   Paoli I.T.

AFFIDAVIT OF MOTHER.

UNITED STATES OF AMERICA, INDIAN TERRITORY, }
Southern   District.

I,   Minnie A Yoakum   , on oath state that I am 27   years of age and a citizen by Intermarriage   , of the   Chickasaw   Nation; that I am the lawful wife of   John T Yoakum   , who is a citizen, by   Blood   of the   Chickasaw   Nation; that a   male child was born to me on   12th day of   July   , 1904 , that said child has been named   George W. Yoakum , and is now living.

                                                     Minnie A Yoakum
Witnesses To Mark:

Subscribed and sworn to before me this   the 13th day of   March   , 1905.

                        AS Kelley
                                  Notary Public.
My commission expires Mch 12-1908

AFFIDAVIT OF ATTENDING PHYSICIAN OR MID-WIFE.

UNITED STATES OF AMERICA, INDIAN TERRITORY, }
Southern   District.

I,   Laura A Yoakum   , a   midwife   , on oath state that I attended on Mrs.   Minnie A Yoakum   , wife of   John T. Yoakum   on the 12th day of   July   , 190 4 ; that there was born to her on said date a   male   child; that said child is now living and is said to have been named George W. Yoakum

                                                     Laura A Yoakum
Witnesses To Mark:

Applications for Enrollment of Chickasaw Newborn
Act of 1905 Volume I

Subscribed and sworn to before me this the 13th day of March , 1905.

AS Kelley
Notary Public.

My commission expires Mch 12-1908

9-372

Muskogee, Indian Territory, March 16, 1905.

John T. Yoakum,
    Paoli, Indian Territory.

Dear Sis:

    Receipt is hereby acknowledged of the affidavits of Minnie A. Yoakum and Laura A. Yoakum to the birth of George W. Yoakum, infant son of John T. and Minnie A. Yoakum, July 12, 1904, and the same have been filed with our records as an application for the enrollment of said child.

                  Respectfully,

                              Chairman.

Chic. N.B - 43
    (Thomas H. Higgins
    Born March 1, 1903)

BIRTH AFFIDAVIT.

DEPARTMENT OF THE INTERIOR,
COMMISSION TO THE FIVE CIVILIZED TRIBES.

    IN RE Application for Enrollment, as a citizen of the Chickasaw Nation, of Thomas H. Higgins , born on the 1 day of March , 1903

Name of Father: Thomas H. Higgins   a citizen of the Chickasaw Nation.
Name of Mother: Frances Higgins   a citizen of the Chickasaw Nation.

                  Post-Office: Tuttle, Ind. Terr.

Applications for Enrollment of Chickasaw Newborn
Act of 1905   Volume I

AFFIDAVIT OF MOTHER.

UNITED STATES OF AMERICA, }
   INDIAN TERRITORY.
So   District.

I, Frances Higgins   , on oath state that I am ....years of age and a citizen by   blood   , of the Chickasaw Nation; that I am the lawful wife of   Thomas H Higgins   , who is a citizen, by   Marriage   of the Chickasaw Nation; that a   male   child was born to me on   1   day of   March   , 1903 , that said child has been named Thomas Howard Higgins   , and is now living.

Frances Higgins

WITNESSES TO MARK:

Subscribed and sworn to before me this 23   day of   Oct   , 190 3

   MY COMMISSION EXPIRES JULY 10, 1904.   A S Taylor
                                                   NOTARY PUBLIC.

AFFIDAVIT OF ATTENDING PHYSICIAN OR MID-WIFE.

UNITED STATES OF AMERICA, }
   INDIAN TERRITORY.
.... District.

I, Katie Pikey   , a   Mid wife   , on oath state that I attended on Mrs. Higgins , wife of Thomas H Higgins   on the   1   day of March   , 190 3; that there was born to her on said date a   male   child; that said child is now living and is said to have been named   Thomas H Higgins

her
Katie x Pikey
mark

WITNESSES TO MARK:
{ A.S. Taylor
  Earl Dobbs

Subscribed and sworn to before me this 23   day of   Oct   , 190 3

   MY COMMISSION EXPIRES JULY 10, 1904.   A S Taylor
                                                   NOTARY PUBLIC.

Applications for Enrollment of Chickasaw Newborn
Act of 1905   Volume I

BIRTH AFFIDAVIT.

DEPARTMENT OF THE INTERIOR.
COMMISSION TO THE FIVE CIVILIZED TRIBES.

IN RE APPLICATION FOR ENROLLMENT, as a citizen of the Chickasaw Nation, of Thomas H Higgins, born on the First day of March, 1903

Name of Father: Thomas H Higgins (now dead) a citizen of the Chickasaw Nation.
(formerly Higgins)
Name of Mother: Francis Fryrear   a citizen of the Chickasaw Nation.

Postoffice   Tuttle, Ind. Terr.

AFFIDAVIT OF MOTHER.

UNITED STATES OF AMERICA, Indian Territory,
   Southern   DISTRICT.

I, Francis Fryrear, on oath state that I am 24 years of age and a citizen by blood, of the Chickasaw Nation; that I am the lawful wife of SB Fryrear, who is a citizen, by marriage of the Chickasaw Nation; that a male child was born to me on First day of March, 1903; that said child has been named Thomas H., and was living March 4, 1905.

Francis Fryrear
Witnesses To Mark:
{   *Formerly Francis Higgins lawful wife of Thomas H Higgins*

Subscribed and sworn to before me this 28 day of Mch, 1905

MY COMMISSION EXPIRES 8/4 1908   A S Taylor
                                          Notary Public.

AFFIDAVIT OF ATTENDING PHYSICIAN OR MID-WIFE.

UNITED STATES OF AMERICA, Indian Territory,
   Southern   DISTRICT.

I, Katie Pikey, a Mid wife, on oath state that I attended on Mrs. Francis Higgins, wife of Thomas H. Higgins on the First day of March, 1903; that there was born to her on said date a male child; that said child was living March 4, 1905, and is said to have been named Thomas H.

her
Katie x Pikey
mark

Applications for Enrollment of Chickasaw Newborn
Act of 1905   Volume I

Witnesses To Mark:
{ *(Name Illegible)*
{ L.K. Bingham

Subscribed and sworn to before me this 28 day of March , 1905

MY COMMISSION EXPIRES 8/4 1908   A S Taylor
                                                         Notary Public.

                                                    Chickasaw 378 &
                                                                379.

                            Muskogee, Indian Territory, April 4, 1905.

A. S. Taylor,
   Minco, Indian Territory.

Dear Sir:

Receipt is hereby acknowledged of your letter of March 30th, enclosing affidavits of Frances Fryrear (formerly Higgins) and Kate Pikey to the birth of Thomas H. Higgins, son of Thomas H. Higgins and Frances Fryrear, March 1, 1903; also the affidavits of Mollie Dobbs (formerly Pikey) and Frances Fryrear to the birth of Martha Ana Dobbs. daughter of E. A. and Mary Dobbs, September 24, 1903: also the affidavits of Katie Pikey and Frances Fryrear to the birth of Delila Pikey, daughter of Katie Pikey, January 15, 1901, and the same have been filed with our records as applications for the enrollment of the above named children.

                          Respectfully,

                                        Commissioner in Charge.

Chic. N.B - 44
       (Martha Ann Dobbs
       Born September 24, 1903)

Applications for Enrollment of Chickasaw Newborn
Act of 1905 Volume I

BIRTH AFFIDAVIT.

DEPARTMENT OF THE INTERIOR.
COMMISSION TO THE FIVE CIVILIZED TRIBES.

IN RE APPLICATION FOR ENROLLMENT, as a citizen of the Chickasaw Nation, of Martha Ann Dobbs , born on the 24 day of Sept , 1904

Name of Father: E. A.Dobbs   a citizen of the U.S. Nation.
Name of Mother: Mollie Dobbs   a citizen of the Chickasaw Nation.

Postoffice   Tuttle Ind Terr

AFFIDAVIT OF MOTHER.

UNITED STATES OF AMERICA, Indian Territory, ⎫
     Southern   DISTRICT. ⎭

I, Mollie Dobbs , on oath state that I am 20 years of age and a citizen by blood , of the Chickasaw Nation; that I am the lawful wife of E. A. Dobbs , who is a citizen, by ——— of the United States Nation; that a Female child was born to me on 24 day of September , 1903; that said child has been named Martha Ann Dobbs , and was living March 4, 1905.

                                           Mollie Dobbs
Witnesses To Mark: *Formerly Mollie Pikey*
{

Subscribed and sworn to before me this 28 day of March , 1905

MY COMMISSION EXPIRES 8/4 1908   A S Taylor
                                            Notary Public.

AFFIDAVIT OF ATTENDING PHYSICIAN OR MID-WIFE.

UNITED STATES OF AMERICA, Indian Territory, ⎫
     Southern   DISTRICT. ⎭

I, Francis Fryrear , a Mid Wife , on oath state that I attended on Mrs. Mollie Dobbs , wife of E.A. Dobbs on the 24 day of September , 1903; that there was born to her on said date a Female child; that said child was living March 4, 1905, and is said to have been named Martha Ann

                                         Francis Fryrear
Witnesses To Mark:
{

Applications for Enrollment of Chickasaw Newborn
Act of 1905   Volume I

Subscribed and sworn to before me this 28 day of March , 1905

MY COMMISSION EXPIRES 8/4 1908   A S Taylor
                                    Notary Public.

Chic. N.B - 45
    (Minnie Ruth Cash
    Born June 24, 1904)

BIRTH AFFIDAVIT.

DEPARTMENT OF THE INTERIOR.
COMMISSION TO THE FIVE CIVILIZED TRIBES.

IN RE APPLICATION FOR ENROLLMENT, as a citizen of the Chickasaw Nation, of Minnie Ruth Cash , born on the 24" day of June , 1904

Name of Father: A. P. Cash   a citizen of the Chickasaw Nation.
Name of Mother: Alice Cash   a citizen of the Chickasaw Nation.

    Postoffice   Maysville, I.T.

AFFIDAVIT OF MOTHER.

UNITED STATES OF AMERICA, Indian Territory,
.... DISTRICT.

    I, Alice Cash , on oath state that I am 23 years of age and a citizen by blood , of the Chickasaw Nation; that I am the lawful wife of A. P. Cash , who is a citizen, by Intermarriage of the Chickasaw Nation; that a female child was born to me on 24" day of June , 1904; that said child has been named Minnie Ruth Cash , and was living March 4, 1905.

                      Alice Cash

Witnesses To Mark:

    Subscribed and sworn to before me this 15th day of May , 1905

                      T. H. Vaughn
                      Notary Public.

Applications for Enrollment of Chickasaw Newborn
Act of 1905   Volume I

AFFIDAVIT OF ATTENDING PHYSICIAN OR MID-WIFE.

UNITED STATES OF AMERICA, Indian Territory, }
.... DISTRICT. }

    I,................................., a ...., on oath state that I attended on Mrs.   Alice Cash   , wife of   A. P. Cash   on the 24" day of June   , 1904; that there was born to her on said date a   female   child; that said child was living March 4, 1905, and is said to have been named Minnie Ruth Cash

                                   Pris[sic] Patterson
Witnesses To Mark:
{

    Subscribed and sworn to before me this   13th day of   May   , 1905

                                   T. H. Vaughn
                                   Notary Public.

BIRTH AFFIDAVIT.
DEPARTMENT OF THE INTERIOR.
COMMISSION TO THE FIVE CIVILIZED TRIBES.

    IN RE APPLICATION FOR ENROLLMENT, as a citizen of the   Chickasaw   Nation, of   Minnie Ruth Cash   , born on the   24   day of   June   , 1904

Name of Father: Albert P. Cash   a citizen of the   Chickasaw   Nation.
Name of Mother: Alice Cash   a citizen of the   Chickasaw   Nation.

                     Postoffice   Maysville, I.T.

AFFIDAVIT OF MOTHER.

UNITED STATES OF AMERICA, Indian Territory, }
    Southern Judicial   DISTRICT. }

    I,   Alice Cash   , on oath state that I am   23   years of age and a citizen by blood   , of the   Chickasaw   Nation; that I am the lawful wife of   Albert P. Cash , who is a citizen, by   intermarriage   of the   Chickasaw   Nation; that a Female   child was born to me on   24   day of   June   , 1904, that said child has been named   Minnie Ruth Cash   , and is now living.

                                   Alice Cash
Witnesses To Mark:
{

Applications for Enrollment of Chickasaw Newborn
Act of 1905   Volume I

Subscribed and sworn to before me this 31st day of Jan , 1905.

My commission } (Name Illegible)
expires Nov 21st 1906 }   Notary Public.

AFFIDAVIT OF ATTENDING PHYSICIAN OR MID-WIFE.

UNITED STATES OF AMERICA, Indian Territory, }
17th DISTRICT. }

I, Price Patterson , a Phisician[sic] , on oath state that I attended on Mrs. Alice Cash , wife of Albert P. Cash on the 24th day of June , 1904; that there was born to her on said date a female child; that said child is now living and is said to have been named Minnie Ruth Cash

Price Patterson M.D.

Witnesses To Mark:
{

Subscribed and sworn to before me this 10th day of March , 1905.

T. J. Austin
Notary Public.

9-381

Muskogee, Indian Territory, March 15, 1905.

Albert P. Cash,
    Maysville, Indian Territory.

Dear Sir:

Receipt is hereby acknowledged of the affidavits of Alice Cash and Price Patterson to the birth of Minnie Ruth Cash infant daughter of Albert P. and Alice Cash, June 24, 1904, and the same have been filed with our records as an application for the enrollment of said child.

Respectfully,

Chairman.

Applications for Enrollment of Chickasaw Newborn
Act of 1905 Volume I

9-N.B. 45.

Muskogee, Indian Territory, May 10, 1905.

A. P. Cash,
Maysville, Indian Territory.

Dear Sir:

There is enclosed you herewith for execution application for the enrollment of your infant child, Minnie Ruth Cash, born June 24, 1904.

The affidavits heretofore filed with the Commission show the child was living on January 31, 1905. It is necessary, for the child to be enrolled, that she was living on March 4, 1905.

In having these affidavits executed care should be exercised to see that all names are written in full, as they appear in the body of the affidavit, and in the event that either of the persons signing the affidavit are unable to write, signatures by mark must be attested by two witnesses. Each affidavit must be executed before a Notary Public and the notarial seal and signature of the officer must be attached to each separate affidavit.

Respectfully,

Chairman.

V. 10/1.

---

9 NB 45.

Muskogee, Indian Territory, May 18, 1905.

A. P. Cash,
Maysville, Indian Territory.

Dear Sir:

Receipt is hereby acknowledged of the affidavits of Alice Cash and Pris Patterson to the birth of Minnie Ruth Cash, daughter of A. P. and Alice Cash, June 24, 1904, and the same have been filed with our records as an application for the enrollment of said child.

Respectfully,

Chairman.

Applications for Enrollment of Chickasaw Newborn
Act of 1905 Volume I

Chic. N.B - 46
(Missouri D. Stanton
Born March 13, 1904)

BIRTH AFFIDAVIT.   No 21

IN RE-APPLICATION FOR ENROLLMENT, as a citizen of the Chickasaw Nation, of Missouri D. Stanton, born on the 13 day of March, 1904

Name of Father: M G Stanton   a citizen of the U.S. Nation.
Name of Mother: Nora L Stanton   a citizen of the Chickasaw Nation.
(enroled[sic] as Nora Rogers[sic])

Postoffice   Pauls Valley I.T.

AFFIDAVIT OF MOTHER.

UNITED STATES OF AMERICA, INDIAN TERRITORY,
Southern   District.

I, Nora Stanton, on oath state that I am 19 years of age and a citizen by blood, of the Chickasaw Nation; that I am the lawful wife of M G Stanton, who is a citizen, by .... of the U.S. Nation; that a female child was born to me on 13th day of March, 1904, that said child has been named Missouri D. Stanton, and is now living.

Nora Rodgers

Witnesses To Mark:
{

Subscribed and sworn to before me this 11 day of Feby, 1905.

J T Blanton
Notary Public.

AFFIDAVIT OF ATTENDING PHYSICIAN OR MID-WIFE.

UNITED STATES OF AMERICA, INDIAN TERRITORY,
Southern   District.

I, R H Salmon, a Physician, on oath state that I attended on Mrs. Nora Stanton, wife of MG Stanton on the 13 day of March, 1904; that there was born to her on said date a female child; that said child is now living and is said to have been named Missouri D Stanton

R.H. Salmon

Witnesses To Mark:
{

Applications for Enrollment of Chickasaw Newborn
Act of 1905   Volume I

Subscribed and sworn to before me this   11   day of   Feby   , 1905.

J T Blanton
Notary Public.

BIRTH AFFIDAVIT.

DEPARTMENT OF THE INTERIOR.
COMMISSION TO THE FIVE CIVILIZED TRIBES.

IN RE APPLICATION FOR ENROLLMENT, as a citizen of the   Chickasaw   Nation, of   Missouri D. Stanton   , born on the 13th day of   March   , 1904

Name of Father: Mirle G. Stanton   a citizen of the .... Nation.
Name of Mother: Nora Lee Stanton (nee Rogers) a citizen of the   Chickasaw   Nation.

Postoffice   Pauls Valley I.T.

AFFIDAVIT OF MOTHER.

UNITED STATES OF AMERICA, Indian Territory,
Southern   DISTRICT.

I,   Nora Lee Stanton (nee Rogers)   , on oath state that I am   19   years of age and a citizen by   Blood   , of the   Chickasaw   Nation; that I am the lawful wife of   Mirle D. Stanton   , who is a   *non*   citizen, by .... of the .... Nation; that a   Female   child was born to me on   13th day of March   , 1904; that said child has been named   Missouri D Stanton   , and was living March 4, 1905.

Nora Lee Stanton
Witnesses To Mark: *(nee Rogers)*

Subscribed and sworn to before me this   23 day of   March   , 1905

Marion Henderson
Notary Public.

Applications for Enrollment of Chickasaw Newborn
Act of 1905   Volume I

AFFIDAVIT OF ATTENDING PHYSICIAN OR MID-WIFE.

UNITED STATES OF AMERICA, Indian Territory, }
Southern   DISTRICT.

I,   Mary A Stanton   , a   mid-wife   , on oath state that I attended on Mrs.   Nora Lee Stanton   , wife of   Mirle D Stanton   on the 13th day of March , 1904; that there was born to her on said date a   Female   child; that said child was living March 4, 1905, and is said to have been named Missouri D Stanton

                                    Mary A Stanton
Witnesses To Mark:
{

    Subscribed and sworn to before me this 23 day of   March   , 1905

                               Marion Henderson
                                 Notary Public.

                                  9-386

                Muskogee, Indian Territory, March 28, 1905.

Mirle G. Stanton,
    Pauls Valley, Indian Territory.

Dear Sir:

    Receipt is hereby acknowledged of the affidavits of Nora Lee Stanton (Rogers) and Mary A. Stanton to the birth of Missouri D. Stanton, daughter of Mirle G. and Nora Lee Stanton, March 13, 1904, and the same have been filed with our records as an application for the enrollment of said child.

                          Respectfully,

                                    Chairman.

Applications for Enrollment of Chickasaw Newborn
Act of 1905   Volume I

Chic. N.B - 47
(Rodie Gibson
Born March 14, 1904)

Indian Territory •
•
•
•
Southern District •

    Before me Geo. T. Putty a notary Public, in and for the Southern District of the Indian Territory personally came and appeared, Silas Gibson, Choctaw Indian by blood, and his wife Minnie Gibson, a Chickasaw Indian by blood, who after being by me duly sworn state that, that[sic] they are Choctaw and Chickasaw Indians respectfully, by blood, and that their child recently born for which they have made application for its enrollment, is their own, born in lawful wedlock, and that they desire to have the same enrolled on the rolls of the Chickasaw Nation.

Witnessed by	Silas Gibson
Geo T. Putty	her
	Minnie x Gibson
	mark

Subscribed and sworn to before me this the 17 day of April, 1905

Com expires	Geo T. Putty
2/18/05.	Notary Public.

    IN RE APPLICATION FOR ENROLLMENT, as a citizen of the   Chickasaw Nation of   Rodie Gibson   born on the   14   day of   March   1904

Name of Father	Silas Gibson	citizen of	Choctaw	Nation
Name of Mother	Minnie Gibson	citizen of	Chickasaw	Nation

Post Office.   Marlow I.T.

AFFIDAVIT OF MOTHER

United States of America Southern District of the Indian Territory:

    I,   Minnie Gibson   on oath state that I am   38   years of age and a citizen by blood   of the   Chickasaw   Nation that I am the lawful wife of   Silas Gibson   who is a citizen by blood of the   Choctaw   Nation that a   Female   Child was born to me on

Applications for Enrollment of Chickasaw Newborn
Act of 1905 Volume I

the 14 day of March 1904 that said Child has been named Rodie Gibson and was living March 4, 1905.

Witnessed by - Geo T. Putty
WC Thompson

Minnie x Gibson
(her mark)

Subscribed and sworn to before me this the 28 day of Mar A.D. 190 *(blank)*

Geo T. Putty
Notary Public.

AFFIDAVIT OF ATTENDING PHYSICIAN

United States of America Southern District of the Indian Territory:

I, W. C. Nation a physician on oath state that I attend[sic] on Mrs Minnie Gibson wife of Silas Gibson on the 14 day of March 1904 and that there was born to her on that date a Female child and that said child was living March 4, 1905, and is said to have been named Rodie Gibson

W. C. Nation M.D.

Subscribed and sworn to before me this the 28 day of Mar 1905.

Geo T. Putty
Notary Public,

Chickasaw 389.

Muskogee, Indian Territory, April 4, 1905.

Silas Gibson,
   Marlow, Indian Territory.

Dear Sir:

Receipt is hereby acknowledged of the affidavits of Minnie Gibson and W. C. Nation to the birth of Rodie Gibson, daughter of Silas and Minnie Gibson, March 14, 1904, and the same have been filed with our records as an application for the enrollment of said child.

Respectfully,

Commissioner in Charge.

Applications for Enrollment of Chickasaw Newborn
Act of 1905 Volume I

COPY. 9 NB 47

9--389
7---24
N B

Muskogee, Indian Territory, April 14, 1905.

Silas Gibson,
    Marlow, Indian Territory.

Dear Sir:

    Referring to the application for the enrollment of your infant child, Rodie Gibson, it appears that you are a citizen by blood of the Choctaw Nation, while your wife is a citizen by blood of the Chickasaw Nation.

    Your attention is called to the provision of the Act of Congress approved June 28, 1898, as follows:

    "The several Tribes may, by agreement, determine the right of persons who for any reason may claim citizenship in two or more tribes, and to allotment of lands and distribution of moneys belonging to each tribe; but if no such agreement be made, then such claimant shall be entitled to such rights in one tribe only, and may elect in which tribe he will take such right; but if he fail or refuse to make such selection in due time, he shall be enrolled in the tribe with whom he has resided, and there be given such allotment and distributions, and not elsewhere."

    It will therefore, be necessary for you and your wife to appear before a Notary Public or other officer authorized to administer oaths, and by affidavit elect in which nation you desire to have said child enrolled, forwarding same, when properly executed, to the Commission.

                Respectfully,

SIGNED
T. B. Needles.
Commissioner in Charge.

Applications for Enrollment of Chickasaw Newborn
Act of 1905 Volume I

COPY

Chickasaw N.B. 117

Muskogee, Indian Territory, April 121[sic], 1905.

Silas Gibson,
    Marlow, Indian Territory.

Dear Sir:

    Receipt is hereby acknowledged of the joint affidavit of Silas and Minnie Gibson, electing to have their child, recently born, for whom enrollment application has been made, enrolled as a citizen of the Chickasaw Nation and the same has been filed with our records in the matter of the enrollment of Rodie Gibson, daughter of Silas and Minnie Gibson.

                  Respectfully,
                  SIGNED

                    Tams Bixby
                       Chairman.

Chic. N.B - 48
    (Douglas Thompson Mitchell
    Born March 19, 1904)

BIRTH AFFIDAVIT.
                    DEPARTMENT OF THE INTERIOR.
             COMMISSION TO THE FIVE CIVILIZED TRIBES.

    IN RE APPLICATION FOR ENROLLMENT, as a citizen of the Chickasaw Nation, of Duglis[sic] Thompson Mitchell, born on the 19 day of March, 1904

Name of Father: Gains A Mitchell   a citizen of the Chickasaw Nation.
Name of Mother: Rilla Mitchell   a citizen of the Chickasaw Nation.

                    Postoffice   Johnson Ind Ter

Applications for Enrollment of Chickasaw Newborn
Act of 1905   Volume I

AFFIDAVIT OF MOTHER.

UNITED STATES OF AMERICA, Indian Territory, }
Sothern[sic]   DISTRICT.

    I, Rilla Mitchell   , on oath state that I am 27   years of age and a citizen by Blood   , of the   Chickasaw   Nation; that I am the lawful wife of   Gains A Mitchell   , who is a citizen, by marage[sic]   of the   Chickasaw   Nation; that a   Boy   child was born to me on   19   day of   March   , 1904; that said child has been named   Duglis Thompson Mitchell   , and was living March 4, 1905.

                                         Rilla Mitchell

Witnesses To Mark:
  { Myrtle Brewer
    Mattie C Dalton

    Subscribed and sworn to before me this 20   day of   March   , 1905

                                        J.W. Gaylord
                                        Notary Public.

AFFIDAVIT OF ATTENDING PHYSICIAN OR MID-WIFE.

UNITED STATES OF AMERICA, Indian Territory, }
Sothern   DISTRICT.

    I,   G.L. Johnson   , a   Physician   , on oath state that I attended on Mrs.   Rilla Mitchell   , wife of   Gains A Mitchell   on the   19th day of   March, 1904; that there was born to her on said date a   male   child; that said child was living March 4, 1905, and is said to have been named Douglas Thompson Mitchell

                                        G.L. Johnson M.D.

Witnesses To Mark:
  { W L Lee

    Subscribed and sworn to before me this 20   day of   March   , 1905

                                        J.W. Gaylord
                                        Notary Public.

Applications for Enrollment of Chickasaw Newborn
Act of 1905 Volume I

9-394

Muskogee, Indian Territory, March 24, 1905.

James A. Mitchell,
    Johnson, Indian Territory.

Dear Sir:

    Receipt is hereby acknowledged of the affidavits of Rilla Mitchell and G. L. Johnson to the birth of Douglis Thompson Mitchell child of James A. and Rilla Mitchell, March 19, 1904, and the same have been filed with our records as an application for the enrollment of said child.

        Respectfully,

            Chairman.

Chic. N.B - 49
    (Ulalia Ruth Howard
    Born February 15, 1903)

BIRTH AFFIDAVIT.

DEPARTMENT OF THE INTERIOR.
COMMISSION TO THE FIVE CIVILIZED TRIBES.

    IN RE APPLICATION FOR ENROLLMENT, as a citizen of the Chickasaw Nation, of Ulalia Ruth Howard, born on the 15th day of February, 1903

Name of Father: William B Howard   a citizen of the Chickasaw Nation.
Name of Mother: Mary I Howard   a citizen of the Chickasaw Nation.

        Postoffice   Norman, O.T.

AFFIDAVIT OF MOTHER.

UNITED STATES OF AMERICA, Indian Territory, }
    Southern   DISTRICT.

    I, Mary I Howard, on oath state that I am 25 years of age and a citizen by blood, of the Chickasaw Nation; that I am the lawful wife of William B

Applications for Enrollment of Chickasaw Newborn
Act of 1905 Volume I

Howard   , who is a citizen, by   intermarriage   of the   Chickasaw   Nation; that a   female   child was born to me on   15th day of   February   , 1903, that said child has been named   Ulalia Ruth Howard   , and is now living.

Mary I Howard

Witnesses To Mark:
{

Subscribed and sworn to before me this   20th day of   March   , 1905.

(Illegible) Carter
Notary Public.

AFFIDAVIT OF ATTENDING PHYSICIAN OR MID-WIFE.

UNITED STATES OF AMERICA, Indian Territory,
   Southern   DISTRICT.

I,   C.P. Kelly[sic]   , a   Physician   , on oath state that I attended on Mrs.   Mary I Howard   , wife of   William B Howard   on the   15th day of February , 1903; that there was born to her on said date a   female   child; that said child is now living and is said to have been named Ulalia Ruth Howard

Dr C P Kelley

Witnesses To Mark:
{

Subscribed and sworn to before me this   27th day of   March   , 1905.

James A. Cowan
Notary Public.

My Commission Expires Feb. 15, 1908.

9-404

Muskogee, Indian Territory, April 4, 1905.

William B. Howard,
    Purcell, Indian Territory.

Dear Sir:

Receipt is hereby acknowledged of your letter of March 20, 1905, enclosing the affidavits of Mary I. Howard and Dr. C. P. Kelly to the birth of Ulalia Ruth Howard,

Applications for Enrollment of Chickasaw Newborn
Act of 1905   Volume I

daughter of William B/[sic] and Mary I. Howard, February 15, 1903, and the same have been filed with our records as an application for the enrollment of said child.

        Respectfully,

                Chairman.

                9 NB 49

      Muskogee, Indian Territory, April 20, 1905.

William B. Howard,
   Norman, Oklahoma.

Dear Sir:

    Receipt is hereby acknowledged of your letter of April 15, 1905, asking if affidavit in regard to the enrollment of your child Eulalia[sic] Ruth Howard has been received.

    In reply to your letter you are informed that the affidavits heretofore forwarded to the birth of your child Eulalia Ruth Howard have been filed with our records as an application for the enrollment of said child.

        Respectfully,

                Chairman.

Chic. N.B - 50
    (Estella M. Friend
    Born November 17, 1902)
    (Douglas H. Friend
    Born August 12, 1904)

Applications for Enrollment of Chickasaw Newborn
Act of 1905 Volume I

BIRTH AFFIDAVIT.

DEPARTMENT OF THE INTERIOR.
COMMISSION TO THE FIVE CIVILIZED TRIBES.

IN RE APPLICATION FOR ENROLLMENT, as a citizen of the Chickasaw Nation, of Estella M. Friend, born on the 17th day of Nov, 1902

by Intermarriage

Name of Father: Thos L. Friend   a citizen of the Chickasaw Nation.
Name of Mother: Retta Friend   a citizen of the Chickasaw Nation.
     Postoffice   Chickasha, Ind. Ter.

AFFIDAVIT OF MOTHER.

UNITED STATES OF AMERICA, Indian Territory, } Southern DISTRICT.

I, Retta Friend, on oath state that I am twenty eight years of age and a citizen by blood, of the Chickasaw Nation; that I am the lawful wife of Thos L. Friend, who is a citizen, by Intermarriage of the Chickasaw Nation; that a Female child was born to me on Seventeenth day of November, 1902, that said child has been named Estella M Friend, and is now living.

                 Retta Friend

Witnesses To Mark:
{

Subscribed and sworn to before me this 21st day of Jany A.D., 1905.

                 R.D. Wilborne
                 Notary Public.

AFFIDAVIT OF ATTENDING PHYSICIAN OR MID-WIFE.

UNITED STATES OF AMERICA, Indian Territory, } Southern DISTRICT.

I, E. L. Dawson, a Physician, on oath state that I attended on Mrs. Retta Friend, wife of Thos L Friend on the 17th day of Nov A.D., 1902; that there was born to her on said date a Female child; that said child is now living and is said to have been named Estella M Friend

                 E. L. Dawson, M.D.

Witnesses To Mark:
{

Applications for Enrollment of Chickasaw Newborn
Act of 1905   Volume I

Subscribed and sworn to before me this 21ˢᵗ day of Jany A.D. , 1905.

R.D. Wilborne
Notary Public.

BIRTH AFFIDAVIT.   #129

DEPARTMENT OF THE INTERIOR.
COMMISSION TO THE FIVE CIVILIZED TRIBES.

IN RE APPLICATION FOR ENROLLMENT, as a citizen of the Chickasaw Nation, of Douglas H. Friend , born on the 12ᵗʰ day of August A.D. , 1904

by Intermarriage

Name of Father: Thos L. Friend   a citizen of the Chickasaw Nation.
Name of Mother: Retta Friend   a citizen of the Chickasaw Nation.

Postoffice   Chickasha, Ind. Ter.

AFFIDAVIT OF MOTHER.

UNITED STATES OF AMERICA, Indian Territory, ⎫
Southern   DISTRICT.   ⎬

I, Retta Friend , on oath state that I am twenty eight years of age and a citizen by blood , of the Chickasaw Nation; that I am the lawful wife of Thos L. Friend , who is a citizen, by Intermarriage of the Chickasaw Nation; that a male child was born to me on 12ᵗʰ day of August A.D. , 1904, that said child has been named Douglas H Friend , and is now living.

Retta Friend

Witnesses To Mark:
{

Subscribed and sworn to before me this 21ˢᵗ day of Jany A.D. , 1905.

R.D. Wilborne
Notary Public.

Applications for Enrollment of Chickasaw Newborn
Act of 1905 Volume I

AFFIDAVIT OF ATTENDING PHYSICIAN OR MID-WIFE.

UNITED STATES OF AMERICA, Indian Territory,
Southern   DISTRICT.

I, E. L. Dawson, a Physician, on oath state that I attended on Mrs. Retta Friend, wife of Thos L Friend on the 12th day of August A.D., 1904; that there was born to her on said date a male child; that said child is now living and is said to have been named Douglas H Friend

E. L. Dawson, M.D.

Witnesses To Mark:

Subscribed and sworn to before me this 21st day of Jany A.D., 1905.

R.D. Wilborne
Notary Public.

BIRTH AFFIDAVIT.

DEPARTMENT OF THE INTERIOR.
COMMISSION TO THE FIVE CIVILIZED TRIBES.

IN RE APPLICATION FOR ENROLLMENT, as a citizen of the Chickasaw Nation, of Douglas H. Friend, born on the 12th day of Aug, 1904

Name of Father: Thomas L Friend   a citizen of the Chickasaw Nation.
Name of Mother: Retta Friend   a citizen of the Chickasaw Nation.

Postoffice Chickasha I T

Box 785

AFFIDAVIT OF MOTHER.

UNITED STATES OF AMERICA, Indian Territory,
Southern   DISTRICT.

I, Retta Friend, on oath state that I am 28 years of age and a citizen by Blood, of the Chickasaw Nation; that I am the lawful wife of Thomas L Friend, who is a citizen, by Intermarriage of the Chickasaw Nation; that a male child was born to me on 12th day of August, 1904; that said child has been named Douglas H. Friend, and was living March 4, 1905.

Retta Friend

Applications for Enrollment of Chickasaw Newborn
Act of 1905 Volume I

Witnesses To Mark:
{

    Subscribed and sworn to before me this 14 day of March , 1905

                          R. M. Cochran
                          Notary Public.

AFFIDAVIT OF ATTENDING PHYSICIAN OR MID-WIFE.

UNITED STATES OF AMERICA, Indian Territory, }
   Southern   DISTRICT. }

    I, E L Dawson , a Physician , on oath state that I attended on Mrs. Retta Friend , wife of Thomas L Friend on the 12th day of August, 1904; that there was born to her on said date a male child; that said child was living March 4, 1905, and is said to have been named Douglas H Friend

                          E L Dawson M D

Witnesses To Mark:
{

    Subscribed and sworn to before me this 14 day of March , 1905

                          R. M. Cochran
                          Notary Public.

BIRTH AFFIDAVIT.

DEPARTMENT OF THE INTERIOR.
COMMISSION TO THE FIVE CIVILIZED TRIBES.

    IN RE APPLICATION FOR ENROLLMENT, as a citizen of the Chickasaw Nation, of Estella M. Friend , born on the 17 day of Nov , 1902

Name of Father: Thomas L Friend   a citizen of the Chickasaw Nation.
Name of Mother: Retta Friend   a citizen of the Chickasaw Nation.

                Postoffice   Chickasha I T
                        Box 785

Applications for Enrollment of Chickasaw Newborn
Act of 1905   Volume I

AFFIDAVIT OF MOTHER.

UNITED STATES OF AMERICA, Indian Territory, }
Southern   DISTRICT.

I, Retta Friend, on oath state that I am 28 years of age and a citizen by Blood, of the Chickasaw Nation; that I am the lawful wife of Thomas L Friend, who is a citizen, by Intermarriage of the Chickasaw Nation; that a Female child was born to me on 17th day of November, 1902; that said child has been named Estella M Friend, and was living March 4, 1905.

Retta Friend

Witnesses To Mark:
{

Subscribed and sworn to before me this 14 day of Mach, 1905

Notary Public.

AFFIDAVIT OF ATTENDING PHYSICIAN OR MID-WIFE.

UNITED STATES OF AMERICA, Indian Territory, }
Southern   DISTRICT.

I, E L Dawson, a Physician, on oath state that I attended on Mrs. Retta Friend, wife of Thomas L Friend on the 17th day of November, 1902; that there was born to her on said date a Female child; that said child was living March 4, 1905, and is said to have been named Estella M Friend

E L Dawson M D

Witnesses To Mark:
{

Subscribed and sworn to before me this 14th day of March, 1905

R M Cochran
Notary Public.

Applications for Enrollment of Chickasaw Newborn
Act of 1905 Volume I

9-406

Muskogee, Indian Territory, March 20, 1905.

Thomas L. Friend,
    Box 785,
        Chickasha, Indian Territory.

Dear Sir:

    Receipt is hereby acknowledged of the affidavits of Retta Friend and E. L. Dawson M. D., to the birth of Douglas H. Friend, child of Thomas L. and Retta Friend, August 12, 1904, and the same have been filed with our records as an application for the enrollment of said child.

Respectfully,

Chairman.

9-406

Muskogee, Indian Territory, March 20, 1905.

Thomas L. Friend,
    Box 785,
        Chickasha, Indian Territory.

Dear Sir:

    Receipt is hereby acknowledged of the affidavits of Retta Friend and E. L. Dawson M.D., to the birth of Estella M. Friend child of Thomas L. and Retta Friend, November 17, 1902, and the same have been filed with our records as an application for the enrollment of said child.

Respectfully,

Chairman.

Applications for Enrollment of Chickasaw Newborn
Act of 1905   Volume I

9-NB-50

Muskogee, Indian Territory, May 18, 1905.

Thomas L. Friend,
    Chickasha, Indian Territory.

Dear Sir:

    There is enclosed herewith application for the enrollment of your infant child, Douglas H. Friend, born August 12, 1904, in which the notary public failed to sign the mothers[sic] affidavit.

    You will please secure the signature of the notary public to this affidavit and return it promptly to this office.

                     Respectfully,

                              Chairman.

---

9 N.B. 50.

Muskogee, Indian Territory, May 26, 1905.

Thomas L. Friend,
    Chickasha, Indian Territory.

Dear Sir:

    Receipt is hereby acknowledged of the application for the enrollment of Douglas H. Friend, which has been corrected by having the signature of the Notary Public affixed to the affidavit of the mother, Reta[sic] Friend, and the same has been filed in the matter of the enrollment of said child.

                     Respectfully,

                              Chairman.

Applications for Enrollment of Chickasaw Newborn
Act of 1905 Volume I

Chic. N.B - 51
    (Tommy C. Myers
    Born May 18, 1904)

BIRTH AFFIDAVIT.   No 63

DEPARTMENT OF THE INTERIOR.
COMMISSION TO THE FIVE CIVILIZED TRIBES.

IN RE APPLICATION FOR ENROLLMENT, as a citizen of the Chickasaw Nation, of Tommy C. Myers, born on the 18th day of May, 1904

Name of Father: Joseph F. Myers   a citizen of the Chickasaw Nation.
Name of Mother: Eula Myers   a citizen of the Chickasaw Nation.

    Postoffice   Pauls Valley Ind Ter

AFFIDAVIT OF MOTHER.

UNITED STATES OF AMERICA, Indian Territory,
Southern District   DISTRICT.

    I, Eula Myers, on oath state that I am 35 years of age and a citizen by Blood, of the Chickasaw Nation; that I am the lawful wife of Joseph F Myers, who is a citizen, by marriage of the Chickasaw Nation; that a girl child was born to me on 18th day of May, 1904, that said child has been named Tommy C. Myers, and is now living.

                Eula Myers
Witnesses To Mark:

    Subscribed and sworn to before me this 31st day of December, 1904

                L. T. Jones
                    Notary Public.

Applications for Enrollment of Chickasaw Newborn
Act of 1905   Volume I

AFFIDAVIT OF ATTENDING PHYSICIAN OR MID-WIFE.

UNITED STATES OF AMERICA, Indian Territory, ⎫
Southern District   DISTRICT. ⎬

I, W.J. Maniss , a Physician , on oath state that I attended on Mrs. Eula Myers , wife of Joseph F Myers on the 18th day of May , 1904; that there was born to her on said date a girl child; that said child is now living and is said to have been named Tommy C. Myers

W.J. Maniss

Witnesses To Mark:
{

Subscribed and sworn to before me this 31st day of December , 1904

L. T. Jones
My commission expires   Notary Public.
March 18th 1905

BIRTH AFFIDAVIT.

IN RE-APPLICATION FOR ENROLLMENT, as a citizen of the   Chickasaw   Nation, of Tommie C. Myers , born on the 18th day of May , 190 4

Name of Father: Joseph F Myers   a citizen of the   Chickasaw   Nation.
Name of Mother: Eula Myers   a citizen of the   "   Nation.

Postoffice   Pauls Valley I.T.

AFFIDAVIT OF MOTHER.

UNITED STATES OF AMERICA, INDIAN TERRITORY, ⎫
Southern Judicial   District. ⎬

I, Eula Myers , on oath state that I am .... years of age and a citizen by Blood , of the Chickasaw Nation; that I am the lawful wife of Joseph F Myers , who is a citizen, by Marriage of the Chickasaw Nation; that a girl child was born to me on 18th day of May , 1904, that said child has been named Tommie C Myers, and is now living.

Eula Myers

Witnesses To Mark:
{ Seila R. Maniss
{ Jessie E. Moore

Applications for Enrollment of Chickasaw Newborn
Act of 1905   Volume I

Subscribed and sworn to before me this 16th day of March, 1905.

                                 L.T. Jones
                                 Notary Public.

AFFIDAVIT OF ATTENDING PHYSICIAN OR MID-WIFE.

UNITED STATES OF AMERICA, INDIAN TERRITORY,
Southern Judicial District.

    I, W.J. Maniss, a Physician, on oath state that I attended on Mrs. Eula Myers, wife of Joseph F Myers on the 18th day of May, 190 4; that there was born to her on said date a girl child; that said child is now living and is said to have been named Tommie C Myers

                               W. J. Maniss M.D.

Witnesses To Mark:
{ R.B. Smith
{ *(Name Illegible)*

Subscribed and sworn to before me this 16th day of March, 1905.

                               L.T. Jones
                               Notary Public.

9-410

Muskogee, Indian Territory, March 24, 1905.

Joseph F. Myers,
    Pauls Valley, Indian Territory.

Dear Sir:

    Receipt is hereby acknowledged of the affidavits of Eula Myers and W. P. Morriss[sic] to the birth of Tommie C. Myers daughter of Joseph F. and Eula Myers, May 18, 1904, and the same have been filed with our records as an application for the enrollment of said child.

                     Respectfully,

                               Chairman.

Applications for Enrollment of Chickasaw Newborn
Act of 1905   Volume I

Chic. N.B - 52
*(Jewel Eugenia Nichols
Born November 2, 1903)*

BIRTH AFFIDAVIT.

DEPARTMENT OF THE INTERIOR,
COMMISSION TO THE FIVE CIVILIZED TRIBES.

In Re Application for Enrollment, as a citizen of the Chickasaw   Nation, of   Jewel Eugenia   , born on the 2   day of   November   , 1903

Name of Father: James Luther Nichols   a citizen of the United States Nation.
Name of Mother: Velary Etta Colbert Nichols   a citizen of the Chickasaw   Nation.

Post-office   Lindsay IT

AFFIDAVIT OF MOTHER.

UNITED STATES OF AMERICA, }
 INDIAN TERRITORY,
Southern   District.

I, Velary Etta Colbert Nichols , on oath state that I am   20   years of age and a citizen by   Blood   , of the   Chickasaw   Nation; that I am the lawful wife of   James Luther Nichols   , who is a citizen, by Birth of the   United States   Nation; that a   Female   child was born to me on   2   day of November   , 1903 , that said child has been named   Jewel Eugenia Nichols   , and is now living.

Velary Etta Colbert Nichols

WITNESSES TO MARK:
{

Subscribed and sworn to before me this   14   day of   May   , 190 4

TM Bell
NOTARY PUBLIC.

Applications for Enrollment of Chickasaw Newborn
Act of 1905 Volume I

AFFIDAVIT OF ATTENDING PHYSICIAN OR MID-WIFE.

UNITED STATES OF AMERICA,
INDIAN TERRITORY,
Southern District.

I, S W Wilson MD , a Physician , on oath state that I attended on Mrs. Velary Etta Colbert Nichols , wife of James Luther Nichols on the 2 day of November , 1904[sic] ; that there was born to her on said date a Female child; that said child is now living and is said to have been named ....

SW Wilson M.D.

WITNESSES TO MARK:

Subscribed and sworn to before me this 14 day of May , 190 4

TM Bell
NOTARY PUBLIC.

BIRTH AFFIDAVIT. #101

DEPARTMENT OF THE INTERIOR,
COMMISSION TO THE FIVE CIVILIZED TRIBES.

In Re Application for Enrollment, as a citizen of the Chickasaw Nation, of Joel[sic] Eugenia Nichols , born on the 2nd day of November , 1903

Intermarried

Name of Father: Luther Nichols — a citizen of the Chickasaw Nation.
Name of Mother: Velary Etta Nichols — a citizen of the Chickasaw Nation.

Post-office Lindsay Ian'd[sic] Territory

AFFIDAVIT OF MOTHER.

UNITED STATES OF AMERICA,
INDIAN TERRITORY,
Southern District.

I, Velary Etta Nichols , on oath state that I am 21 years of age and a citizen by Blood , of the Chickasaw Nation; that I am the lawful wife of Luther Nichols , who is a citizen, by Intermarriage of the Chickasaw Nation; that a Female child was born to me on the 2nd day of November , 1903 , that said child has been named Joel Eugenia Nichols , and is now living.

Applications for Enrollment of Chickasaw Newborn
Act of 1905 Volume I

Velary Etta Nichols

WITNESSES TO MARK:
{

Subscribed and sworn to before me this 17th day of February , 190 5

F.E. Rice
My Com expires   **NOTARY PUBLIC.**
Dec 4" 1907

AFFIDAVIT OF ATTENDING PHYSICIAN OR MID-WIFE.

UNITED STATES OF AMERICA, }
  INDIAN TERRITORY,
Southern   District. }

I, S W Wilson , a Practicing Physician , on oath state that I attended on Mrs. Velary Etta Nichols , wife of Luther Nichols on the 2nd day of November , 1903 ; that there was born to her on said date a female child; that said child is now living and is said to have been named Joel Eugenia Nichols

SW Wilson M.D.

WITNESSES TO MARK:
{

Subscribed and sworn to before me this 17th day of February , 190 5

F.E. Rice
My Com expires Dec 4" 1907   **NOTARY PUBLIC.**

BIRTH AFFIDAVIT.

DEPARTMENT OF THE INTERIOR.
COMMISSION TO THE FIVE CIVILIZED TRIBES.

IN RE APPLICATION FOR ENROLLMENT, as a citizen of the Chickasaw Nation, of Jerrel Eugenia Nichols , born on the 2nd day of November , 1903

Name of Father: Luther Nichols   a citizen of the .... Nation.
Name of Mother: Velary[sic] Etta Nichols   a citizen of the Chickasaw Nation.

Postoffice   Lindsay, Indian Territory

Applications for Enrollment of Chickasaw Newborn
Act of 1905   Volume I

AFFIDAVIT OF MOTHER.

UNITED STATES OF AMERICA, Indian Territory, }
Southern   DISTRICT.

    I, Velary Etta Nichols, on oath state that I am 21 years of age and a citizen by Blood, of the Chickasaw Nation; that I am the lawful wife of Luther Nichols, who is a citizen, by ——— of the ——— Nation; that a female child was born to me on 2nd day of November, 1903; that said child has been named Jerrel Eugenia Nichols, and was living March 4, 1905.

                                                    Velary Etta Nichols

Witnesses To Mark:
{

    Subscribed and sworn to before me this 27th day of March, 1905

                                                    F.E. Rice
                                                    Notary Public.

AFFIDAVIT OF ATTENDING PHYSICIAN OR MID-WIFE.

UNITED STATES OF AMERICA, Indian Territory, }
Southern   DISTRICT.

    I, S.W. Wilson, a Physician, on oath state that I attended on Mrs. Velary Etta Nichols, wife of Luther Nichols on the 2nd day of November, 1903; that there was born to her on said date a female child; that said child was living March 4, 1905, and is said to have been named Jerrel Eugenia Nichols

                                                  S W Wilson M.D.

Witnesses To Mark:
{

    Subscribed and sworn to before me this 28th day of March, 1905

                                                      F.E. Rice
                                                    Notary Public.

Applications for Enrollment of Chickasaw Newborn
Act of 1905 Volume I

9-412

Muskogee, Indian Territory, April 4, 1905.

F. E. Rice,
    Lindsay, Indian Territory.

Dear Sir:

    Receipt is hereby acknowledged of the affidavits of Velary Etta Nichols and S. W. Wilson to the birth of Jerrel Eugenia Nichols daughter of Luther and Velary Etta Nichols, November 2, 1903, and the same have been filed with our records as an application for the enrollment of said child.

Respectfully,

Chairman.

Chic. N.B - 53
    (Gladys Monnie Gooch
    Born January 10, 1905)

BIRTH AFFIDAVIT.

DEPARTMENT OF THE INTERIOR,
COMMISSION TO THE FIVE CIVILIZED TRIBES.

IN RE APPLICATION FOR ENROLLMENT, as a citizen of the Chickasaw Nation of Gladys Monnie Gooch, born on the 10th day of January 1905

Intermarried

Name of Father: Dean Gooch   a citizen of the Chickasaw Nation
Name of Mother: Cora Eugenia Gooch, a citizen of the Chickasaw Nation

Post-office   Lindsay, Indian Territory

Applications for Enrollment of Chickasaw Newborn
Act of 1905   Volume I

AFFIDAVIT OF MOTHER.

United States of America,
Indian Territory,
Southern District.

I,   Cora Eugenia Gooch   , on oath state that I am   19   years of age and a citizen, by Blood   of the   Chickasaw   nation that I am the lawful wife of   Dean Gooch   who is a citizen by   Intermarriage   of the   Chickasaw Nation; that a   female   child was born to me on the   10th   day of   January   190 5, that said child has been named   Gladys Monnie Gooch   , and is now living.
Witnesses to mark.   Cora Eugenia Gooch

Subscribed and sworn to before me this   2   day of   March   1905.

F. E. Rice
Notary Public.

AFFIDAVIT OF ATTENDING PHYSICIAN, OR MID-WIFE.

United States of America,
Indian Territory,
   Southern   District.

I,   SW Wilson   , a Practicing Physician, on oath state that I attended on Mrs.   Cora Eugenia Gooch   , wife of   Dean Gooch   on the   10th   day of   January   190 5; that there was born to her on said date a   female   child; that said child is now living and is said to have been named   Gladys Monnie Gooch

S W Wilson M.D.

Subscribed and sworn to before me this   2nd   day of   March   1905.

My Commission expires   F. E. Rice
   Dec 4th 1907   Notary Public.

(The above affidavit given again.)

Applications for Enrollment of Chickasaw Newborn
Act of 1905   Volume I

BIRTH AFFIDAVIT.

DEPARTMENT OF THE INTERIOR,
COMMISSION TO THE FIVE CIVILIZED TRIBES.

In Re Application for Enrollment, as a citizen of the Chickasaw Nation, of Gladys Monnie Gooch, born on the 10th day of January, 1905

Intermarried

Name of Father: Dean Gooch   a citizen of the Chickasaw Nation.
Name of Mother: Cora Eugenia Gooch   a citizen of the Chickasaw Nation.

Post-office   Lindsay, Indian Territory

AFFIDAVIT OF MOTHER.

UNITED STATES OF AMERICA, }
INDIAN TERRITORY,
Southern   District.

I, Cora Eugenia Gooch, on oath state that I am 19 years of age and a citizen by Blood, of the Chickasaw Nation; that I am the lawful wife of Dean Gooch, who is a citizen, by Intermarriage of the Chickasaw Nation; that a female child was born to me on the 10th day of January, 1905, that said child has been named Gladys Monnie Gooch, and is now living.

Cora Eugenia Gooch

WITNESSES TO MARK:
{

Subscribed and sworn to before me this 2nd day of March, 1905

F. E. Rich

NOTARY PUBLIC.

AFFIDAVIT OF ATTENDING PHYSICIAN OR MID-WIFE.

UNITED STATES OF AMERICA, }
INDIAN TERRITORY,
Southern   District.

I, S W Wilson, a Practicing Physician, on oath state that I attended on Mrs. Cora Eugenia Gooch, wife of Dean Gooch on the 10th day of January, 1905; that there was born to her on said date a female child; that said child is now living and is said to have been named Gladys Monnie Gooch

S W Wilson M.D.

Applications for Enrollment of Chickasaw Newborn
Act of 1905 Volume I

WITNESSES TO MARK:
{

Subscribed and sworn to before me this 2nd day of March, 1905

My commission expires F. E. Rich
Dec 4 1907 **NOTARY PUBLIC.**

BIRTH AFFIDAVIT.

DEPARTMENT OF THE INTERIOR.
COMMISSION TO THE FIVE CIVILIZED TRIBES.

IN RE APPLICATION FOR ENROLLMENT, as a citizen of the Chickasaw Nation, of Gladys Monnie Gooch , born on the 10th day of January , 1905

Name of Father: Dean Gooch a citizen of the .... Nation.
Name of Mother: Cora Eugenia Gooch a citizen of the Chickasaw Nation.

Postoffice Lindsay Ind Territory

AFFIDAVIT OF MOTHER.

UNITED STATES OF AMERICA, Indian Territory, }
Southern DISTRICT. }

I, Cora Eugenia Gooch , on oath state that I am 20 years of age and a citizen by blood , of the Chickasaw Nation; that I am the lawful wife of Dean Gooch , who is a citizen, by Intermarriage of the .... Nation; that a female child was born to me on 10th day of January , 1905; that said child has been named Gladys Monnie Gooch , and was living March 4, 1905.

Cora Eugenia Gooch

Witnesses To Mark:
{

Subscribed and sworn to before me this 13th day of April , 1905

F. E. Rice
Notary Public.

Applications for Enrollment of Chickasaw Newborn
Act of 1905   Volume I

AFFIDAVIT OF ATTENDING PHYSICIAN OR MID-WIFE.

UNITED STATES OF AMERICA, Indian Territory, }
Southern   DISTRICT. }

I, S.W. Wilson, a Physician, on oath state that I attended on Mrs. Cora Eugenia Gooch, wife of Dean Gooch on the 10th day of January, 1905; that there was born to her on said date a female child; that said child was living March 4, 1905, and is said to have been named Gladys Monnie Gooch

S W Wilson MD

Witnesses To Mark:
{

Subscribed and sworn to before me this 13th day of April, 1905.

F. E. Rice
Notary Public.

9-412

Muskogee, Indian Territory, April 20, 1905.

F. E. Rice,
Lindsay, Indian Territory.

Dear Sir:

Receipt is hereby acknowledged of your letter of April 13, 1905, transmitting affidavits of Cora Eugenia Gooch and S. W. Wilson to the birth of Gladys Monnie Gooch, daughter of Dean and Cora Eugenia Gooch, January 10, 1905, and the same have been filed with our records as an application for the enrollment of said child.

Respectfully,

Chairman.

Applications for Enrollment of Chickasaw Newborn
Act of 1905   Volume I

Chic. N.B - 54
   (Mattie Hull
   Born October 23, 1902)

BIRTH AFFIDAVIT.   9 n 1354

Department of the Interior,
COMMISSION TO THE FIVE CIVILIZED TRIBES.

IN RE APPLICATION FOR ENROLLMENT, as a citizen of the   Chickasaw   Nation, of   Mattie Hull   , born on the   23   day of   October   , 190 2

Name of Father: Jesse Hull   a citizen of the Chickasaw   Nation.
Name of Mother: Belle Hull   a citizen of the Chickasaw   Nation.

Post-Office: Whitebead I.T.

AFFIDAVIT OF MOTHER.

UNITED STATES OF AMERICA,
   INDIAN TERRITORY,
Southern   District.

I,   Belle Hull   , on oath state that I am 24   years of age and a citizen by   marriage   , of the   Chickasaw   Nation; that I am the lawful wife of   Jesse Hull   , who is a citizen, by Blood   of the   Chickasaw   Nation; that a female   child was born to me on 23 day of   October   , 1902, that said child has been named   Mattie Hull   , and is now living.

                                    Belle Hull
WITNESSES TO MARK:
{

Subscribed and sworn to before me this   11   day of   November   , 1902

                              C.S. Hannin
                                    Notary Public.

221

Applications for Enrollment of Chickasaw Newborn
Act of 1905   Volume I

AFFIDAVIT OF ATTENDING PHYSICIAN OR MID-WIFE.

UNITED STATES OF AMERICA, }
   INDIAN TERRITORY,
  Southern   District.

I, T.C. Branum, a Doctor, on oath state that I attended on Mrs. Belle Hull, wife of Jesse Hull on the 23 day of October, 190 2; that there was born to her on said date a female child; that said child is now living and is said to have been named Mattie Hull

                        T.C. Branum M.D.

WITNESSES TO MARK:
{

Subscribed and sworn to before me this 11 day of November, 1902

                      C.S. Hannin
                        Notary Public.

BIRTH AFFIDAVIT.

DEPARTMENT OF THE INTERIOR.
COMMISSION TO THE FIVE CIVILIZED TRIBES.

IN RE APPLICATION FOR ENROLLMENT, as a citizen of the Chickasaw Nation, of Mattie Hull, born on the 23rd day of October, 1902

Name of Father: Jesse Hull   a citizen of the Chickasaw Nation.
Name of Mother: Belle Langdon Hull   a citizen of the Chickasaw Nation.

            Postoffice   ~~Whitebead~~ I.T.
                         Wagner — —

AFFIDAVIT OF MOTHER.

UNITED STATES OF AMERICA, Indian Territory, }
  Southern   DISTRICT.

I, Belle Langdon Hull, on oath state that I am 27 years of age and a citizen by marriage, of the Chickasaw Nation; that I am the lawful wife of Jesse Hull, who is a citizen, by blood of the Chickasaw Nation; that a female child was born to me on 23rd day of October, 1902; that said child has been named Mattie Hull, ~~and was living March 4, 1905~~.
                          Died on Oct. 18th 1904

Applications for Enrollment of Chickasaw Newborn
Act of 1905   Volume I

Witnesses To Mark:

{

Subscribed and sworn to before me this .... day of ...., 190.....

....
Notary Public.

AFFIDAVIT OF ATTENDING PHYSICIAN OR MID-WIFE.

UNITED STATES OF AMERICA, Indian Territory, }
.... DISTRICT. }

I, ..., a ...., on oath state that I attended on Mrs. Belle Langdon Hull , wife of Jesse Hull on the 23rd day of October, 1902; that there was born to her on said date a   female   child; that said child was living March 4, 1905, and is said to have been named Mattie Hull

Witnesses To Mark:

{

Subscribed and sworn to before me this .... day of ...., 190.....

....
Notary Public.

It appearing from the within affidavits that Mattie Hull born October 23, 1902, for whose enrollment as a citizen by blood of the Chickasaw Nation application was made under the Act of Congress approved March 3, 1905, (33 Stats., 1071), died October 18, 1904, it is hereby ordered that the application for the enrollment of said Mattie Hull, as a citizen by blood of the Chickasaw Nation be dismissed.

Tams Bixby   Commissioner,

Muskogee, Indian Territory,
NOV 16 1905

Applications for Enrollment of Chickasaw Newborn
Act of 1905   Volume I

DEPARTMENT OF THE INTERIOR.
COMMISSION TO THE FIVE CIVILIZED TRIBES.

In the matter of the death of   Mattie Hull   a citizen of the   Chickasaw Nation, who formerly resided at or near   Wayne   , Ind. Ter., and died on the   18th   day of October , 1904

AFFIDAVIT OF RELATIVE.

UNITED STATES OF AMERICA, Indian Territory,
Southern   DISTRICT.

I, Jesse Hull , on oath state that I am   25   years of age and a citizen by blood , of the Chickasaw Nation; that my postoffice address is   Wayne   , Ind. Ter.; that I am   father   of   Mattie Hull   who was a citizen, by blood   , of the Chickasaw Nation and that said   Mattie Hull   died on the   18th   day of   October , 1904

Jesse Hull

Witnesses To Mark:
{

Subscribed and sworn to before me this   13th   day of   September   , 1905.

T.J. Austin
Notary Public.

AFFIDAVIT OF ACQUAINTANCE.

UNITED STATES OF AMERICA, Indian Territory,
Southern   DISTRICT.

I,   William Hull   , on oath state that I am   61   years of age, and a citizen by intermarriage   of the Chickasaw   Nation; that my postoffice address is   White Bead   , Ind. Ter.; that I was personally acquainted with   Mattie Hull   who was a citizen, by blood , of the Chickasaw Nation; and that said   Mattie Hull   died on the   18th   day of   October   , 1904

William Hull

Witnesses To Mark:
{

Subscribed and sworn to before me this   14th   day of   September   , 1905.

Marion Henderson
Notary Public.

Applications for Enrollment of Chickasaw Newborn
Act of 1905   Volume I

9, N.B. 54.

Muskogee, Indian Territory, May 10, 1905.

Jesse Hull,
    Whitebead, Indian Territory.

Dear Sir:

    There is enclosed you herewith for execution application for the enrollment of your infant child, Mattie Hull, born October 23, 1902.

    The affidavits heretofore filed with the Commission show the child was living on November 11, 1902. It is necessary, for the child to be enrolled, that she was living on March 4, 1905.

    In having these affidavits executed care should be exercised to see that all names are written in full, as they appear in the body of the affidavit, and in the event that either of the persons signing the affidavit are unable to write, signatures by mark must be attested by two witnesses. Each affidavit must be executed before a Notary Public and the notarial seal and signature of the officer must be attached to each separate affidavit.

                    Respectfully,

                                    Chairman.

V. 10/7.

7-NB-54.

Muskogee, Indian Territory, June 10, 1905.

Jesse Hull,
    Whitebead, Indian Territory.

Dear Sir:

    There is enclosed herewith for execution application the enrollment of your infant child, Mattie Hull, born October 23, 1902.

    Your attention is called to the Commission's letter of May 10, 1905, in which was enclosed an application similar to the one above mentioned, to which you have failed to reply.

    The affidavits heretofore filed with the Commission show the child was living on November 11, 1902. Before this matter can be finally disposed of, it will be necessary

Applications for Enrollment of Chickasaw Newborn
Act of 1905   Volume I

that you have the enclosed affidavits executed, showing that the child was living on March 4, 1905.

In having these affidavits executed care should be exercised to see that all names are written in full, as they appear in the body of the affidavit, and in the event that either of the persons signing the affidavit are unable to write, signatures by mark must be attested by two witnesses. Each affidavit must be executed before a Notary Public and the notarial seal and signature of the officer must be attached to each separate affidavit.

Respectfully,

Chairman.

9-NB-54

Muskogee, Indian Territory, August 14, 1905.

Jesse Hull,
    Whitebead, Indian Territory.

Dear Sir:

On May 10, 1905 and June 10, 1905, the Commission to the Five Civilized Tribes addressed letters to you requesting you to furnish this Office with proof of birth of your minor daughter, Mattie Hull, and each time enclosed you a blank for proof of birth, properly filled out. To those letters no reply has been received.

You are again requested to furnish the proof desired, and you are advised that until the same is filed with the records of this Office, nothing further can be done in the matter of the enrollment of your said daughter as a citizen of the Chickasaw Nation.

Respectfully,

Acting Commissioner.

Applications for Enrollment of Chickasaw Newborn
Act of 1905   Volume I

9-NB-54

Muskogee, Indian Territory, September 5, 1905.

Jesse Hull,
    Wayne, Indian Territory.

Dear Sir:

    Receipt is hereby acknowledged of the application for the enrollment of your infant child, Mattie Hull, born October 23, 1902, returned by you unexecuted with pencil notation on same that said child died October 18, 1904. You request to be informed if any further evidence is required.

    There is inclosed you herewith an affidavit to the death of said child on October 18, 1904, which you are requested to execute, first filling in the blank spaced left in said affidavits. When the affidavits are executed please return them to this office i the inclosed envelope which requires no postage.

                             Respectfully,

Vr. 5-1.   Acting Commissioner.
Env.

9-NB-54

Muskogee, Indian Territory, November 18, 1905.

Jesse Hull,
    Wayne, Indian Territory.

Dear Sir:

    You are hereby advised that is appearing from the records of this office that your infant child, Mattie Hull, died prior to March 4, 1905, the Commissioner to the Five Civilized Tribes, on November 16, 1905, dismissed the application for her enrollment as a citizen by blood of the Chickasaw Nation.

                             Respectfully,

                             W. O. Beall

                             Acting Commissioner.

Applications for Enrollment of Chickasaw Newborn
Act of 1905   Volume I

Chic. N.B - 55
    (James P. Dulin
    Born July 18, 1904)

436

CERTIFICATE OF RECORD OF MARRIAGE

UNITED STATES OF AMERICA,
   INDIAN TERRITORY,   } sct.
   SOUTHERN DISTRICT.

I, C. M. CAMPBELL, Clerk of the United States Court, in the Territory and District aforesaid Do HEREBY CERTIFY, that the License for and Certificate of Marriage of

MR   Simpson Dulin   and

M   Fannie Johnson

were filed in my office in said Territory and District the   8   day of   Oct. A.D., 190 3   and duly recorded in Book   G. of Marriage Record, Page 436

WITNESS my hand and Seal of said Court, at Ardmore, this   8   day of   Oct   A.D. 190 3

    C. M. Campbell
                      CLERK.

Return this License to the United States Clerk at Ardmore, that it may be recorded, when it will be mailed to the proper address.

Ardmoreite Steam Print.

FILED
AT ARDMORE
OCT 8 1903 8AM
C. M. CAMPBELL, Clerk.
and Exofficio Recorder.
District No. 2, Ind. Ter.

Applications for Enrollment of Chickasaw Newborn
Act of 1905   Volume I

No person is authorized to perform the Marriage Ceremony in the Indian Territory unless the proper credentials have first been recorded in the Clerk's office.

MARRIAGE LICENSE.

No. 2342

UNITED STATES OF AMERICA,
INDIAN TERRITORY,   } SS.   To Any Person Authorized by Law to Solemnize
SOUTHERN DISTRICT.   Marriage, Greeting:

YOU ARE HEREBY COMMANDED to solemnize the Rite and publish the Banns of Matrimony between Mr. Simpson Dulin of Paoli in the Indian Territory, aged 29 years, and M iss Fannie Johnson of Paoli in the Indian Territory, aged 22 years, according to law; and do you officially sign and return this license to the parties therein named.

WITNESS my hand and official Seal, this 3rd day of October A. D. 190 3

C. M. CAMPBELL
Clerk of the United States Court.
by S H Woolton Dpty

Certificate of Marriage.

UNITED STATES OF AMERICA,
INDIAN TERRITORY,   } SS.
SOUTHERN DISTRICT.   I, J.K. Florence an ordnd minister of the gospel

do hereby certify that on the 8 day of October A. D. 190 3 , I did duly and according to law, as commanded in the foregoing License, solemnize the Rite and publish the Banns of Matrimony between the parties therein named.

WITNESS my hand this 3 day of Oct. A. D. 190 3

My credentials are recorded in the office of the Clerk of the United States Court, Indian Territory, Southern District, at Ardmore, Book A , Page 66

J. K. Florence

a Minister of the gospel

NOTE. (a)- This License and Certificate of Marriages must be returned to the office of the Clerk of the United States Court in the Indian Territory, at Ardmore, within sixty days from the date thereof, or the party to whom the License was issued will be liable in the amount of ONE HUNDRED DOLLARS ($100).

Applications for Enrollment of Chickasaw Newborn
Act of 1905   Volume I

BIRTH AFFIDAVIT.

DEPARTMENT OF THE INTERIOR,
COMMISSION TO THE FIVE CIVILIZED TRIBES.

In Re Application for Enrollment, as a citizen of the Chickasaw Nation, of James P Dulin , born on the 18th day of July , 1904

Name of Father: Simpson Dulin   a citizen of the Chickasaw Nation.
Name of Mother: Fanny Dulin   a citizen of the United States Nation.

Post-office   Paoli I.T.

AFFIDAVIT OF MOTHER.

UNITED STATES OF AMERICA,
 INDIAN TERRITORY,
Southern   District.

I, Fanny[sic] Dulin , on oath state that I am 23 years of age and a citizen by .... , of the United States Nation; that I am the lawful wife of Simpson Dulin , who is a citizen, by Blood of the Chickasaw Nation; that a male child was born to me on 18 day of July , 1904 , that said child has been named James P Dulin , and is now living.

Fannie Dulin

WITNESSES TO MARK:

Subscribed and sworn to before me this 27th day of July , 190 4

My commission   A.S. Kelley
expires Feb 6-1908   NOTARY PUBLIC.

AFFIDAVIT OF ATTENDING PHYSICIAN OR MID-WIFE.

UNITED STATES OF AMERICA,
 INDIAN TERRITORY,
Southern   District.

I, W C Hottle , a Physician , on oath state that I attended on Mrs. Fanny Dulin , wife of Simpson Dulin on the 18 day of July , 1904 ; that there was born to her on said date a male child; that said child is now living and is said to have been named James P Dulin

W.C. Hottle MD

Applications for Enrollment of Chickasaw Newborn
Act of 1905 Volume I

WITNESSES TO MARK:

Subscribed and sworn to before me this 27th day of July, 1904

My commission
expires Feb 6-1908

A.S. Kelley
NOTARY PUBLIC.

BIRTH AFFIDAVIT.

DEPARTMENT OF THE INTERIOR.
COMMISSION TO THE FIVE CIVILIZED TRIBES.

IN RE APPLICATION FOR ENROLLMENT, as a citizen of the Chickasaw Nation, of James P Dulin, born on the 18th day of July, 1904

Name of Father: Simpson Dulin   a citizen of the Chickasaw Nation.
Name of Mother: Fannie Dulin   a citizen of the United States Nation.

Postoffice Paoli I.T.

AFFIDAVIT OF MOTHER.

UNITED STATES OF AMERICA, Indian Territory,
Southern DISTRICT.

I, Fannie Dulin, on oath state that I am 23 years of age and a citizen by ...., of the United States ~~Nation~~; that I am the lawful wife of Simpson Dulin, who is a citizen, by blood of the Chickasaw Nation; that a male child was born to me on 18th day of July, 1904; that said child has been named James P Dulin, and was living March 4, 1905.

Fannie Dulin

Witnesses To Mark:

Subscribed and sworn to before me this 11th day of May, 1905

My commission expires Mch 12-1908   A.S. Kelley
Notary Public.

Applications for Enrollment of Chickasaw Newborn
Act of 1905 Volume I

AFFIDAVIT OF ATTENDING PHYSICIAN OR MID-WIFE.

UNITED STATES OF AMERICA, Indian Territory, }
Southern DISTRICT.

I, W C Hottle , a M.D. , on oath state that I attended on Mrs. Fannie Dulin , wife of Simpson Dulin on the 18th day of July , 1904; that there was born to her on said date a male child; that said child was living March 4, 1905, and is said to have been named James P Dulin

WC Hottle M.D.

Witnesses To Mark:
{

Subscribed and sworn to before me this 11th day of May , 1905

A.S. Kelley
Notary Public.

Chickasaw 438.

Muskogee, Indian Territory, July 27, 1904.

Simpson Dulin,
    Paoli, Indian Territory.

Dear Sir:

    Receipt is hereby acknowledged of your letter of July 19, asking how to have a child born July 18, 1904, enrolled.

    In reply to your letter, you are advised that, under the provisions of the Act of Congress approved July 1, 1902, the Commission is without authority to enroll infant children born to citizens and freedmen of the Choctaw and Chickasaw Nations subsequent to September 25, 1902, the date of the final ratification by the Choctaw and Chickasaw Nations of the Act of Congress above referred to.

Respectfully,

Commissioner in Charge.

Applications for Enrollment of Chickasaw Newborn
Act of 1905   Volume I

9-438

Muskogee, Indian Territory, March 28, 1905.

Simpson Dulin,
    Paoli, Indian Territory.

Dear Sir:

    Receipt is hereby acknowledged of your letter of March 16, 1905, asking if the birth certificate heretofore filed is sufficient for the enrollment of your child born in July 18, 1904.

    In reply you are informed that the affidavits heretofore forwarded to the birth of your child James P. Dulin have been filed with our records as an application for the enrollment of said child.

                             Respectfully,

                                            Chairman.

9-N.B. 55.

Muskogee, Indian Territory, May 10, 1905.

Simpson Dulin,
    Paoli, Indian Territory.

Dear Sir:

    There is enclosed you herewith for execution application for the enrollment of your infant child, James P. Dulin, born July 18, 1904.

    The affidavits heretofore filed with the Commission show the child was living on July 27, 1904. It is necessary, for the child to be enrolled, that he was living on March 4, 1905.

    In having these affidavits executed care should be exercised to see that all names are written in full, as they appear in the body of the affidavit, and in the event that either of the persons signing the affidavit are unable to write, signatures by mark must be attested by two witnesses. Each affidavit must be executed before a Notary Public and the notarial seal and signature of the officer must be attached to each separate affidavit.

                             Respectfully,

                                            Chairman.

Applications for Enrollment of Chickasaw Newborn
Act of 1905   Volume I

Chickasaw N B 55

Muskogee, Indian Territory, May 16, 1905.

Simpson Dulin,
 Paoli, Indian Territory.

Dear Sir:

    Receipt is hereby acknowledged of the affidavits of Fannie Dulin and W. C. Hattle[sic] to the birth of your child, James P. Dulin, July 18, 1904, and the same have been filed with our records in the matter of the enrollment of said child.

                  Respectfully,

                  Chairman.

9-NB-55.

Muskogee, Indian Territory, June 10, 1905.

Simpson Dulin,
 Paoli, Indian Territory.

Dear Sir:

    Referring to the application for the enrollment of your infant child, James P. Dulin, born July 18, 1904, it is noted from the affidavits heretofore filed in this office that the applicant claims through you.

    If this is correct it will be necessary that you file in this office, either the original or a certified copy of the marriage license and certificate of your marriage to the applicant's mother, Fannie Dulin.

    This matter should receive your immediate attention as no further action can be taken until these affidavits are filed in this office.

                  Respectfully,

                  Chairman.

Applications for Enrollment of Chickasaw Newborn
Act of 1905   Volume I

9 NB 55

Muskogee, Indian Territory, June 18, 1905.

Simpson Dulin,
    Paoli, Indian Territory.

Dear Sir:

    Receipt is hereby acknowledged of the marriage license and certificate between yourself and Fannie Johnson which you offer in support of the application for the enrollment of your child James P. Dulin as a citizen by blood of the Chickasaw Nation.

Respectfully,

Chairman.

Chic. N.B - 56
    (Eddie Lee Fryrear
    Born October 27, 1902)

BIRTH AFFIDAVIT.

Department of the Interior,
COMMISSION TO THE FIVE CIVILIZED TRIBES.

    IN RE APPLICATION FOR ENROLLMENT, as a citizen of the Chickasaw Nation, of Eddie Lee, born on the 27 day of Oct., 1902

Name of Father: S. Burl Fryrear   a citizen of the Chickasaw Nation.
Name of Mother: Rosa Fryrear   a citizen of the Chickasaw Nation.

Post-Office: Tuttle Ind. Terr.

AFFIDAVIT OF ~~MOTHER~~. *Husband*

UNITED STATES OF AMERICA,
  INDIAN TERRITORY,
  Southern District.

    I, S. Burl Fryrear, on oath state that I am 41 years of age and a citizen by Marriage, of the Chickasaw Nation; that I am the lawful ~~wife of~~

Applications for Enrollment of Chickasaw Newborn
Act of 1905   Volume I

Husband of Rosa Fryrear, who is *was* a citizen, by blood of the Chickasaw Nation; that a male child was born to ~~me~~ *her* on 27 day of Oct , 190 2, that said child has been named Eddie Lee , and is now living. *That Rosa Fryrear its mother died April 5, 1903*

S. Burl Fryrear

WITNESSES TO MARK:
{

Subscribed and sworn to before me this 28 day of Sept , 1903

MY COMMISSION EXPIRES JULY 10, 1904.   A S Taylor
Notary Public.

AFFIDAVIT OF ATTENDING PHYSICIAN OR MID-WIFE.

UNITED STATES OF AMERICA,
    INDIAN TERRITORY,
Southern District.

I, Sophia Waldon , a Mid wife , on oath state that I attended on Mrs. Rosa Fryrear , wife of S. Burl Fryrear on the 27 day of Oct , 190 2; that there was born to her on said date a male child; that said child is now living and is said to have been named Eddie Lee

her
Sophia x Waldon
mark

WITNESSES TO MARK:
{ Allen McDaniels
  Byrd Waldon

Subscribed and sworn to before me this 28 day of Sept , 1903

A S Taylor
Notary Public.
MY COMMISSION EXPIRES JULY 10, 1904.

BIRTH AFFIDAVIT.

DEPARTMENT OF THE INTERIOR.
COMMISSION TO THE FIVE CIVILIZED TRIBES.

IN RE APPLICATION FOR ENROLLMENT, as a citizen of the Chickasaw Nation, of Eddie Lee Fryrear , born on the 27th day of Oct , 1902

Name of Father: S. Burrel[sic] Fryrear   a citizen of the Chickasaw Nation.
Name of Mother: Rosa Fryrear   a citizen of the Chickasaw Nation.

Applications for Enrollment of Chickasaw Newborn
Act of 1905 Volume I

Postoffice Tuttle I.T.

AFFIDAVIT OF ~~MOTHER~~. Father

UNITED STATES OF AMERICA, Indian Territory, }
Southern   DISTRICT.   }

I, S. Burrel Fryrear, on oath state that I am 43 years of age and a citizen by adoption, of the Chickasaw Nation; that I am the lawful ~~wife~~ husband of Rosa Fryrear, who is a citizen, by Blood of the Chickasaw Nation; that a male child was born to ~~me~~ her on 27th day of Oct, 1902; that said child has been named Eddie Lee Fryrear, and was living March 4, 1905.

S. Burrel Fryrear

Witnesses To Mark:
{

Subscribed and sworn to before me this 24th day of Mar, 1905

J. H. Carlisle
Notary Public.

AFFIDAVIT OF ATTENDING PHYSICIAN OR MID-WIFE.

UNITED STATES OF AMERICA, Indian Territory, }
Southern   DISTRICT.   }

I, Sophie Waldon, a mid-wife, on oath state that I attended on Mrs. Rosa Fryrear, wife of S. Burrel Fryrear on the 27th day of Oct, 1902; that there was born to her on said date a male child; that said child was living March 4, 1905, and is said to have been named Eddie Lee

Sophie Waldon
Her mark x

Witnesses To Mark:
{ Bill Hartin
{ M.A. Carlisle

Subscribed and sworn to before me this 24th day of Mar, 1905

J. H. Carlisle
Notary Public.

Applications for Enrollment of Chickasaw Newborn
Act of 1905 Volume I

Tuttle I. T.
Mar 24th 1905

This is to certify that my wife, Rosa Fryrear, died on the 25th day of April 1903.

S Burl Fryrear

Subscribed and sworn to before me this 24th day of Mar 1905

J.H. Carlisle
Notary Public

My Com Ex Jan 26th 1907.

INDIAN TERRITORY,)
              ;SS.   AFFIDAVIT.
SOUTHERN DISTRICT.)

Personally appeared before me, A. S. Taylor, a notary public within and for the Southern District of Indian Territory, Sallie Fry and Georgia Davidson, well known to me to be reputable persons, who after being by me duly sworn, depose and say:

That they are well acquainted with S B. Fryrear and were acquainted with his former wife, Rosa Fryrear; and that there was born to Rosa Fryrear and S. B. Fryrear on October 27th, 1902, a male child named Eddie Lee Fryrear, and that said child is now living.

That the said Rosa Fryrear, wife of S. B. Fryrear, died on the 25th day of April, 1903.

Sallie Fry

Georgia Davidson

Subscribed and sworn to before me this 3rd day of June, 1905.

A. S. Taylor
Notary Public.

My notarial commission expires 8/4/1908

Applications for Enrollment of Chickasaw Newborn
Act of 1905 Volume I

9-439

Muskogee, Indian Territory, March 29, 1905.

S. Burl Tryrear[sic],
    Tuttle, Indian Territory.

Dear Sir:

    Receipt is hereby acknowledged of your affidavit and the affidavit of Sophia Waldon to the birth of Eddie Lee Tryrear[sic], son of S. Burl and Rosa Tryrear, October 27, 1902, and the same have been filed with our records as an application for the enrollment of said child.

    Receipt is also acknowledged of your affidavit to the death of your wife Rosa Tryear[sic], April 25, 1903, and the same have been filed with our records as evidence of death of the above named person.

                  Respectfully,

                          Chairman.

9-N.B. 56.

Muskogee, Indian Territory, May 10, 1905.

S. Burl Fryrear,
    Tuttle, Indian Territory.

Dear Sir:

    In the matter of the application for the enrollment of your infant child, Eddie Lee Fryrear, it is noted from the affidavit heretofore filed with the Commission that the mother of the applicant is dead.

    If this is the case, it will be necessary for you to secure the affidavits of two disinterested persons who have actual knowledge of the facts that the child was born, the date of it's[sic] birth; that it was living on March 4, 1905, and that Rosa Fryrear was his mother.

                  Respectfully,

                          Chairman.

Applications for Enrollment of Chickasaw Newborn
Act of 1905   Volume I

9-NB-56

Muskogee, Indian Territory, June 12, 1905.

S. B. Fryrear,
    Minco, Indian Territory.

Dear Sir:

    Receipt is hereby acknowledged of your letter of June 2, 1905, inclosing the joint affidavit of Sallie Fry and Georgia Davidson to the birth of Eddie Lee Fryrear, son of S. B. and Rosa Fryrear, October 27, 1902, and the same has been filed with our records in the matter of the enrollment of said child.

                    Respectfully,

                                Chairman.

9-NB-56.

Muskogee, Indian Territory, June 21, 1905.

Burrell S. Fryrear[sic],
    Tuttle, Indian Territory.

Dear Sir:

    There is returned herewith the joint affidavit of Sallie Fry and Georgia Davison[sic] to the birth of your infant child, Eddie Lee Fryrear, for the reason that the Notary Public before whom the affidavit was executed failed to affix his seal. You will please have this seal attached and then return the affidavit to this office.

                    Respectfully,

                                Chairman.

DeB 3/21.

Applications for Enrollment of Chickasaw Newborn
Act of 1905 Volume I

Chickasaw NB 56

Muskogee, Indian Territory, June 28, 1905.

S. B. Fryrear,
    Tuttle, Indian Territory.

Dear Sir:

    Receipt is hereby acknowledged of the joint affidavit of Sallie Fry and Georgia Davidson to the birth of Eddie Lee Fryrear, daughter[sic] of Burrell S. and Rosa Fryrear, corrected by having the seal of the Notary Public affixed thereto, and the same has been filed with our records in the matter of the enrollment of said child.

Respectfully,

Chairman.

Chic. N.B - 57
    (Clara May Bell
    Born January 26, 1904)

BIRTH AFFIDAVIT.

DEPARTMENT OF THE INTERIOR.
COMMISSION TO THE FIVE CIVILIZED TRIBES.

IN RE APPLICATION FOR ENROLLMENT, as a citizen of the Chickasaw Nation, of Clara May Bell , born on the 26th day of January , 1904

intermarried

Name of Father: J. E. Bell   a^citizen of the Chickasaw Nation.
Name of Mother: Alta Pearl Bell   a citizen of the Chickasaw Nation.

Postoffice   Purcell I.T.

Applications for Enrollment of Chickasaw Newborn
Act of 1905   Volume I

AFFIDAVIT OF MOTHER.

UNITED STATES OF AMERICA, Indian Territory, }
Southern   DISTRICT.

    I, Alta Pearl Bell, on oath state that I am 23 years of age and a citizen by blood, of the Chickasaw Nation; that I am the lawful wife of J. E. Bell, who is a citizen, by marriage of the Chickasaw Nation; that a female child was born to me on the 26th day of January, 1904, that said child has been named Clara May Bell, and is now living.

                                Alta Pearl Bell

Witnesses To Mark:
{

    Subscribed and sworn to before me this 31st day of January, 1905.

                                Geo W Miller
                                Notary Public.

My commission expires 4/18 1908

AFFIDAVIT OF ATTENDING PHYSICIAN OR MID-WIFE.

UNITED STATES OF AMERICA, Indian Territory, }
Southern   DISTRICT.

    I, G. M. Tralle, a Physician, on oath state that I attended on Mrs. Alta Pearl Bell, wife of J. E. Bell on the 26th day of January, 1904; that there was born to her on said date a female child; that said child is now living and is said to have been named Clara May Bell

                                  G. M. Tralle

Witnesses To Mark:
{

    Subscribed and sworn to before me this 31st day of January, 1905.

                                Geo W Miller
                                Notary Public.

T G Walker
    Stonewall

Applications for Enrollment of Chickasaw Newborn
Act of 1905 Volume I

BIRTH AFFIDAVIT.

DEPARTMENT OF THE INTERIOR.
COMMISSION TO THE FIVE CIVILIZED TRIBES.

IN RE APPLICATION FOR ENROLLMENT, as a citizen of the Chickasaw Nation, of Clara May Bell, born on the 26th day of January, 1904

Name of Father: James Edgar Bell   a citizen of the Chickasaw Nation.
by intermarriage   *adoption*
Name of Mother: Alta Pearl Bell   a citizen of the Chickasaw Nation.

Postoffice   Purcell I.T.

AFFIDAVIT OF MOTHER.

UNITED STATES OF AMERICA, Indian Territory,
Southern   DISTRICT.

I, Alta Pearl Bell, on oath state that I am 24 years of age and a citizen by blood, of the Chickasaw Nation; that I am the lawful wife of James Edgar Bell, who is a citizen, by intermarriage of the Chickasaw Nation; that a female child was born to me on 26th day of January, 1904; that said child has been named Clara May Bell, and was living March 4, 1905.

Alta Pearl Bell

Witnesses To Mark:

Subscribed and sworn to before me this 27th day of March, 1905

Geo W Miller
Notary Public.

AFFIDAVIT OF ATTENDING PHYSICIAN OR MID-WIFE.

UNITED STATES OF AMERICA, Indian Territory,
Southern   DISTRICT.

I, G. M. Tralle, a physician, on oath state that I attended on Mrs. Alta Pearl Bell, wife of James Edgar Bell on the 26th day of January, 1904; that there was born to her on said date a female child; that said child was living March 4, 1905, and is said to have been named Clara May Bell

G.M. Tralle, M.D.

Applications for Enrollment of Chickasaw Newborn
Act of 1905 Volume I

Witnesses To Mark:

{

Subscribed and sworn to before me this 27th day of March , 1905

Geo W Miller
Notary Public.

Chic. N.B - 58
*(Elmer Franklin Asbury
Born March 5, 1904)*

BIRTH AFFIDAVIT. # 88

IN RE-APPLICATION FOR ENROLLMENT, as a citizen of the Chickasaw Nation, of Elmer Franklin Asbury , born on the 5th day of March , 190 4

Name of Father: Allen S. Asbury   a citizen of the Chickasaw Nation.
Name of Mother: Alice Asbury   a citizen of the Chickasaw Nation.

Postoffice   Chism Chickasaw Nation

AFFIDAVIT OF MOTHER.

UNITED STATES OF AMERICA, INDIAN TERRITORY,
Southern   District.

I, Alice Asbury , on oath state that I am 35 years of age and a citizen by blood , of the Chickasaw Nation; that I am the lawful wife of Allen S Asbury , who is a citizen, by Intermarriage of the Chickasaw Nation; that a male child was born to me on 5th day of March , 1904 , that said child has been named Elmer Franklin Asbury , and is now living.

Alice Asbury

Witnesses To Mark:
{

Subscribed and sworn to before me this 17th day of Feb , 1905.

R Walter Small
Notary Public.

244

Applications for Enrollment of Chickasaw Newborn
Act of 1905 Volume I

AFFIDAVIT OF ATTENDING PHYSICIAN OR MID-WIFE.

UNITED STATES OF AMERICA, INDIAN TERRITORY, }
Southern District.

I, Mrs. A. H. Bragg, a mid-wife, on oath state that I attended on Mrs. Alice Asbury, wife of Allen S. Asbury on the 5th day of March, 1904; that there was born to her on said date a male child; that said child is now living and is said to have been named Elmer Franklin Asbury

                                  her
                          Mrs. A. H. x Bragg
Witnesses To Mark: mark
{ J B Small
{ *(Name Illegible)*

Subscribed and sworn to before me this 17th day of Feb, 1905.

                        R Walter Small
                          Notary Public.

BIRTH AFFIDAVIT.

DEPARTMENT OF THE INTERIOR.
COMMISSION TO THE FIVE CIVILIZED TRIBES.

IN RE APPLICATION FOR ENROLLMENT, as a citizen of the Chickasaw Nation, of Elmer Franklin Asbury, born on the 5th day of March, 1904

Name of Father: Allen S. Asbury   a citizen of the Chickasaw Nation.
Name of Mother: Alice Asbury   a citizen of the Chickasaw Nation.

                  Postoffice   Chism Ind. Ter.

AFFIDAVIT OF MOTHER.

UNITED STATES OF AMERICA, Indian Territory, }
Southern DISTRICT.

I, Alice Asbury, on oath state that I am 35 years of age and a citizen by Blood, of the Chickasaw tion; that I am the lawful wife of Allen S Asbury, who is a citizen, by Intermarriage of the Chickasaw Nation; that a male child was born to me on 5th day of March, 1904; that said child has been named Elmer Franklin Asbury, and was living March 4, 1905.

                        Alice Asbury

Applications for Enrollment of Chickasaw Newborn
Act of 1905 Volume I

Witnesses To Mark:
{

    Subscribed and sworn to before me this 25th day of   March   , 1905

                      R Walter Small
                      Notary Public.

AFFIDAVIT OF ATTENDING PHYSICIAN OR MID-WIFE.

UNITED STATES OF AMERICA, Indian Territory, }
  Southern   **DISTRICT.**

    I, Mrs A. H. Bragg , a midwife , on oath state that I attended on Mrs. Alice Asbury , wife of Allen S. Asbury on the 5th day of March , 1904; that there was born to her on said date a male child; that said child was living March 4, 1905, and is said to have been named Elmer Franklin Asbury

                      her
               A. H. x Bragg
Witnesses To Mark: mark
{ W P Ward
  J B Small

    Subscribed and sworn to before me this 25th day of   March   , 1905

                      R Walter Small
                      Notary Public.

                                    Chickasaw 446

            Muskogee, Indian Territory, March 31, 1905.

Allen S. Asbury,
    Chism, Indian Territory.

Dear Sir:

    Receipt is hereby acknowledged of your letter of March 26, inclosing affidavits of Alice Asbury and A. H. Bragg to the birth of Elmer Franklin Asbury, son of Allen S. and Alice Asbury, March 5, 1905[sic], and the same have been filed with our records as an application for the enrollment of said child.

    Replying to that portion of your letter in which you ask if you can have land reserved for this child, you are advised that no reservation can be made or allotments

Applications for Enrollment of Chickasaw Newborn
Act of 1905 Volume I

selected for children enrolled under the provisions of the act of Congress of March 3, 1905, until their enrollment has been approved by the Secretary of the Interior.

Respectfully,

Chairman.

9 NB 58

Muskogee, Indian Territory, April 17, 1905.

Allen Asbury,
    Chism, Indian Territory.

Dear Sir:

    Receipt is hereby acknowledged of your letter of April 10, 1905, in which you state that the date of the birth of your child was March 5, 1904, instead of March 5, 1905 as it appears in our letter; you ask if the affidavits show the child to have been born on March 5, 1905.

    In reply to your letter you are informed that the affidavits of Alice Asbury and A. H. Bragg heretofore forwarded to the birth of your child Elmer Franklin Asbury show that said child was born March 5, 1904.

Respectfully,

Chairman.

Chic. N.B - 59
    (John Dean Love
    Born May 3, 1904)

BIRTH AFFIDAVIT.   *#87*

    IN RE-APPLICATION FOR ENROLLMENT, as a citizen of the Chickasaw Nation, of John Dean Love, born on the 3rd day of May, 190 4

Name of Father: Buck Love   a citizen of the Chickasaw Nation.
Name of Mother: Hattie S. Love   a citizen of the ———— Nation.

Applications for Enrollment of Chickasaw Newborn
Act of 1905 Volume I

Postoffice Purcell Ind Ter

AFFIDAVIT OF MOTHER.

UNITED STATES OF AMERICA, INDIAN TERRITORY,
  Southern   District.

I, Hattie S. Love, on oath state that I am 20 years of age and a citizen by ——, of the ———— Nation; that I am the lawful wife of Buck Love, who is a citizen, by Blood of the Chickasaw Nation; that a male child was born to me on 3rd day of May, 1904, that said child has been named John Dean Love, and is now living.

Hattie S Love

Witnesses To Mark:

Subscribed and sworn to before me this 18th day of February, 1905.

Emra C Brown
Notary Public.

AFFIDAVIT OF ATTENDING PHYSICIAN OR MID-WIFE.

UNITED STATES OF AMERICA, INDIAN TERRITORY,
....District.

I, J.S. Childs, a Physician, on oath state that I attended on Mrs. Hattie S. Love, wife of Buck Love on the 3rd day of May, 190 4; that there was born to her on said date a male child; that said child is now living and is said to have been named John Dean Love

JS Childs MD

Witnesses To Mark:

Subscribed and sworn to before me this 18th day of February, 1905.

Emra C Brown
Notary Public.

Applications for Enrollment of Chickasaw Newborn
Act of 1905   Volume I

DEPARTMENT OF THE INTERIOR,
Commission to the Five Civilized Tribes.

---o-o---

IN RE APPLICATION FOR ENROLLMENT, as a citizen of the   Chickasaw Nation of   John Dean Love , born on the   3rd day of   May , 190 4

Name of Father: Buck Love , a citizen of the   Chickasaw   Nation.
Name of Mother: Hattie S. Love , a citizen of the   ———— Nation.

Postoffice: Purcell, I.T.

---o-o---
AFFIDAVIT OF MOTHER.
UNITED STATES OF AMERICA, |
INDIAN TERRITORY, | SS.
SOUTHERN DISTRICT. |

I,   Hattie S Love , on oath state that I am   20   years of age and a citizen by ———— of the ———— Nation; that I am the lawful wife of   Buck Love   who is a citizen by   Blood   of the   Chickasaw   Nation; that a   Male   child was born to me on the   3rd day of   May , 190 4; that said child has been named   John Dean Love   and is now living.

Hattie S. Love

Witnesses to Mark.

_____

_____

Subscribed and sworn to before me, this   8th day of   March , 190 5

Emra C Brown
Notary Public.

---o-o---
AFFIDAVIT OF ATTENDING PHYSICIAN, OR MID-WIFE.
UNITED STATES OF AMERICA, |
INDIAN TERRITORY, | SS.
SOUTHERN DISTRICT. |

I,   Joseph S Child , a   Physician , on oath state that I attended on Mrs.   Hattie S. Love , wife of   Buck Love , on the   3rd day of   May , 190 4; that there was born to her on said date a   Male   child; that said child is now living and is said to have been named   John Dean Love

Joseph S Childs M.D.

Witnesses to Mark.

_____

_____

Applications for Enrollment of Chickasaw Newborn
Act of 1905 Volume I

Subscribed and sworn to before me, this 8th day of March , 190 5

Emra C Brown

My commission expires Jan 18-1908   Notary Public.

9-448

Muskogee, Indian Territory, March 15, 1905.

Buck Love,
    Purcell, Indian Territory.

Dear Sir:

    Receipt is hereby acknowledged of your letter of March 8, 1905, enclosing the affidavits of Hattie S. Love and Joseph S. Childs to the birth of John Dean Love, infant son of Buck and Hattie S. Love, May 3, 1904, and the same have been filed with our records as an application for the enrollment of said child.

    Respectfully,

    Chairman.

9-448

Muskogee, Indian Territory, March 20, 1905.

Buck Love,
    Purcell, Indian Territory.

Dear Sir:

    Receipt is hereby acknowledged of your letter of March 13, 1905, stating that on March 8, 1905, you forwarded an application for the enrollment of your child John Dean Love; you wish to be advised if this is considered an application if it will be necessary for you to appear and make personal application for this child

    In reply to your letter you are informed that the affidavits heretofore forwarded for the enrollment of John Dean Love, son of Buck and Hattie S. Love, have been filed as an application for the enrollment of said child and it will not be necessary for you to make personal appearance in this matter unless you so desire.

    Respectfully,

    Chairman.

Applications for Enrollment of Chickasaw Newborn
Act of 1905 Volume I

Chic. N.B - 60
*(John L. W. Hogue
Born January 19, 1903)*

BIRTH AFFIDAVIT.

DEPARTMENT OF THE INTERIOR.
COMMISSION TO THE FIVE CIVILIZED TRIBES.

IN RE APPLICATION FOR ENROLLMENT, as a citizen of the Chickasaw Nation, of John L. W. Hogue, born on the 19th day of January, 1903

Name of Father: Henry A Hogue   a citizen of the Chickasaw Nation.
Name of Mother: Beulah Hogue   a citizen of the Chickasaw Nation.

Postoffice   **RUSH SPRINGS, IND. TER.**

AFFIDAVIT OF MOTHER.

UNITED STATES OF AMERICA, Indian Territory, }
    Southern   DISTRICT.

I, Beulah Hogue, on oath state that I am 20 years of age and a citizen by Intermarriage, of the Chickasaw Nation; that I am the lawful wife of Henry A Hogue, who is a citizen, by Blood of the Chickasaw Nation; that a male child was born to me on 19th day of January, 1903; that said child has been named John L. W. Hogue, and was living March 4, 1905.

                                   Beulah Hogue
Witnesses To Mark:
{

Subscribed and sworn to before me this 29th day of March, 1905

                     (Illegible) Brown
                          Notary Public.

AFFIDAVIT OF ATTENDING PHYSICIAN OR MID-WIFE.

UNITED STATES OF AMERICA, Indian Territory, }
    Southern   DISTRICT.

I, Mrs Kitty Howard, a mid-wife, on oath state that I attended on Mrs. Beulah Hogue, wife of Henry Hogue on the 19th day of January,

Applications for Enrollment of Chickasaw Newborn
Act of 1905 Volume I

1903; that there was born to her on said date a male child; that said child was living March 4, 1905, and is said to have been named John L. W. Hogue

Kitty Howard

Witnesses To Mark:

{

    Subscribed and sworn to before me this 29th day of March , 1905

Stephen Brown
Notary Public.

(The letter below typed as given.)

Bank of Rush Springs,
Rush Springs, I.T.
ROBT.F.LINDSEY, PRESIDENT STEPHEN BROWN, CASHIER.
J.L.LINDSEY, ASST.CASHIER.

United Staes of America,
    Southern District,
Indian Territory.

    Before me the undersigned, a Notary Public in and for the Southern Dist. Ind. Ter. personally came and appeared, Mrs. Ida Gilbreath to me well known to be the person she represents herself to be and who after being duly sworn according to law deposes and says that she is the wife of W.W. Gilbreath, that she lives just across the street from Henry Hogue and family, in Rush Springs I.T. that she sees the members of the Hogue family frequently, that she has frequently visited the family, that she has known them for about two years that she knows Mrs. Bulah Hogue, wife of Henry Hogue and their Child John W.L.Hogue, that aid Child is now living and was living on the 4th day of March 19o5, the Child was born prior to the time they moved to Rush Springs but she has every reason to believe that it is the same Child mentioned in the attached Affidavit of mother in Application for enrollment of said John W.L.Hogue.
    Rush Springs Ind. Ter. March 29th. 19o5

Mrs Ida Gilbreath

Subscribed and sworn to before me this the 29th. day of March 19o5

Stephen Brown
Notary Public.

Applications for Enrollment of Chickasaw Newborn
Act of 1905 Volume I

9-453

Muskogee, Indian Territory, April 4, 1905.

Henry Hogue,
    Rush Springs, Indian Territory.

Dear Sir:

    Receipt is hereby acknowledged of the affidavits of Mrs. Ida Gilbreath, Beulah Hogue and Kitty Howard to the birth of John L. W. Hogue, son of Henry A. and Beulah Hogue, January 19, 1903, and the same have been filed with our records as an application for the enrollment of said child.

Respectfully,

Chairman.

---

9 NB 60

Muskogee, Indian Territory, April 21, 1905.

H. A. Hogue,
    Rush Springs, Indian Territory.

Dear Sir:

    Receipt is hereby acknowledged of your letter of April 6, 1905, and replying to that portion of it in which you ask that you be advised of the approval of the enrollment of your baby for whom application has recently been made, you are advised that you will be notified when the enrollment of your son, John L. W. Hogue, has been approved by the Secretary of the Interior.

Respectfully,

Chairman.

Applications for Enrollment of Chickasaw Newborn
Act of 1905 Volume I

Chic. N.B - 61
*(Lenoir Gretell Burkes
Born October 18, 1904)*

BIRTH AFFIDAVIT.

No 62[sic]

DEPARTMENT OF THE INTERIOR.
COMMISSION TO THE FIVE CIVILIZED TRIBES.

Chickasaw

IN RE APPLICATION FOR ENROLLMENT, as a citizen of the ~~Lenoir Gretell Burks~~ Nation, of Lenoir Gretell Burks , born on the 18 day of Oct , 1904

Name of Father: Royden E Burks   a citizen of the Chickasaw Nation.
Name of Mother: Nora Burks   a citizen of the United States Nation.

Postoffice   Pauls Valley I.T.

AFFIDAVIT OF MOTHER.

UNITED STATES OF AMERICA, Indian Territory,
    Southern   DISTRICT.

I, Nora Burks , on oath state that I am .... years of age and a citizen by ———— , of the United States ~~Nation~~; that I am the lawful wife of Royden E Burks , who is a citizen, by blood of the Chickasaw Nation; that a female child was born to me on 18 day of Oct. , 1904, that said child has been named Lenoir Gretell Burks , and is now living.

                            Mrs Nora Burks

Witnesses To Mark:
{

Subscribed and sworn to before me this 5 day of January , 1905.

                       JT Blanton
                           Notary Public.

Applications for Enrollment of Chickasaw Newborn
Act of 1905 Volume I

AFFIDAVIT OF ATTENDING PHYSICIAN OR MID-WIFE.

UNITED STATES OF AMERICA, Indian Territory,
Southern DISTRICT.

I, JA Young, a Physician, on oath state that I attended on Mrs. Nora Burks, wife of Royden E Burks on the 18th day of Oct, 1904; that there was born to her on said date a female child; that said child is now living and is said to have been named Lenoir Gretell Burks

James A Young M.D.

Witnesses To Mark:
{

Subscribed and sworn to before me this 5 day of January, 1905.

JT Blanton
Notary Public.

BIRTH AFFIDAVIT.

DEPARTMENT OF THE INTERIOR.
COMMISSION TO THE FIVE CIVILIZED TRIBES.

IN RE APPLICATION FOR ENROLLMENT, as a citizen of the Chickasaw Nation, of Gretell Lenoir Burks, born on the 18 day of Oct, 1904

Name of Father: Royden E Burks   a citizen of the Chickasaw Nation.
Name of Mother: Lenoir Burks   a citizen of the U S Nation.

Postoffice   Pauls Valley I.T.

AFFIDAVIT OF MOTHER.

UNITED STATES OF AMERICA, Indian Territory,
Southern DISTRICT.

I, Lenoir Burks, on oath state that I am 21 years of age and a citizen ~~by~~ ...., of the U.S. ~~Nation~~; that I am the lawful wife of Royden Burks, who is a citizen, by blood of the Chickasaw Nation; that a female child was born to me on 18th day of Oct, 1904, that said child has been named Gretell Lenoir Burks, and is now living.

Mrs Lenoir Burks

Applications for Enrollment of Chickasaw Newborn
Act of 1905   Volume I

Witnesses To Mark:
{

Subscribed and sworn to before me this 27th day of March, 1905.

JT Blanton
Notary Public.

AFFIDAVIT OF ATTENDING PHYSICIAN OR MID-WIFE.

UNITED STATES OF AMERICA, Indian Territory, }
Southern   DISTRICT.   }

I, JA Young, a Physician, on oath state that I attended on Mrs. Lenoir Burks, wife of Royden Burks on the 18th day of Oct, 1904; that there was born to her on said date a female child; that said child is now living and is said to have been named Gretell Lenoir Burks

James A Young

Witnesses To Mark:
{

Subscribed and sworn to before me this 27 day of March, 1905.

J.T. Blanton
Notary Public.

BIRTH AFFIDAVIT.

DEPARTMENT OF THE INTERIOR.
COMMISSION TO THE FIVE CIVILIZED TRIBES.

IN RE APPLICATION FOR ENROLLMENT, as a citizen of the Chickasaw Nation, of Gretell Lenoir Burks, born on the 18 day of Oct, 1904

Name of Father: Roydon Burks   a citizen of the Chickasaw Nation.
Name of Mother: Nora Burks   a citizen of the   U.S.   Nation.

Postoffice   Pauls Valley Ind. Ter.

Applications for Enrollment of Chickasaw Newborn
Act of 1905   Volume I

AFFIDAVIT OF MOTHER.

UNITED STATES OF AMERICA, Indian Territory, ⎫
Southern   DISTRICT.   ⎭

I, Nora Burks, on oath state that I am 21 years of age and a citizen by —————, of the United States ~~Nation~~; that I am the lawful wife of Roydon Burks, who is a citizen, by blood of the Chickasaw Nation; that a female child was born to me on 18th day of October, 1904; that said child has been named Gretell Lenoir Burks, and was living March 4, 1905.

Nora Burks

Witnesses To Mark:
{

Subscribed and sworn to before me this 13th day of July, 1905

JT Blanton
Notary Public.

AFFIDAVIT OF ATTENDING PHYSICIAN OR MID-WIFE.

UNITED STATES OF AMERICA, Indian Territory, ⎫
Southern   DISTRICT.   ⎭

I, James A Young, a Physician, on oath state that I attended on Mrs. Nora Burks, wife of Roydon Burks on the 18th day of Oct, 1904; that there was born to her on said date a female child; that said child was living March 4, 1905, and is said to have been named Gretell Lenoir Burks

James A Young

Witnesses To Mark:
{

Subscribed and sworn to before me this 13th day of July, 1905

JT Blanton
Notary Public.

Applications for Enrollment of Chickasaw Newborn
Act of 1905   Volume I

CERTIFICATE OF RECORD OF MARRIAGE

UNITED STATES OF AMERICA,
  INDIAN TERRITORY,   } sct.
  SOUTHERN DISTRICT.

I, C. M. CAMPBELL, Clerk of the United States Court, in the Territory and District aforesaid DO HEREBY CERTIFY, that the License for and Certificate of Marriage of

MR   R E Burks   and

M   Nora Carter

were filed in my office in said Territory and District the 23 day of December A.D., 1903 and duly recorded in Book G of Marriage Record, Page 571

WITNESS my hand and Seal of said Court, at Ardmore, this 23 day of Dec A.D. 1903

C. M. Campbell
CLERK.

Return this License to the United States Clerk at Ardmore, that it may be recorded, when it will be mailed to the proper address.

Pauls Valley

DEPARTMENT OF THE INTERIOR,
COMMISSION TO THE FIVE CIVILIZED TRIBES.
FILED
MAY 16 1905
Tams Bixby   CHAIRMAN

FILED
AT ARDMORE.
DEC 23 1903 8AM
C. M. CAMPBELL, Clerk
and Exofficio Recorder.
District No 21 Ind. Ter.

9-NB 61

No person is authorized to perform the Marriage Ceremony in the Indian Territory unless the proper credentials have first been recorded in the Clerk's office.

MARRIAGE LICENSE.

№   2430

United States of America,
  Indian Territory,   } ss
  Southern District.

To Any Person Authorized by Law to Solemnize Marriage, Greeting:

Applications for Enrollment of Chickasaw Newborn
Act of 1905 Volume I

𝔜ou are hereby Commanded to solemnize the Rite and publish the Banns of Matrimony between Mr.   R E Burks   of   Pauls Valley   in the Indian Territory, aged   21 years, and Miss Nora Carter of   Pauls Valley   in the Indian Territory, aged   20   years, according to law; and do you officially sign and return this license to the parties therein named.

Witness my hand and official Seal, this   19th   day of   December   A. D. 190 3

C.M. CAMPBELL
Clerk of the United States Court.

By JH Wootten

Certificate of Marriage.

United States of America,
Indian Territory,   } ss
Southern District.

I,   J.B. Reaves a minister of the gospel do hereby certify that on the   20"   day of   December   A. D. 190 3   , I did duly and according to law, as commanded in the foregoing License, solemnize the Rite and publish the Banns of Matrimony between the parties therein named.

Witness my hand this   22"   day of   December   A. D. 190 3

My credentials are recorded in the office of the Clerk of the United States Court, Indian Territory, Southern District, at Ardmore, Book C   , Page 23

J.B. Reaves
a minister of the gospel

NOTE. (a)- This License and Certificate of Marriages must be returned to the office of the Clerk of the United States Court in the Indian Territory, at Ardmore, within sixty days from the date thereof, or the party to whom the License was issued will be liable in the amount of ONE HUNDRED DOLLARS ($100).

United States of America,
Indian Territory,
Southern Judicial District.

Royden E. Burks, being first duly sworn on oath deposes and says that he is the person whose name is mentioned in affidavits heretofore filed with the Commission to the Five Civilized Tribes in re application of Gretell Lenoir Burks for enrollment as a citizen by blood of the Chickasaw Nation blood of the Chickasaw Nation, as Royden Burks, and whose name appears in his marriage lisence[sic] on file with said Commission as R. E. Burks and that R. E. Burks and Royden Burks are one and the same person, and that he, Royden E. Burks is that person.

Royden E. Burks

Applications for Enrollment of Chickasaw Newborn
Act of 1905   Volume I

Subscribed and sworn to before me this 5th day of July, 1905.

(Name Illegible)
My Commission
Expires in 1908
Notary Public.

9- NB 61.

Muskogee, Indian Territory, May 11, 1905.

Royden E. Burks,
    Pauls Valley, Indian Territory.

Dear Sir:

    Referring to the application for the enrollment of your infant child, Lenoir Gretell Burks, born October 18, 1904, it is noted that the applicant claims through you. In this event it will be necessary for you to file with the Commission either the original of a certified copy of the license and certificate of your marriage to Nora Burks.

    Please give this matter your immediate attention.

Respectfully,

Chairman.

---

9 NB 61

Muskogee, Indian Territory, May 18, 1905.

R. E. Burks,
    Pauls Valley, Indian Territory.

Dear Sir:

    Receipt is hereby acknowledged of marriage license and certificate between R. E. Burks and Miss Nora Carter, which are offered in support of the application of your child Gretell Lenoir Burks for enrollment as a citizen by blood of the Chickasaw Nation and the same have been filed with the record in this case.

Respectfully,

Chairman.

Applications for Enrollment of Chickasaw Newborn
Act of 1905 Volume I

9-NB-61.

Muskogee, Indian Territory, July 3, 1905.

Royden Burks,
    Pauls Valley, Indian Territory.

Dear Sir:

    Referring to the application for the enrollment of your infant child, Gretell Lenoir Burks, born October 18, 1904, it is noted in the affidavits heretofore filed in this office that your name is given as Royden Burks, while it appears on the marriage license also on file, as R. E. Burks.

    Before further action can be taken in this case, it will be necessary for you to submit your affidavit to this office to the fact that Royden Burks and R. E. Burks is one and the same person, and that you are that person.

                      Respectfully,

                                      Commissioner.

9-NB-61

Muskogee, Indian Territory, July 10, 1905.

Roydon Burks,
    Pauls Valley, Indian Territory.

Dear Sir:

    Referring to the application for the enrollment of your infant child, Gretell Lenoir Burks, born October 18, 1904, it appears from the license and certificate of marriage filed in this case that the maiden name of your wife was Nora Carter, and that the affidavit to the birth of said child executed by her January 1, 1905, is signed "Nora Burks"; in the affidavit executed by her March 25, 1905, she signs as "Lenoir Burks."

    There is inclosed you herewith for execution application for the enrollment of said child, in which the name of your wife is inserted as Nora Burks, in conformity to the license and certificate of marriage filed by you. Please have the same properly executed and return to this office.

    You should give this matter your immediate attention as no further action can be taken relative to the enrollment of your child until the evidence requested is supplied.

Applications for Enrollment of Chickasaw Newborn
Act of 1905 Volume I

Respectfully,

LM 10-1

Commissioner.

9-NB-61

Muskogee, Indian Territory, July 11, 1905.

W. M. Waide,
    Pauls Valley, Indian Territory.

Dear Sir:

    Receipt is hereby acknowledged of the affidavit of Royden E. Burks in the matter of the application for the enrollment of Gretell Lenoir Burks and the same has been filed with the records in this case.

Respectfully,

Commissioner.

9-NB-61

Muskogee, Indian Territory, July 21, 1905.

Roydon Burks,
    Pauls Valley, Indian Territory.

Dear Sir:

    Receipt is hereby acknowledged of the affidavits of Nora Burks and James A. Young to the birth of Gretell Lenoir Burks, daughter of Roydon and Nora Burks, October 8, 1904, and the same have been filed with the record in this case.

Respectfully,

Commissioner.

Applications for Enrollment of Chickasaw Newborn
Act of 1905   Volume I

9-NB-61

Muskogee, Indian Territory, August 7, 1905.

Royden Burks,
    Pauls Valley, Indian Territory.

Dear Sir:

    Receipt is hereby acknowledged of your letter of August 3, 1905, asking if Gretell Lenoir Burks has been approved.

    In reply to your letter you are advised that the name of your child Gretell Lenoir Burks has not yet been placed upon a schedule of citizens by blood of the Chickasaw Nation prepared for forwarding to the Secretary of the Interior, but you will be advised in the event further evidence is necessary to determine her right to enrollment.

    Respectfully,

    Acting Commissioner.

9-NB-61

Muskogee, Indian Territory, August 25, 1905.

Blanton & Andrews,
    Attorneys at law,
        Pauls Valley, Indian Territory.

Gentlemen:

    Receipt is hereby acknowledged of your letter of August 10, 1905, asking the status of the application for the enrollment of Gretelle[sic] Burks.

    In reply to your letter you are advised that the name of Gretell Lenoir Burks has been placed upon a schedule of citizens by blood of the Chickasaw Nation which has been preapred[sic] for forwarding to the Secretary of the Interior.

    Respectfully,

    Commissioner.

Applications for Enrollment of Chickasaw Newborn
Act of 1905   Volume I

Chic. N.B - 62
(Julia Rebekah Clayton
Born July 7, 1903)

BIRTH AFFIDAVIT.

DEPARTMENT OF THE INTERIOR.
COMMISSION TO THE FIVE CIVILIZED TRIBES.

IN RE APPLICATION FOR ENROLLMENT, as a citizen of the Chickasaw Nation, of Julia Rebekah Clayton, born on the 7" day of July, 1903

by marriage

Name of Father: William S Clayton   a citizen of the Chickasaw Nation.^
Name of Mother: Tamsey A. Clayton   a citizen of the Chickasaw Nation.

Postoffice   Pauls Valley, Indian Tery

AFFIDAVIT OF MOTHER.

UNITED STATES OF AMERICA, Indian Territory, }
    Southern   DISTRICT.

I, Tamsey A. Clayton, on oath state that I am thirty six years of age and a citizen by blood, of the Chickasaw Nation; that I am the lawful wife of William S Clayton, who is a citizen, by marriage of the Chickasaw Nation; that a girl child was born to me on seventh day of July, 1903, that said child has been named Julia Rebekah Clayton, and is now living.

Tamsey A. Clayton

Witnesses To Mark:
{

Subscribed and sworn to before me this 6" day of February, 1905.

C.H. Thomason
Notary Public.

AFFIDAVIT OF ATTENDING PHYSICIAN OR MID-WIFE.

UNITED STATES OF AMERICA, Indian Territory, }
.... DISTRICT.

I, James R. Callaway, a Physician, on oath state that I attended on Mrs. Tamsey A Clayton, wife of Wm S Clayton on the 7th day of July,

Applications for Enrollment of Chickasaw Newborn
Act of 1905   Volume I

1903; that there was born to her on said date a   Female   child; that said child is now living and is said to have been named Julia Rebekah Clayton

James R. Callaway M.D.

Witnesses To Mark:
{

Subscribed and sworn to before me this 6" day of February , 1905.

C.H. Thomason
Notary Public.

9-463

Muskogee, Indian Territory, February 11, 1905.

William S. Clayton,
    Pauls Valley, Indian Territory.

Dear Sir:

    Receipt is hereby acknowledged of the affidavits of Tansy[sic] A. Clayton and James R. Callaway to the birth of Julia Rebekah Clayton, daughter of William S. and Tansy A. Clayton July 7, 1903, which it is presumed have been forwarded as an application for the enrollment of said child.

    You are advised that under the provisions of the act of Congress approved July 1, 1902, no children born to citizens of the Choctaw and Chickasaw Nations subsequent to September 25, 1902, the date of the ratification of said act, are entitled to enrollment and allotment in the Choctaw and Chickasaw Nations.

Respectfully,

Chairman.

Applications for Enrollment of Chickasaw Newborn
Act of 1905   Volume I

9-463

Muskogee, Indian Territory, March 22, 1905.

W. S. Clayton,
    Pauls Valley, Indian Territory.

Dear Sir:

    Receipt is hereby acknowledged of your letter of March 16, 1905, stating that sometime ago you made out an application for the enrollment of your child Julia Rebekah Clayton and you wish to be advised if this is sufficient application for said child.

    In reply to your letter you are informed that the affidavits heretofore forwarded to the birth of Julia Rebekah Clayton have been filed as an application for the enrollment of said child. If further evidence is necessary in this matter you will be duly notified.

Respectfully,

Chairman.

Chic. N.B - 63
    (Marrley M. Stanton
    Born June 13, 1903)

BIRTH AFFIDAVIT.

IN RE-APPLICATION FOR ENROLLMENT, as a citizen of the   Chickasaw   Nation, of   Marrley M. Stanton , born on the   13th day of   June , 190 3
intermarried into
Name of Father: R.D. Stanton   a citizen of the ~~the~~ Chickasaw Nation.
Name of Mother: Maggie May Sealy   a citizen of the   Chickasaw   Nation.

Postoffice   Pauls Valley I.T.

Applications for Enrollment of Chickasaw Newborn
Act of 1905   Volume I

AFFIDAVIT OF MOTHER.

UNITED STATES OF AMERICA, INDIAN TERRITORY,
Southern District.

I, Maggie May Sealy, on oath state that I am 21 years of age and a citizen by Blood, of the Chickasaw Nation; that I am the lawful wife of R. D. Stanton, who is a citizen, by marriage of the Chickasaw Nation; that a female child was born to me on 13th day of June, 1903, that said child has been named Marrley M Stanton, and is now living.

Maggie May Sealy

Witnesses To Mark:
- Victor Suggs
- R.M. Mellaw

Subscribed and sworn to before me this 14 day of Feb, 1905.

Victor Suggs
Notary Public.

AFFIDAVIT OF ATTENDING PHYSICIAN OR MID-WIFE.

UNITED STATES OF AMERICA, INDIAN TERRITORY,
Southern District.

I, Mary A Stanton, a citizen of W.S., on oath state that I attended on Mrs. Maggie May Stanton, wife of R.D. Stanton on the 13 day of June, 1903; that there was born to her on said date a female child; that said child is now living and is said to have been named Marrley M. Stanton

Mary A Stanton

Witnesses To Mark:

Subscribed and sworn to before me this 21st day of March, 1905.

Victor Suggs
Notary Public.

Applications for Enrollment of Chickasaw Newborn
Act of 1905   Volume I

BIRTH AFFIDAVIT.

DEPARTMENT OF THE INTERIOR.
COMMISSION TO THE FIVE CIVILIZED TRIBES.

IN RE APPLICATION FOR ENROLLMENT, as a citizen of the   Chickasaw   Nation, of   Marrley M. Stanton   , born on the 13" day of June , 1903

Name of Father: R. D. Stanton   a citizen of the   U.S.   Nation.
Name of Mother: Maggie Stanton   a citizen of the Chickasaw   Nation.

Postoffice   Pauls Valley, I.T.

AFFIDAVIT OF MOTHER.

UNITED STATES OF AMERICA, Indian Territory, ⎫
       Southern   DISTRICT.   ⎭

I,   Maggie Stanton   , on oath state that I am   21   years of age and a citizen by   blood   , of the   Chickasaw   Nation; that I am the lawful wife of   R.D. Stanton   , who is a citizen, ~~by~~ .... of the   Chickasaw   Nation; that a female   child was born to me on   13"   day of June   , 1903; that said child has been named   Marrley M Stanton   , and was living March 4, 1905.

Maggie May Stanton

Witnesses To Mark:
{

Subscribed and sworn to before me this 16th day of   May   , 1905

Victor Suggs
Notary Public.

AFFIDAVIT OF ATTENDING PHYSICIAN OR MID-WIFE.

UNITED STATES OF AMERICA, Indian Territory, ⎫
       Southern   DISTRICT.   ⎭

I,   Mary A. Stanton   , a   citizen   , on oath state that I attended on Mrs.   Maggie Stanton   , wife of   R. D. Stanton   on the 13 day of June , 1903; that there was born to her on said date a   female   child; that said child was living March 4, 1905, and is said to have been named   Marrley M Stanton

Mary A Stanton

Witnesses To Mark:
{

Applications for Enrollment of Chickasaw Newborn
Act of 1905   Volume I

Subscribed and sworn to before me this 16th day of May , 1905

Victor Suggs
Notary Public.

BIRTH AFFIDAVIT.

DEPARTMENT OF THE INTERIOR.
COMMISSION TO THE FIVE CIVILIZED TRIBES.

IN RE APPLICATION FOR ENROLLMENT, as a citizen of the Chickasaw Nation, of Marrley M. Stanton , born on the 13 day of June , 1903

Name of Father: R. D. Stanton   a citizen of the U.S. Nation.
Name of Mother: Maggie Stanton   a citizen of the Chickasaw Nation.

Postoffice   Pauls Valley, I.T.

AFFIDAVIT OF MOTHER.

UNITED STATES OF AMERICA, Indian Territory, }
.... DISTRICT. }

I, Maggie Stanton , on oath state that I am 21 years of age and a citizen by blood , of the Chickasaw Nation; that I am the lawful wife of R.D. Stanton , who is a citizen, ~~by~~ ——— of the United States Nation; that a female child was born to me on 13 day of June , 1903; that said child has been named Marrley M Stanton , and was living March 4, 1905.

Maggie Stanton

Witnesses To Mark:
{

Subscribed and sworn to before me this 1st day of July , 1905

Victor Suggs
Notary Public.

AFFIDAVIT OF ATTENDING PHYSICIAN OR MID-WIFE.

UNITED STATES OF AMERICA, Indian Territory, }
.... DISTRICT. }

I, Mary A. Stanton , a citizen , on oath state that I attended on Mrs. Maggie Stanton , wife of R. D. Stanton on the 13 day of June ,

Applications for Enrollment of Chickasaw Newborn
Act of 1905 Volume I

1903; that there was born to her on said date a female child; that said child was living March 4, 1905, and is said to have been named Marrley M Stanton

Mary A Stanton

Witnesses To Mark:

{ Subscribed and sworn to before me this 30 day of June , 1905

Victor Suggs
Notary Public.

9-N.B. 63.

Muskogee, Indian Territory, May 11, 1905.

R. D. Stanton,
    Pauls Valley, Indian Territory.

Dear Sir:

    There is enclosed you herewith for execution application for the enrollment of your infant child, Marrley M. Stanton, born June 13, 1903.

    The affidavit of the mother, heretofore filed with the Commission, shows the child living on February 14, 1905. It is necessary, for the child to be enrolled, that she was living on March 4, 1905.

    In having these affidavits executed care should be exercised to see that all names are written in full, as they appear in the body of the affidavit, and in the event that either of the persons signing the affidavit are unable to write, signatures by mark must be attested by two witnesses. Each affidavit must be executed before a Notary Public and the notarial seal and signature of the officer must be attached to each separate affidavit.

Respectfully,

V.11/2.   Chairman.

Applications for Enrollment of Chickasaw Newborn
Act of 1905 Volume I

9 NB 63

Muskogee, Indian Territory, May 19, 1905.

R. D. Stanton,
    Pauls Valley, Indian Territory.

Dear Sir:

    Receipt is hereby acknowledged of the affidavits of Maggie May Stanton and Mary A. Stanton to the birth of Marrley M. Stanton daughter of R. D. and Maggie Stanton, June 13, 1903, and the same have been filed with our records as an application for the enrollment of said child.

                              Respectfully,

                                          Chairman.

Muskogee, Indian Territory, June 21, 1905.

R. D. Stanton,
    Pauls Valley, Indian Territory.

Dear Sir:

    There is enclosed herewith for execution application the enrollment of your infant child, Marrley M. Stanton, born June 13, 1903.

    In the affidavits heretofore filed in this office your wife signs her name as Maggie May Stanton. Her name appears upon the records of the Commission as Maggie Sealy. In the enclosed affidavits her name is inserted as Maggie Stanton which it would be since her marriage to you, and in which manner you will please have her to sign.

    In having these affidavits executed care should be exercised to see that all names are written in full, as they appear in the body of the affidavit, and in the event that either of the persons signing the affidavit are unable to write, signatures by mark must be attested by two witnesses. Each affidavit must be executed before a Notary Public and the notarial seal and signature of the officer must be attached to each separate affidavit.

    You are requested to give this matter your immediate attention, as no further action can be taken until these affidavits are filed in this office.

                              Respectfully,

DeB--2/21.   Chairman.

Applications for Enrollment of Chickasaw Newborn
Act of 1905   Volume I

9-NB-63

Muskogee, Indian Territory, August 1, 1905.

R. D. Stanton,
    Pauls Valley, Indian Territory.

Dear Sir:

    Receipt is hereby acknowledged of your letter of July 27, 1905, asking if your child Marrley Stanton has been enrolled.

    In reply to your letter you are advised that the name of your child Marrley M. Stanton has been placed upon a schedule of citizens by blood of the Chickasaw Nation which has been forwarded the Secretary of the Interior and you will be notified when her enrollment is approved by the Department.

                      Respectfully,

                              Commissioner.

Chic. N.B - 64
    (Tishie Hortense Nolen
    Born September 17, 1903)

BIRTH AFFIDAVIT.

Department of the Interior,
COMMISSION TO THE FIVE CIVILIZED TRIBES.

IN RE APPLICATION FOR ENROLLMENT, as a citizen of the .... Nation, of   Tishie Hortense Nolen   , born on the   17th day of   September   , 190 3

Name of Father: Robert L Nolen   a citizen of the United States Nation.
                            Nee Bourland
Name of Mother: Clemmie Nolen   a citizen of the Chickasaw   Nation.

                    Post-Office: Willis Ind Ter

Applications for Enrollment of Chickasaw Newborn
Act of 1905 Volume I

AFFIDAVIT OF MOTHER.

UNITED STATES OF AMERICA, }
INDIAN TERRITORY,
Southern District.

Nee Bourland

I, Clemmie Nolen, on oath state that I am 20 years of age and a citizen by blood, of the Chickasaw Nation; that I am the lawful wife of Robert L Nolen, who is a citizen, by Intermarriage of the Chickasaw Nation; that a Female child was born to me on 17th day of September, 190 3, that said child has been named Tishie Hortense Nolen, and is now living.

Clemmie Nolen

WITNESSES TO MARK:
{

Subscribed and sworn to before me this 23rd day of March, 1905

C. H. Thomes
Notary Public.

AFFIDAVIT OF ATTENDING PHYSICIAN OR MID-WIFE.

UNITED STATES OF AMERICA, }
INDIAN TERRITORY,
Southern District.

I, J. P. Collins, a Physician, on oath state that I attended on Mrs. Clemmie Nolen, wife of Robert L Nolen on the 17th day of September, 190 3; that there was born to her on said date a Female child; that said child is now living and is said to have been named Tishie Hortense Nolen

J.P. Collins

WITNESSES TO MARK:
{

Subscribed and sworn to before me this 25th day of March, 1905

C.H. Thomes
Notary Public.

Applications for Enrollment of Chickasaw Newborn
Act of 1905   Volume I

Chickasaw-488.

Muskogee, Indian Territory, April 3, 1905.

Robert L. Nolen,
   Willis, Indian Territory.

Dear Sir:

   Receipt is hereby acknowledged of the affidavits of Clemmie Nolen (Bourland) and J. P. Collins to the birth of Tishie Hortense Nolen, daughter of Robert L. and Clemmie Nolen, September 17, 1903, and the same have been filed with our records as an application for the enrollment of said child.

Respectfully,

Chairman.

Chic. N.B - 65
   (Allie or Ollie May Maxwell
   Born August 14, 1904)

BIRTH AFFIDAVIT.

Department of the Interior,
COMMISSION TO THE FIVE CIVILIZED TRIBES.

   IN RE APPLICATION FOR ENROLLMENT, as a citizen of the Chickasaw Nation, of   Alie[sic] May Maxwell   , born on the   14th day of Aug   , 190 4

Name of Father: Wisdom Maxwell   a citizen of the Chickasaw Nation.
Name of Mother: Malindy   "   a citizen of the Chickasaw Nation.

Post-Office: Berwyn, Indian Territory

AFFIDAVIT OF MOTHER.

UNITED STATES OF AMERICA,
   INDIAN TERRITORY,
   Southern   District.

   I,   Malindy[sic] Maxwell   , on oath state that I am   27   years of age and a citizen by   Blood , of the   Chickasaw   Nation; that I am the lawful wife

Applications for Enrollment of Chickasaw Newborn
Act of 1905 Volume I

of   Wisdom Maxwell   , who is a citizen, by   Blood   of the   Chickasaw Nation; that a   Female   child was born to me on   14th day of   Aug   , 190 4, that said child has been named   Alie May Maxwell   , and is now living.

Malinda Maxwell

WITNESSES TO MARK:
{

Subscribed and sworn to before me this   24th day of   September   , 1904

S. T. Wiggins
Notary Public.

AFFIDAVIT OF ATTENDING PHYSICIAN OR MID-WIFE.

UNITED STATES OF AMERICA, }
  INDIAN TERRITORY,
  Southern   District.

I,   Sallie Kyles   , a   Mid-wife   , on oath state that I attended on Mrs.   Maxwell   , wife of   Wisdom Maxwell   on the   14th day of   Aug.   , 190 4; that there was born to her on said date a   Female   child; that said child is now living and is said to have been named   Alie May Maxwell

Sallie Kyles

WITNESSES TO MARK:
{

Subscribed and sworn to before me this   24th day of   September   , 1904

S. T. Wiggins
Notary Public.

BIRTH AFFIDAVIT.

DEPARTMENT OF THE INTERIOR.

COMMISSION TO THE FIVE CIVILIZED TRIBES.

IN RE APPLICATION FOR ENROLLMENT, as a citizen of the   CHICKASAW   Nation, of   Ollie May Maxwell   , born on the   14th   day of   August   , 1904

Name of Father: Wisdom Maxwell   a citizen of the CHICKASAW   Nation.
Name of Mother: Malinda Maxwell   a citizen of the CHICKASAW   Nation.

Postoffice   Berwyn Ind Ter

Applications for Enrollment of Chickasaw Newborn
Act of 1905   Volume I

AFFIDAVIT OF MOTHER.

UNITED STATES OF AMERICA, Indian Territory, }
Southern   DISTRICT.

    I,   Malinda Maxwell   , on oath state that I am   26   years of age and a citizen by   blood   , of the   CHICKASAW   Nation; that I am the lawful wife of Wisdom Maxwell   , who is a citizen, by blood   of the   CHICKASAW   Nation; that a   female   child was born to me on   14th day of   August   , 1904; that said child has been named   Ollie May Maxwell   , and was living March 4, 1905.

                                Malinda Maxell[sic]

Witnesses To Mark:
{

    Subscribed and sworn to before me this 20th day of   March   , 1905

                                H.C. Miller
                                Notary Public.

BIRTH AFFIDAVIT.

DEPARTMENT OF THE INTERIOR.
COMMISSION TO THE FIVE CIVILIZED TRIBES.

    IN RE APPLICATION FOR ENROLLMENT, as a citizen of the   Chickasaw   Nation, of   Ollie May Maxwell   , born on the   4th[sic] day of   August   , 1904

Name of Father: Wisdom Maxwell   a citizen of the   Chickasaw   Nation.
Name of Mother: Malinda Maxwell   a citizen of the   Chickasaw   Nation.

                    Postoffice   Berwyn Ind Ter

AFFIDAVIT OF MOTHER.

UNITED STATES OF AMERICA, Indian Territory, }
....DISTRICT.

    I,   Malinda Maxwell   , on oath state that I am   26   years of age and a citizen by   blood   , of the   Chickasaw Nation; that I am the lawful wife of Wisdom Maxwell   , who is a citizen, by blood   of the   Chickasaw Nation; that a   female   child was born to me on   14th day of   August   , 1904; that said child has been named   Ollie May Maxwell   , and was living March 4, 1905.

                                Mrs Malinda Maxwell

Applications for Enrollment of Chickasaw Newborn
Act of 1905   Volume I

Witnesses To Mark:
{

  Subscribed and sworn to before me this 15   day of   May   , 1905

         Jas H Malkey
         Notary Public.

AFFIDAVIT OF ATTENDING PHYSICIAN OR MID-WIFE.

UNITED STATES OF AMERICA, Indian Territory, }
.... DISTRICT. }

  I,   Sallie Kyles   , a .... , on oath state that I attended on Mrs.   Malinda Maxwell   , wife of   Wisdom Maxwell   on the   14th day of   August   , 1904; that there was born to her on said date a   female   child; that said child was living March 4, 1905, and is said to have been named   Ollie May Maxwell

        Sallie Kyles

Witnesses To Mark:
{

  Subscribed and sworn to before me this 15   day of   May   , 1905

         Jas H Malkey
         Notary Public.

$W^m O.B.$

| COMMISSIONERS:
TAMS BIXBY,
THOMAS B. NEEDLES,
C.R. BRECKINRIDGE.

WM. O. BEALL
Secretary | DEPARTMENT OF THE INTERIOR,
COMMISSIONER TO THE FIVE CIVILIZED TRIBES. | REFER IN REPLY TO THE FOLLOWING:
9-1578
9-489 |

ADDRESS ONLY THE
COMMISSION TO THE FIVE CIVILIZED TRIBES.

        Muskogee, Indian Territory, September 29, 1904.

Wisdom Maxwell,
  Ardmore, Indian Territory.

Dear Sir:-

  Receipt is hereby acknowledged of your letter of the 24th instant, enclosing the affidavits of Malinda Maxwell and Sallie Kyles relative to the birth of your infant daughter Alie May Maxwell August 14, 1904, which it is presumed have been forwarded

Applications for Enrollment of Chickasaw Newborn
Act of 1905   Volume I

to this office as an application for enrollment of said child as a citizen by blood of the Chickasaw Nation.

The act of Congress approved July 1, 1902, which was ratified by the citizens of the Choctaw and Chickasaw Nations September 25, 1902 among other things provides that no child born to a citizen of the Choctaw or Chickasaw Nation subsequent to the date of said ratification shall be entitled to enrollment or to participate in the distribution of the tribal property of the Choctaw and Chickasaws.

Respectfully,

Tams Bixby
Chairman.

9-489

Muskogee, Indian Territory, March 30, 1905.

Wisdom Maxwell,
    Berwyn, Indian Territory.

Dear Sir:

Receipt is hereby acknowledged of your letter of March 22, 1905, stating that prior to the passage of the act of Congress for the enrollment of Indian children you sent to the office of the Commission affidavits to the birth of your child Ollie May Maxwell; you state that it will be a saving of expense and time if this office will send the said affidavits to the chickasaw Land Office at Ardmore, Indian Territory and you ask to be advised of our action in this matter.

In reply to your letter you are informed that the affidavits heretofore forwarded to the birth of your daughter Allie May Maxwell, August 14, 1904, have been filed with our records as an application for the enrollment of said child. You are advised, however, that no selection of allotment can be permitted for children for whom application was made under the provisions of the act of Congress of March 3, 1905, until their enrollment has been approved by the Secretary of the Interior.

Respectfully,

Chairman.

Applications for Enrollment of Chickasaw Newborn
Act of 1905   Volume I

9-N.B/ 65.

Muskogee, Indian Territory, May 11, 1905.

Wisdom Maxwell,
    Berwyn, Indian Territory.

Dear Sir:

    There is enclosed you herewith for execution application for the enrollment of your infant child, Ollie May Maxwell, born August 14, 1904.

    The affidavit of the physician, heretofore filed with the Commission, shows the child living on September 24, 1904. It is necessary, for the applicant to be enrolled, that this affidavit show that she was living on March 4, 1905.

    In having these affidavits executed care should be exercised to see that all names are written in full, as they appear in the body of the affidavit, and in the event that either of the persons signing the affidavit are unable to write, signatures by mark must be attested by two witnesses. Each affidavit must be executed before a Notary Public and the notarial seal and signature of the officer must be attached to each separate affidavit.

        Respectfully,

                      Chairman.

V. 11/1.

Chickasaw NB 65

Muskogee, Indian Territory, May 19, 1905.

Wisdom Maxwell,
    Berwyn, Indian Territory.

Dear Sir:

    Receipt is hereby acknowledged of your letter of May 16, transmitted affidavits of Malinda Maxwell and Sallie Kyles to the birth of Ollie May Maxwell, daughter of Wisdom and Malinda Maxwell, August 4, 1904, and the same have been filed with our records in the matter of the enrollment of said child.

        Respectfully,

                      Chairman.

Applications for Enrollment of Chickasaw Newborn
Act of 1905 Volume I

Chic. N.B - 66
(Ula Johnson
Born February 26, 1905)
(Cecil Elihu Johnson
Born September 29, 1902)

BIRTH AFFIDAVIT.

DEPARTMENT OF THE INTERIOR.
COMMISSION TO THE FIVE CIVILIZED TRIBES.

IN RE APPLICATION FOR ENROLLMENT, as a citizen of the Chickasaw Nation, of Ula Johnson, born on the 26 day of Feby, 1905

Name of Father: H Z Johnson   a citizen of the Chickasaw Nation.
Name of Mother: Rella Johnson   a citizen of the Chickasaw Nation.

Postoffice   Marietta I T

AFFIDAVIT OF MOTHER.

UNITED STATES OF AMERICA, Indian Territory, }
    Southern   DISTRICT.

     I, Rella Johnson, on oath state that I am 37 years of age and a citizen by Bood[sic], of the Chickasaw Nation; that I am the lawful wife of H Z Johnson, who is a citizen, by Adoption of the Chickasaw Nation; that a Female child was born to me on 26 day of Feby, 1905; that said child has been named Ula Johnson, and was living March 4, 1905.

                              Rella Johnson
Witnesses To Mark:
{

     Subscribed and sworn to before me this 17 day of Mch, 1905.

                              D G Bartlett
                                   Notary Public.

Applications for Enrollment of Chickasaw Newborn
Act of 1905   Volume I

AFFIDAVIT OF ATTENDING PHYSICIAN OR MID-WIFE.

UNITED STATES OF AMERICA, Indian Territory,
Southern   DISTRICT.

I, B S Gardner, a Physician, on oath state that I attended on Mrs. Rella Johnson, wife of H Z Johnson on the 26 day of Feby, 1905; that there was born to her on said date a Female child; that said child was living March 4, 1905, and is said to have been named Ula Johnson

B.S. Gardner MD

Witnesses To Mark:

Subscribed and sworn to before me this 17 day of Mch, 1905

D G Bartlett
Notary Public.

BIRTH AFFIDAVIT.

DEPARTMENT OF THE INTERIOR.
COMMISSION TO THE FIVE CIVILIZED TRIBES.

IN RE APPLICATION FOR ENROLLMENT, as a citizen of the Chickasaw Nation, of Cecil Elihu Johnson, born on the 29 day of Sept, 1902

Name of Father: H Z Johnson   a citizen of the Chickasaw Nation.
Name of Mother: Rella Johnson (Wolfenbarger)   a citizen of the Chickasaw Nation.

Postoffice   Marietta I T

AFFIDAVIT OF MOTHER.

UNITED STATES OF AMERICA, Indian Territory,
Southern   DISTRICT.

I, Rella Johnson (Wolfenbarger), on oath state that I am 37 years of age and a citizen by Blood, of the Chickasaw Nation; that I am the lawful wife of H Z Johnson, who is a citizen, by Intermarriage of the Chickasaw Nation; that a Male child was born to me on 29 day of Sept, 1902; that said child has been named Cecil Elihu Johnson, and was living March 4, 1905.

Rella Johnson (Wolfenbarger)

Witnesses To Mark:

Applications for Enrollment of Chickasaw Newborn
Act of 1905   Volume I

Subscribed and sworn to before me this   28   day of   Mch   , 1905

                              D G Bartlett
                              Notary Public.

AFFIDAVIT OF ATTENDING PHYSICIAN OR MID-WIFE.

UNITED STATES OF AMERICA, Indian Territory, }
   Southern   DISTRICT.

      I,   E F Graham   , a   Physician   , on oath state that I attended on Mrs.   Rella Johnson (Wolfenbarger)   , wife of   H Z Johnson   on the 29   day of   Sept   , 1902; that there was born to her on said date a .... child; that said child was living March 4, 1905, and is said to have been named   Cecil Elihu Johnson

                              E F Graham MD
Witnesses To Mark:
{

Subscribed and sworn to before me this   28   day of   Mch   , 1905

                              D G Bartlett
                              Notary Public.

BIRTH AFFIDAVIT.
                  DEPARTMENT OF THE INTERIOR.
          COMMISSION TO THE FIVE CIVILIZED TRIBES.

     IN RE APPLICATION FOR ENROLLMENT, as a citizen of the   Chickasaw   Nation, of   Ula Johnson   , born on the   26   day of   Feby   , 1905

Name of Father: H Z Johnson   a citizen of the   adoption   Nation.
Name of Mother: Rella Johnson (Wolfenbarger) a citizen of the   Chickasaw   Nation.

                   Postoffice   Marietta I T

AFFIDAVIT OF MOTHER.

UNITED STATES OF AMERICA, Indian Territory, }
   Southern   DISTRICT.

     I,   Rella Johnson Wolfenbarger   , on oath state that I am   37   years of age and a citizen by   Blood   , of the   Chickasaw   Nation; that I am the lawful wife of H Z Johnson , who is a citizen, by   adoption   of the   Chickasaw   Nation; that a

Applications for Enrollment of Chickasaw Newborn
Act of 1905 Volume I

Female child was born to me on 26 day of Feby, 1905; that said child has been named Ula Johnson, and was living March 4, 1905.

         Rella Johnson (Wolfenbarger)

Witnesses To Mark:
{

  Subscribed and sworn to before me this 28 day of Mch, 1905

         D G Bartlett
         Notary Public.

AFFIDAVIT OF ATTENDING PHYSICIAN OR MID-WIFE.

UNITED STATES OF AMERICA, Indian Territory, }
 Southern   DISTRICT.

  I, B S Gardner, a Physician, on oath state that I attended on Mrs. Rella Johnson (Wolfenbarger), wife of H Z Johnson on the 26 day of Feby, 1905; that there was born to her on said date a Female child; that said child was living March 4, 1905, and is said to have been named Ula Johnson

         B.S. Gardner MD

Witnesses To Mark:
{

  Subscribed and sworn to before me this 28 day of Mch, 1905

         D G Bartlett
         Notary Public.

BIRTH AFFIDAVIT.

      DEPARTMENT OF THE INTERIOR.
    COMMISSION TO THE FIVE CIVILIZED TRIBES.

  IN RE APPLICATION FOR ENROLLMENT, as a citizen of the Chickasaw Nation, of Cecil Elihu Johnson, born on the 29 day of Sept, 1902

Name of Father: H Z Johnson   a citizen of the Chickasaw Nation.
Name of Mother: Rella Johnson   a citizen of the Chickasaw Nation.

     Postoffice   Marietta I T

Applications for Enrollment of Chickasaw Newborn
Act of 1905 Volume I

AFFIDAVIT OF MOTHER.

UNITED STATES OF AMERICA, Indian Territory, }
Southern   DISTRICT.

    I, Rella Johnson , on oath state that I am 37 years of age and a citizen by Blood , of the Chickasaw Nation; that I am the lawful wife of H Z Johnson , who is a citizen, by adoption of the Chickasaw Nation; that a Male child was born to me on 29 day of Sept , 1902; that said child has been named Cecil Elihu Johnson , and was living March 4, 1905.

                                     Rella Johnson

Witnesses To Mark:
{
  Subscribed and sworn to before me this 17 day of March , 1905

                                     D G Bartlett
                                     Notary Public.

AFFIDAVIT OF ATTENDING PHYSICIAN OR MID-WIFE.

UNITED STATES OF AMERICA, Indian Territory, }
Southern   DISTRICT.

    I, E F Graham , a Physician , on oath state that I attended on Mrs. Rella Johnson , wife of H Z Johnson on the 29 day of Sept , 1902; that there was born to her on said date a Male child; that said child was living March 4, 1905, and is said to have been named Cecil Elihu Johnson

                                     E F Graham MD

Witnesses To Mark:
{
  Subscribed and sworn to before me this 17 day of March , 1905

                                     D G Bartlett
                                     Notary Public.

Applications for Enrollment of Chickasaw Newborn
Act of 1905 Volume I

9-493

Muskogee, Indian Territory, March 27, 1905.

D. G. Bartlett,
    Marietta, Indian Territory.

Dear Sir:

    Receipt is hereby acknowledged of your letter of March 17, 1905, enclosing affidavits of Rella Johnson and B. S. Gardner to the birth of Eula[sic] Johnson, daughter of H. Z. and Rella Johnson, February 26, 1905, and the same have been filed with our records as an application for the enrollment of said child.

                Respectfully,

                            Chairman.

9-493

Muskogee, Indian Territory, April 4, 1905.

D. G. Bartlett,
    Marietta, Indian Territory.

Dear Sir:

    Receipt is hereby acknowledged of the affidavits of Rella Johnson (Wolfenbarger) and E. F. Graham to the birth of Cecile[sic] Elihu Johnson, son of H. Z. Johnson and Rella Johnson (Wolfenbarger), September 29, 1902; also the affidavits of Rella Johnson (Wolfenbarger[sic] and B. S. Gardner to the birth of Ula Johnson, daughter of H. Z. Johnson and Rella Johnson (Wolfenbarger) February 28, 1905, and the same have been filed with our records as an application for the enrollment of said child.

                Respectfully,

                            Chairman.

Applications for Enrollment of Chickasaw Newborn
Act of 1905 Volume I

Chic. N.B - 67
(Bessie May Watkins
Born November 25, 1903)

BIRTH AFFIDAVIT.

DEPARTMENT OF THE INTERIOR.
COMMISSION TO THE FIVE CIVILIZED TRIBES.

IN RE APPLICATION FOR ENROLLMENT, as a citizen of the Chickasaw Nation, of Bessie May Watkins, born on the 25th day of November, 1903

Name of Father: James Watkins   a citizen of the Chickasaw Nation.
Name of Mother: Norah[sic] Watkins   a citizen of the Chickasaw Nation.

Postoffice   Ardmore, I.T.

AFFIDAVIT OF MOTHER.

UNITED STATES OF AMERICA, Indian Territory, }
     Southern   DISTRICT.

I, Norah Watkins, on oath state that I am 24 years of age and a citizen by Intermarriage, of the Chickasaw Nation; that I am the lawful wife of James Watkins, who is a citizen, by blood of the Chickasaw Nation; that a female child was born to me on 25th day of November, 1903; that said child has been named Bessie May Watkins, and was living March 4, 1905.

                               Nora Watkins
Witnesses To Mark:
{

Subscribed and sworn to before me this 17th day of March, 1905

                             JE Williams
                             Notary Public.

AFFIDAVIT OF ATTENDING PHYSICIAN OR MID-WIFE.

UNITED STATES OF AMERICA, Indian Territory, }
     Southern   DISTRICT.

I, W Hardy, a physician, on oath state that I attended on Mrs. Nora Watkins, wife of James Watkins on the 25th day of November, 1903; that there was born to her on said date a female child; that

Applications for Enrollment of Chickasaw Newborn
Act of 1905   Volume I

said child was living March 4, 1905, and is said to have been named Bessie May Watkins

W. Hardy M.D.

Witnesses To Mark:
{

Subscribed and sworn to before me this 17th day of   March   , 1905

JE Williams
Notary Public.

9-494

Muskogee, Indian Territory, March 21, 1905.

James Watkins,
    Ardmore, Indian Territory.

Dear Sir:

Receipt is hereby acknowledged of the affidavits of Nora Watkins and W. Hardy to the birth of Bessie May Watkins, daughter of James and Nora Watkins, November 25, 1903, and the same have been filed with our records as an application for the enrollment of said child.

Respectfully,

Chairman.

Chic. N.B - 69
   (Willie Laura Allison
   Born February 1, 1905)

Applications for Enrollment of Chickasaw Newborn
Act of 1905   Volume I

BIRTH AFFIDAVIT.

DEPARTMENT OF THE INTERIOR.
COMMISSION TO THE FIVE CIVILIZED TRIBES.

IN RE APPLICATION FOR ENROLLMENT, as a citizen of the Chickasaw Nation, of Willie Laura Allison, born on the 1st day of February 1905, 1........

Name of Father: Will Alison[sic]   a citizen of the *by marriage Chickasaw* Nation.
Name of Mother: Mrs Nancy Allison   a citizen of the Chickasaw Nation.

Postoffice   Marietta I.T.

AFFIDAVIT OF MOTHER.

UNITED STATES OF AMERICA, Indian Territory, }
Southern   DISTRICT.

I, Mrs Nancy Allison, on oath state that I am 27 years of age and a citizen by blood, of the Chickasaw Nation; that I am the lawful wife of *widow of Will Allison, deceased died on the 25 Dec 1904*, who is a citizen, by *marriage* of the Chickasaw Nation; that a Female child was born to me on 1st day of Feby 1905, 1..........; that said child has been named Willie Laura Watkins, and was living March 4, 1905.

Nancy Allison

Witnesses To Mark:
{ *(Name Illegible)*
{ *(Name Illegible)*

Subscribed and sworn to before me this 15 day of March, 1905

Guy A Sigler
Notary Public.

AFFIDAVIT OF ATTENDING PHYSICIAN OR MID-WIFE.

UNITED STATES OF AMERICA, Indian Territory, }
Southern   DISTRICT.

I, R J Dice, a Physician, on oath state that I attended on Mrs. Nancy Allison, wife of Will Allison on the 1st day of Feb, 1905; that there was born to her on said date a female child; that said child was living March 4, 1905, and is said to have been named Willie Laura Allison

R. J. Dice M.D.

Applications for Enrollment of Chickasaw Newborn
Act of 1905 Volume I

Witnesses To Mark:
{ *(Name Illegible)*
{ *(Name Illegible)*

Subscribed and sworn to before me this 16th day of   March   , 1905

(Name Illegible)
Notary Public.

9-495

Muskogee, Indian Territory, March 23, 1905.

E. S. Wiseman,
  Marietta, Indian Territory.

Dear Sir:

   Receipt is hereby acknowledged of your letter of March 18, 1905, enclosing affidavits of Nancy Allison and R. J. Dice to the birth of Willie Laura Allison, daughter of Will and Nancy Allison, February 1, 1905, and the same have been filed with our records as an application for the enrollment of said child.

Respectfully,

Chairman.

Chic. N.B - 69
   (John B. Turnbull
   Born March 7, 1904)

Applications for Enrollment of Chickasaw Newborn
Act of 1905 Volume I

BIRTH AFFIDAVIT.

DEPARTMENT OF THE INTERIOR,
COMMISSION TO THE FIVE CIVILIZED TRIBES.

In Re Application for Enrollment, as a citizen of the Chickasaw Nation, of John B Turnbull , born on the 7th day of March , 1904

Name of Father: Dick Turnbull   a citizen of the Chickasaw Nation.

Name of Mother: Maude Turnbull   *by Intermarriage* a citizen of the Chickasaw Nation.

Post-office   Lindsey, Indian Territory

AFFIDAVIT OF MOTHER.

UNITED STATES OF AMERICA, }
INDIAN TERRITORY,
Southern   District.

I, Maude Turnbull , on oath state that I am 29 years of age and a citizen by Intermarriage , of the Chickasaw Nation; that I am the lawful wife of Dick Turnbull , who is a citizen, by Blood of the Chickasaw Nation; that a male child was born to me on 7th day of March , 1904 , that said child has been named John B Turnbull , and is now living.

                               Maude Turnbull

WITNESSES TO MARK:

Subscribed and sworn to before me this 21st day of September , 190 4

                               F.E. Rice
                               NOTARY PUBLIC.

AFFIDAVIT OF ATTENDING PHYSICIAN OR MID-WIFE.

UNITED STATES OF AMERICA, }
INDIAN TERRITORY,
Southern   District.

I, S.W. Wilson , a Practicing Physician , on oath state that I attended on Mrs. Maude Turnbull , wife of Dick Turnbull on the 7th day of March , 1904 ; that there was born to her on said date a male child; that said child is now living and is said to have been named John B. Turnbull

Applications for Enrollment of Chickasaw Newborn
Act of 1905 Volume I

SW Wilson MD

WITNESSES TO MARK:

Subscribed and sworn to before me this 22nd day of September , 190 4

F.E. Rice
NOTARY PUBLIC.

(The above affidavit given again.)

BIRTH AFFIDAVIT.

IN RE-APPLICATION FOR ENROLLMENT, as a citizen of the Chickasaw Nation, of John B Turnbull , born on the 7th day of March , 190 4

Name of Father: Richard Turnbull   a citizen of the Chickasaw Nation.
                                           Intermarried
Name of Mother: Maude Turnbull   a citizen of the Chickasaw Nation.

Postoffice   Lindsey, Indian Territory

AFFIDAVIT OF MOTHER.

UNITED STATES OF AMERICA, INDIAN TERRITORY,
    Southern   District.

I, Maude Turnbull , on oath state that I am 31 years of age and a citizen by Intermarriage , of the Chickasaw Nation; that I am the lawful wife of Richard Turnbull , who is a citizen, by Blood of the Chickasaw Nation; that a male child was born to me on 7th day of March , 1904 , that said child has been named John B. Turnbull , and is now living.

Maude Turnbull

Witnesses To Mark:

Subscribed and sworn to before me this 16th day of February , 1905.

My Commission expires   F.E. Rice
Dec 4, 1907   Notary Public.

AFFIDAVIT OF ATTENDING PHYSICIAN OR MID-WIFE.

Applications for Enrollment of Chickasaw Newborn
Act of 1905   Volume I

UNITED STATES OF AMERICA, INDIAN TERRITORY, ⎱
 Southern   District. ⎰

 I, S W Wilson   , a   Physician   , on oath state that I attended on Mrs. Maude Turnbull , wife of Richard Turnbull   on the 7th day of March , 190 4; that there was born to her on said date a   male   child; that said child is now living and is said to have been named John B Turnnull

                                                S W Wilson M.D.
Witnesses To Mark:
 {

 Subscribed and sworn to before me this 16th day of February   , 1905.

My Commission expires Dec 4, 1907   F.E. Rice
                                                 Notary Public.

BIRTH AFFIDAVIT.

DEPARTMENT OF THE INTERIOR.
COMMISSION TO THE FIVE CIVILIZED TRIBES.

 IN RE APPLICATION FOR ENROLLMENT, as a citizen of the   Chickasaw   Nation, of   John B Turnbull   , born on the 7th day of March , 1904

Name of Father: Dick Turnbull   a citizen of the Chickasaw   Nation.
                                           Intermarried
Name of Mother: Maude Turnbull   a citizen of the Chickasaw   Nation.

                       Postoffice   Lindsey, Indian Territory

---

AFFIDAVIT OF MOTHER.

UNITED STATES OF AMERICA, Indian Territory, ⎱
 Southern   DISTRICT. ⎰

 I, Maude Turnbull   , on oath state that I am 30   years of age and a citizen by   Intermarriage   , of the   Chickasaw   Nation; that I am the lawful wife of Dick Turnbull   , who is a citizen, by Blood   of the   Chickasaw   Nation; that a   male   child was born to me on 7th day of   March   , 1904; that said child has been named   John B. Turnbull   , and was living March 4, 1905.

                                         Maude Turnbull

Witnesses To Mark:

Applications for Enrollment of Chickasaw Newborn
Act of 1905 Volume I

Subscribed and sworn to before me this 25th day of March, 1905

F. E. Rice
Notary Public.

AFFIDAVIT OF ATTENDING PHYSICIAN OR MID-WIFE.

UNITED STATES OF AMERICA, Indian Territory,
Southern DISTRICT.

I, S W Wilson, a Physician, on oath state that I attended on Mrs. Maude Turnbull, wife of Dick Turnbull on the 7th day of March, 1904; that there was born to her on said date a male child; that said child was living March 4, 1905, and is said to have been named John B. Turnbull

S W Wilson M.D.

Witnesses To Mark:

Subscribed and sworn to before me this 25th day of March, 1905

F. E. Rice
Notary Public.

(The above affidavit given again.)

9-497
7-3342

Muskogee, Indian Territory, March 31, 1905.

F. E. Rice,
Lindsey, Indian Territory.

Dear Sir:

Receipt is hereby acknowledged of the affidavits of Maude Turnbull and S. H[sic]. Wilson to the birth of John B. Turnbull, son of Dick and Maud[sic] Turnbull, March 7, 1904; also the affidavits of Lula McKinnon and Thomas M. Gipson to the birth of Edith *(Illegible)* McKinnon daughter of G. G. and Lula McKinnon, August 11, 1904, and the same have been filed with our records as an application for the enrollment of said children.

Applications for Enrollment of Chickasaw Newborn
Act of 1905   Volume I

Respectfully,

Chairman.

Chic. N.B - 70
(Ruth Williams
Born November 15, 1902)

BIRTH AFFIDAVIT.

DEPARTMENT OF THE INTERIOR.
COMMISSION TO THE FIVE CIVILIZED TRIBES.

IN RE APPLICATION FOR ENROLLMENT, as a citizen of the Chickasaw Nation, of Ruth Williams , born on the 15 day of Nov , 1902

Name of Father: G. M. Williams   a citizen of the (white non) Nation.
Name of Mother: Ella Williams   a citizen of the Chickasaw Nation.

Postoffice   Ardmore Ind. Ter.

AFFIDAVIT OF MOTHER.

UNITED STATES OF AMERICA, Indian Territory, }
Southern   DISTRICT.

I, Ella Williams , on oath state that I am 33 years of age and a citizen by blood , of the Chickasaw Nation; that I am the lawful wife of G.M. Williams , who is a citizen, by —— of the ——— Nation; that a female child was born to me on 15th day of Nov , 1902; that said child has been named Ruth Williams, and was living March 4, 1905.

                                Ella Williams
Witnesses To Mark:
{

Subscribed and sworn to before me this 25 day of March , 1905

                        U.T. Rexroat
                        Notary Public.

AFFIDAVIT OF ATTENDING PHYSICIAN OR MID-WIFE.

Applications for Enrollment of Chickasaw Newborn
Act of 1905 Volume I

UNITED STATES OF AMERICA, Indian Territory, ⎫
  Southern   DISTRICT. ⎭

    I, Robt Wilson , a Practicing Physician , on oath state that I attended on Mrs. Ella Williams , wife of G.M. Williams on the 15 day of Nov , 1902; that there was born to her on said date a female child; that said child was living March 4, 1905, and is said to have been named Ruth Williams

                                    J.R. Wilson

Witnesses To Mark:
  ⎰ R.J. Stanton
  ⎱ W.W. Williams

    Subscribed and sworn to before me this 23 day of March , 1905

                                    J B Privitt
                                    Notary Public.

---

                                    9 NB 70

                Muskogee, Indian Territory, June 16, 1905.

Ella Williams,
    Care of H. H. Matthews,
        Ardmore, Indian Territory.
Dear Madam:

    Receipt is hereby acknowledged of your letter of June 12, 1905, in which you state that you made out proof of the birth of your child Ruth Williams and gave it to the Commission at Ardmore to be forwarded this office, but have received no acknowledgment of it and you wish to know if the application was in proper form and when the child will be approved so that selection of allotment may be made for her; you state that you are about to by some improvements for this child and you want to know if you can have certain land reserved for her.

    In reply to your letter you are advised that the name of Ruth Williams has been placed upon a schedule of citizens by blood of the Chickasaw Nation which has been forwarded the Secretary of the Interior for approval, but the Commission has not yet been advised of Departmental action thereon. You will be notified when her enrollment is approved by the Department.

    You are further advised that pending the approval of her enrollment no reservation of land or selection of allotment can be made for said child.
                                  Respectfully,
                                                  Chairman.

Chic. N.B - 71
    (Douglas H. Johnson Burris

Applications for Enrollment of Chickasaw Newborn
Act of 1905 Volume I

Born February 5, 1905)

BIRTH AFFIDAVIT.

DEPARTMENT OF THE INTERIOR.
COMMISSION TO THE FIVE CIVILIZED TRIBES.

IN RE APPLICATION FOR ENROLLMENT, as a citizen of the Chickasaw Nation, of Duglass[sic] H. Johnson Burris , born on the 5th day of Feby 1905 , 1.......

Name of Father: Melton Burris   a citizen of the Chickasaw Nation.
Name of Mother: Letha Burris   a citizen of the " Nation.

Postoffice   Marietta I.T.

AFFIDAVIT OF MOTHER.

UNITED STATES OF AMERICA, Indian Territory, }
   Southern   DISTRICT. }

I, Letha Burris , on oath state that I am 29 years of age and a citizen by marriage , of the Chickasaw Nation; that I am the lawful wife of Melton Burris , who is a citizen, by blood of the Chickasaw Nation; that a male child was born to me on 5th day of February 1905 , 1..........; that said child has been named Douglas H. Johnson Burris , and was living March 4, 1905.

                                  Letha Burris

Witnesses To Mark:
  { *(Name Illegible)*

Subscribed and sworn to before me this 15 day of March , 1905

                                  Guy H Sigler
                                  Notary Public.

AFFIDAVIT OF ATTENDING PHYSICIAN OR MID-WIFE.

Applications for Enrollment of Chickasaw Newborn
Act of 1905 Volume I

UNITED STATES OF AMERICA, Indian Territory, }
Southern DISTRICT.

I, D. Autry, a practicing physician, on oath state that I attended on Mrs. Letha Burris, wife of Melton Burris on the 5th day of February 1905, 19___; that there was born to her on said date a male child; that said child was living March 4, 1905, and is said to have been named Douglas H. Johnson Burris

D. Autry Md.

Witnesses To Mark:
{ *(Name Illegible)*

Subscribed and sworn to before me this 15 day of March, 1905

Guy H Sigler
Notary Public.

Mail notice back to E.S. Wiseman Marietta I.T.

9-510

Muskogee, Indian Territory, March 20, 1905.

Melton Burris,
Marietta, Indian Territory.

Dear Sir:

Receipt is hereby acknowledged of the affidavits of Letha Burris and D. Autrey[sic] to the birth of Douglas H. Johnson Burris, son of Melton and Letha Burris, February 3[sic], 1905, and the same have been filed with our records as an application for the enrollment of said child.

Respectfully,

Chairman.

9-510

Applications for Enrollment of Chickasaw Newborn
Act of 1905   Volume I

Muskogee, Indian Territory, March 30, 1905.

E. S. Wiseman,
    Marietta, Indian Territory.

Dear Sir:
\

    Receipt is hereby acknowledged of your two letters of March 22, 1905, in which you state that you have been appointee curator for Douglas H. Johnson Burris, child of Melton Burris and you ask if you can now select an allotment for said child.

    In reply to your letter you are informed that the affidavits heretofore forwarded to the birth of Douglas H. Johnson Burris, child of Melton and Lethia[sic] Burris, February 5, 1905, have been filed with our records as an application for the enrollment of said child.

    You are advised, however, that no selection of allotment can be permitted for children for whom application is made under the act of Congress approved March 3, 1905, until their enrollment has been approved by the Secretary of the Interior.

Respectfully,

Chairman.

Chic. N.B - 72
    (Delter Harlin
    Born August 14, 1904)

BIRTH AFFIDAVIT.

DEPARTMENT OF THE INTERIOR.
COMMISSION TO THE FIVE CIVILIZED TRIBES.

IN RE APPLICATION FOR ENROLLMENT, as a citizen of the Chickasaw Nation, of Delter Harlin, born on the 14th day of Aug, 1904

Name of Father: George Harlin   a citizen of the Chickasaw Nation.
Name of Mother: Pearl L. Harlin   a citizen of the Chickasaw Nation.

Postoffice   Ravia, Indian Territory

Applications for Enrollment of Chickasaw Newborn
Act of 1905   Volume I

AFFIDAVIT OF MOTHER.

UNITED STATES OF AMERICA, Indian Territory, }
   Southern   DISTRICT.

    I, Pearl L Harlin, on oath state that I am Thirty-five years of age and a citizen by Marriage, of the Chickasaw Nation; that I am the lawful wife of George Harlin, who is a citizen, by blood of the Chickasaw Nation; that a Girl child was born to me on 14th day of Aug, 1904, that said child has been named Delter, and is now living.

                                      her
                              Pearl L x Harlin
                                  mark

Witnesses To Mark:
{ G J Paden
  W.H. Anderson

    Subscribed and sworn to before me this 18th day of March, 1905.

                              W.T. Brady
                                    Notary Public.

AFFIDAVIT OF ATTENDING PHYSICIAN OR MID-WIFE.

UNITED STATES OF AMERICA, Indian Territory, }
   Southern   DISTRICT.

    I, S.E. Cummings, a Physician, on oath state that I attended on Mrs. Pearl L Harlin, wife of George Harlin on the 14th day of Aug, 1904; that there was born to her on said date a female child; that said child is now living and is said to have been named Delter Harlin

                              S.E. Cummings

Witnesses To Mark:
{ State of Missouri }
  City of St Louis   S.S.

    Subscribed and sworn to before me this 20th day of March, 1905.
    My Commission
    Expires Jany 11th 1909   Chas *(Illegible)*
                                      Notary Public.

                                          Chickasaw 524.

Applications for Enrollment of Chickasaw Newborn
Act of 1905 Volume I

Muskogee, Indian Territory, April 7, 1905.
George Harlin,
    Ravia, Indian Territory.

Dear Sir:

    Receipt is hereby acknowledged of your letter of March 25, in which you state that the Commission has refused to enroll your daughter, Delta[sic] Harlin, because her mother, Pearl Harlin, was refused by the Citizenship Court. You state that you are a citizen by blood of the Chickasaw Nation and request to be advised if it is necessary for both parents to be enrolled citizens by blood of the Chickasaw Nation in order for the child to be enrolled.

    In reply to your letter you are informed that it is not necessary that both parents be enrolled citizens by blood of the Choctaw or Chickasaw Nations in order for the child to be enrolled, and as you have been identified upon our records as an enrolled citizen by blood of the Chickasaw Nation, the affidavits of Pearl L. Harlin and S. E. Cummings to the birth of Delter Harlin, daughter of George and Pearl L. Harlin, August 14, 1904, have been received and filed with our records as an application for the enrollment of said child.

    Respectfully,

    Commissioner in Charge.

9-NB-72

Muskogee, Indian Territory, August 4, 1905.
George Harlin,
    Ravia, Indian Territory.

Dear Sir:

    Receipt is hereby acknowledged of your letter of July 31, 1905, asking if your daughter Delta Harlin has been approved by the Secretary of the Interior.

    In reply to your letter you are advised that the name of your child, Delter Harlin has been placed upon a schedule of citizens by blood of the Chickasaw Nation which has been forwarded the Secretary of the Interior and you will be notified when her enrollment is approved by the Department.

    Respectfully,

    Commissioner.

Chic. N.B - 73

Applications for Enrollment of Chickasaw Newborn
Act of 1905   Volume I

(Jerry R McCoy
Born June 9, 1904)

BIRTH AFFIDAVIT.

DEPARTMENT OF THE INTERIOR.
COMMISSION TO THE FIVE CIVILIZED TRIBES.

IN RE APPLICATION FOR ENROLLMENT, as a citizen of the Chickasaw Nation, of   Jerry R McCoy , born on the 9th day of June , 1904

Name of Father: C.J. McCoy   a ~~non~~ citizen of the   ——— Nation.
Name of Mother: Hattie Brown McCoy   a citizen of the Chickasaw Nation.

Postoffice   Ardmore, I.T.

AFFIDAVIT OF MOTHER.

UNITED STATES OF AMERICA, Indian Territory, }
   Southern   DISTRICT.

I, Hattie Brown McCoy , on oath state that I am 17 years of age and a citizen by blood , of the Chickasaw Nation; that I am the lawful wife of C J McCoy , who is a citizen, by .... of the .... Nation; that a male child was born to me on 9th day of June , 1904; that said child has been named Jerry R McCoy , and was living March 4, 1905.

Hattie Brown McCoy

Witnesses To Mark:
{

Subscribed and sworn to before me this 14th day of March , 1905

J E William
Notary Public.

AFFIDAVIT OF ATTENDING PHYSICIAN OR MID-WIFE.

UNITED STATES OF AMERICA, Indian Territory, }
   Southern   DISTRICT.

I, Adeline Brown , a mid-wife , on oath state that I attended on Mrs. Hattie Brown McCoy , wife of C J McCoy on the 9th day of June , 1904; that there was born to her on said date a male child; that said child was living March 4, 1905, and is said to have been named Jerry R McCoy

Applications for Enrollment of Chickasaw Newborn
Act of 1905 Volume I

Adaline[sic] Brown

Witnesses To Mark:
{

Subscribed and sworn to before me this 14 day of March , 1905

JE Williams
Notary Public.

9-525

Muskogee, Indian Territory, March 20, 1905.

Hattie Brown McCoy,
    Ardmore, Indian Territory.

Dear Madam:

    Receipt is hereby acknowledged of the affidavits of Hattie Brown McCoy and Adeline Brown to the birth of Jerry R. McCoy, son of C. J. and Hattie Brown McCoy, June 9, 1904, and the same have been filed with our records as an application for the enrollment of said child.

Respectfully,

Chairman.

Chic. N.B - 74
    (Charles Ruben Young
    Born March 11, 1904)

BIRTH AFFIDAVIT.
    DEPARTMENT OF THE INTERIOR.

Applications for Enrollment of Chickasaw Newborn
Act of 1905 Volume I

COMMISSION TO THE FIVE CIVILIZED TRIBES.

IN RE APPLICATION FOR ENROLLMENT, as a citizen of the Chickasaw Nation, of Charles Ruben Young, born on the 11 day of March, 1904

Name of Father: Granville Walker Young   a citizen of the Chickasaw Nation.
Name of Mother: Adaline   a citizen of the Chickasaw Nation.

Postoffice Berwyn

AFFIDAVIT OF MOTHER.

UNITED STATES OF AMERICA, Indian Territory, Southern DISTRICT.

I, Adaline Young, on oath state that I am 40 years of age and a citizen by Blood, of the Chickasaw Nation; that I am the lawful wife of Granville Walker Young, who is a citizen, by intermarriage of the Chickasaw Nation; that a male child was born to me on 11 day of March, 1904; that said child has been named Charles Ruben, and was living March 4, 1905.

Adeline Young

Witnesses To Mark:

Subscribed and sworn to before me this 22 day of march, 1905

Jnow.[sic] Massey
Notary Public.

AFFIDAVIT OF ATTENDING PHYSICIAN OR MID-WIFE.

UNITED STATES OF AMERICA, Indian Territory, DISTRICT.

I, S. N. Earp MD, a Physician, on oath state that I attended on Mrs. Adalia[sic] Young, wife of G.W. Young on the 11 day of March, 1904; that there was born to her on said date a boy child; that said child was living March 4, 1905, and is said to have been named Charles Rheuben[sic] Young

S.N. Earp MD

Witnesses To Mark:
T.A. Brown

Applications for Enrollment of Chickasaw Newborn
Act of 1905 Volume I

W. T. Tuck

Subscribed and sworn to before me this 28 day of   March   , 1905

W.S. James
Notary Public.

———

9-530

Muskogee, Indian Territory, March 31, 1905.

G. W. Young,
Berwyn, Indian Territory.

Dear Sir:

    Receipt is hereby acknowledged of your letter of March 24, 1905, enclosing the affidavits of Adeline Young and S. M[sic]. Earl, M. D., to the birth of Charles Reuben Young, son of Granville Walker and Adeline Young, March 11, 1904, and the same have been filed with our records as an application for the enrollment of said child.

Respectfully,

Chairman.

Chic. N.B - 75
   (Vivian Nail Doak
   Born April 28, 1904)

Applications for Enrollment of Chickasaw Newborn
Act of 1905 Volume I

BIRTH AFFIDAVIT.

DEPARTMENT OF THE INTERIOR.
COMMISSION TO THE FIVE CIVILIZED TRIBES.

IN RE APPLICATION FOR ENROLLMENT, as a citizen of the CHICKASAW Nation, of Vivian Nail Doak, born on the 28th day of April, 1904

Name of Father: Dudley Nail Doak a citizen of the CHICKASAW Nation.
Name of Mother: Lovie Le Doak a citizen of the CHICKASAW Nation.

Postoffice Velma, Ind. Ter.

AFFIDAVIT OF MOTHER.

UNITED STATES OF AMERICA, Indian Territory,
Southern DISTRICT.

I, Lovie Lee Doak, on oath state that I am 27 years of age and a citizen by blood, of the CHICKASAW Nation; that I am the lawful wife of Dudley Nail Doak, who is a citizen, by Intermarriage of the CHICKASAW Nation; that a female child was born to me on 28th day of April, 1904; that said child has been named Vivian Nail Doak, and was living March 4, 1905.

Lovie Lee Doak

Witnesses To Mark:

Subscribed and sworn to before me this 23rd day of March, 1905

H.C. Miller
Notary Public.

BIRTH AFFIDAVIT.

DEPARTMENT OF THE INTERIOR.
COMMISSION TO THE FIVE CIVILIZED TRIBES.

IN RE APPLICATION FOR ENROLLMENT, as a citizen of the Chickasaw Nation, of Vivian Nail Doak, born on the 28 day of April, 1904

Name of Father: Dudley Nail Doak a citizen of the Chickasaw Nation.
Name of Mother: Lovie Lee Doak a citizen of the Chickasaw Nation.

Postoffice Velma Ind. Ter.

Applications for Enrollment of Chickasaw Newborn
Act of 1905   Volume I

AFFIDAVIT OF MOTHER.

UNITED STATES OF AMERICA, Indian Territory, }
Southern   DISTRICT.

I, Lovie Lee Doak, on oath state that I am 26 years of age and a citizen by Blood, of the Chickasaw Nation; that I am the lawful wife of Dudley Nail Doak, who is a citizen, by intermarriage of the Chickasaw Nation; that a Female child was born to me on 28 day of April, 1904, that said child has been named Vivian Nail Doak, and is now living.

Lovie Lee Doak

Witnesses To Mark:
{

Subscribed and sworn to before me this 21 day of Dec, 1904

T.J Nichols
Notary Public.

AFFIDAVIT OF ATTENDING PHYSICIAN OR MID-WIFE.

UNITED STATES OF AMERICA, Indian Territory, }
Southern   DISTRICT.

I, W S Spears, a physician, on oath state that I attended on Mrs. Lovie Lee Doak, wife of Dudley Nail Doak on the 28 day of April, 1904; that there was born to her on said date a female child; that said child is now living and is said to have been named Vivian Nail Doak

W.S. Spears M.D.

Witnesses To Mark:
{

Subscribed and sworn to before me this 21 day of December, 1904

T.J. Nichols
Notary Public.

Applications for Enrollment of Chickasaw Newborn
Act of 1905 Volume I

BIRTH AFFIDAVIT.

DEPARTMENT OF THE INTERIOR.
COMMISSION TO THE FIVE CIVILIZED TRIBES.

IN RE APPLICATION FOR ENROLLMENT, as a citizen of the   Chickasaw   Nation, of   Vivian Nail Doak   , born on the 28   day of   April   , 1904

Name of Father: Dudley Nail Doak   a citizen of the Chickasaw Nation.
Name of Mother: Lovie Lee Doak   a citizen of the Chickasaw Nation.

Postoffice   Velma, Ind. Ter.

AFFIDAVIT OF MOTHER.

UNITED STATES OF AMERICA, Indian Territory, }
Southern   DISTRICT. }

I, Lovie Lee Doak , on oath state that I am 27 years of age and a citizen by   Blood , of the   Chickasaw   Nation; that I am the lawful wife of   Dudley Nail Doak , who is a citizen, by Intermarriage of the Chickasaw Nation; that a   Female   child was born to me on 28   day of April   , 1904; that said child has been named   Vivian Nail Doak   , and was living March 4, 1905.

Lovie Lee Doak

Witnesses To Mark:
{

Subscribed and sworn to before me this 27 day of   March   , 1905

T.J. Nichols
Notary Public.

AFFIDAVIT OF ATTENDING PHYSICIAN OR MID-WIFE.

UNITED STATES OF AMERICA, Indian Territory, }
Southern   DISTRICT. }

I,   W S Spears   , a   physician   , on oath state that I attended on Mrs. Lovie Lee Doak , wife of   Dudley Nail Doak n the 28   day of   April , 1904; that there was born to her on said date a   Female   child; that said child was living March 4, 1905, and is said to have been named   Vivian Nail Doak

W. S. Spears

Witnesses To Mark:
{

Applications for Enrollment of Chickasaw Newborn
Act of 1905 Volume I

Subscribed and sworn to before me this 27 day of March , 1905

T.J. Nichols
Notary Public.

Chickasaw 531

Muskogee, Indian Territory, December 27, 1904.

Dudley Nail Doak,
    Velma, Indian Territory.

Dear Sir:

    Receipt is hereby acknowledged of the affidavits of Lovie Lee Doak and W. S. Spears relative to the birth of Vivian Nail Doak, infant daughter of Dudley Nail Doak and Lovie Lee Doak, April 28, 1904, which it is presumed have been forwarded as an application for the enrollment of said child.

    You are advised that under the provisions of the act of Congress approved July 1, 1902, no child born to a citizen of the Choctaw or Chickasaw Nation subsequent to September 25, 1902, the date of the passage of said act, is entitled to enrollment and allotment.

Respectfully,

Chairman.

Choctaw 521.

Muskogee, Indian Territory, April 1, 1905.

Dudley Nail Doak,
    Velma, Indian Territory.

Dear Sir:

    Receipt is hereby acknowledged of the affidavits of Lovie Lee Doak and W. S. Spears to the birth of Vivian Nail Doak, daughter of Dudley Nail Doak and Lovie Lee Doak, April 28, 1904, and the same have been filed with our records as an application for the enrollment of said child.

Respectfully,

Chairman.

Applications for Enrollment of Chickasaw Newborn
Act of 1905 Volume I

Chickasaw NB 75

Muskogee, Indian Territory, June 25, 1905.

D. N. Doak,
    Velma, Indian Territory.

Dear Sir:

    Receipt is hereby acknowledged of your letter of June 23, asking if the enrollment of Vivian Nail Doak has been approved and in reply you are advised that the name of Vivian Nail Doak has been placed upon a schedule of citizens by blood of the Chickasaw Nation which has been forwarded the Secretary of the Interior, but the Commission has not yet been notified of Departmental action thereon.

    You will be informed when her enrollment is approved by the Department.

Respectfully,

Chairman.

Chic. N.B - 76
    (Clover Merchant
    Born January 27, 1905)

BIRTH AFFIDAVIT.

DEPARTMENT OF THE INTERIOR.
COMMISSION TO THE FIVE CIVILIZED TRIBES.

    IN RE APPLICATION FOR ENROLLMENT, as a citizen of the Chickasaw Nation, of Clover Merchant, born on the 27th day of January, 1905

Name of Father: E.E. Merchant   a citizen of the Chickasaw Nation.
Name of Mother: Malvina Merchant   a citizen of the Chickasaw Nation.

Postoffice   Marlow, IT

Applications for Enrollment of Chickasaw Newborn
Act of 1905   Volume I

AFFIDAVIT OF MOTHER.

UNITED STATES OF AMERICA, Indian Territory, ⎫
Southern   DISTRICT. ⎭

I,   Malvina Merchant   , on oath state that I am   28   years of age and a citizen by   blood   , of the   Chickasaw   Nation; that I am the lawful wife of E.E. Merchant   , who is a citizen, by   marriage   of the   Chickasaw   Nation; that a   female   child was born to me on   27th   day of   January   , 1905; that said child has been named   Clover Merchant   , and was living March 4, 1905.

                                            Malvina Merchant

Witnesses To Mark:
{

    Subscribed and sworn to before me this 27th   day of   March   , 1905

                                      W^m A Proctor
                                      Notary Public.

AFFIDAVIT OF ATTENDING PHYSICIAN OR MID-WIFE.

UNITED STATES OF AMERICA, Indian Territory, ⎫
Southern   DISTRICT. ⎭

I,   Thomas C Barnes   , a Medical Doctor   , on oath state that I attended on Mrs.   Malvina Merchant   , wife of   E.E. Merchant   on the   27th   day of   January   , 1905; that there was born to her on said date a   Female   child; that said child was living March 4, 1905, and is said to have been named   Clover Merchant

                                        Thos C Barnes MD

Witnesses To Mark:
{

    Subscribed and sworn to before me this 27th   day of   March   , 1905

                                      W^m A Proctor
                                      Notary Public.

Applications for Enrollment of Chickasaw Newborn
Act of 1905 Volume I

Chickasaw 534.

Muskogee, Indian Territory, April 4, 1905.

E. E. Merchant,
    Marlow, Indian Territory.

Dear Sir:

    Receipt is hereby acknowledged of the affidavits of Malvina Merchant and Thomas C. Barnes to the birth of Clover Merchant, daughter of E. E. and Malvina Merchant, January 27, 1905, and the same have been filed with our records as an application for the enrollment of said child.

    Respectfully,

    Commissioner in Charge.

Chic. N.B - 77
    (Finis Coffey
    Born April 18, 1903)

Applications for Enrollment of Chickasaw Newborn
Act of 1905   Volume I

DEPARTMENT OF THE INTERIOR,
COMMISSION TO THE FIVE CIVILIZED TRIBES.
FILED
APR 15 1905
TamsBixby CHAIRMAN.

Certificate of Record of Marriage

UNITED STATES OF AMERICA, ⎫
INDIAN TERRITORY,   ⎬ SCT.
SECOND JUDICIAL DIVISION. ⎭

I, JOSEPH W. PHILLIPS, Clerk of the United States Court, in the Territory and Division aforesaid

DO HEREBY CERTIFY, that the License for and certificate of the Marriage of

Mr   J I Coffey   and

M iss Stella Masterson

were filed in my office in said Territory and District the   11   day of   Jany A.D., 189 6   and duly recorded in Book   A of Marriage Records, Page   450

WITNESS my hand and Seal of said Court, at Ardmore, this   12   day of   Feby   A.D. 189 6

JOSEPH W. PHILLIPS,   Clerk.

By .... Deputy.

FILED

Jan 11 1898
Joseph W Phillips

Applications for Enrollment of Chickasaw Newborn
Act of 1905   Volume I

NUMBER

MARRIAGE LICENSE

United States of America,
   INDIAN TERRITORY. } SS.
SECOND JUDICIAL DIVISION.

To Any Person Authorized by Law to

Solemnize Marriage--Greeting.

You are hereby commanded to solemnize the Rite and publish the Banns of Matrimony between
Mr.   J.I. Coffey   *of*   Ardmore
in the Indian Territory aged 20 *years, and M* iss Stella Masterson
of   Ardmore   *in the Indian Territory, aged* 18 *years, according to law, and do you officially sign and return this License to the parties therein named.*

WITNESS my hand and Official Seal this   27   day of   Dec   A.D. 189 5

Jos. W. Phillips
CLERK OF THE U. S. COURT

BY .... DEPUTY.

CERTIFICATE OF MARRIAGE.

UNITED STATES OF AMERICA,
  INDIAN TERRITORY. } SS.
SECOND JUDICIAL DIVISION.

I,   J A Clowdus

a   Minister of the Gospel

DO HEREBY CERTIFY, That on the   28   day of   Dec   A. D. 189 5 , I did duly and according to law, as commanded in the foregoing License, solemnize the Rite and publish the Banns of Matrimony between the parties therein mentioned.

WITNESS my hand this   28   day of   Dec   A. D. 189 5
My credentials are recorded in the office of the Clerk of the United States Court
Indian Territory,   2   Judicial Division, Book   A , Page 231 .

JA Clowdus
a   Minister of the Gospel

Applications for Enrollment of Chickasaw Newborn
Act of 1905 Volume I

BIRTH AFFIDAVIT.

DEPARTMENT OF THE INTERIOR.
COMMISSION TO THE FIVE CIVILIZED TRIBES.

IN RE APPLICATION FOR ENROLLMENT, as a citizen of the Chickasaw Nation, of Finis Coffey, born on the 18th day of April, 1903

Name of Father: Ivy Coffey   a citizen of the Chickasaw Nation.
Name of Mother: Stella Coffey   a citizen of the U.S. Nation.

Postoffice   Brock I.T.

AFFIDAVIT OF MOTHER.

UNITED STATES OF AMERICA, Indian Territory, }
Southern DISTRICT. }

I, Stella Coffey, on oath state that I am 28 years of age and a citizen ~~by~~ ——, of the United States ~~Nation~~; that I am the lawful wife of Ivy Coffey, who is a citizen, by Blood of the Chickasaw Nation; that a male child was born to me on 18th day of April, 1903; that said child has been named Finis Coffey, and was living March 4, 1905.

                                Stella Coffey
Witnesses To Mark:
{

Subscribed and sworn to before me this 22 day of March, 1905

                                R. H. Reed
                                Notary Public.

AFFIDAVIT OF ATTENDING PHYSICIAN OR MID-WIFE.

UNITED STATES OF AMERICA, Indian Territory, }
Southern DISTRICT. }

I, S.P. Winston, a Physician, on oath state that I attended on Mrs. Stella Coffey, wife of Ivy Coffey on the 18th day of April, 1903; that there was born to her on said date a male child; that said child was living March 4, 1905, and is said to have been named Finis Coffey

                                S.P. Winston M.D.
Witnesses To Mark:
{

Applications for Enrollment of Chickasaw Newborn
Act of 1905 Volume I

Subscribed and sworn to before me this 21 day of Mar , 1905

Joe Simpson
Notary Public.

$W^m O.B.$

| COMMISSIONERS:
TAMS BIXBY,
THOMAS B. NEEDLES,
C.R. BRECKINBRIDGE.

WM. O. BEALL
Secretary | DEPARTMENT OF THE INTERIOR,
COMMISSIONER TO THE FIVE CIVILIZED TRIBES. | REFER IN REPLY TO THE FOLLOWING:

9 NB 77 |

ADDRESS ONLY THE
COMMISSION TO THE FIVE CIVILIZED TRIBES.

Muskogee, Indian Territory, April 17, 1905.

Ivy Coffey,
    Ardmore, Indian Territory.

Dear Madam[sic]:

    Receipt is hereby acknowledged of your letter of April 13, 1905, in which you state that you forwarded marriage certificate of J. I. Coffey and Stella Masterson in the matter of the application for the enrollment of your child Finis Coffey and the same has been filed with the record in this case.

Respectfully,
Tams Bixby
Chairman.

<u>Chic. N.B - 78</u>
    (Elihu Bennett Johnson
    Born November 21, 1904)

Applications for Enrollment of Chickasaw Newborn
Act of 1905 Volume I

BIRTH AFFIDAVIT.

DEPARTMENT OF THE INTERIOR.
COMMISSION TO THE FIVE CIVILIZED TRIBES.

IN RE APPLICATION FOR ENROLLMENT, as a citizen of the Chickasaw Nation, of Elihu Bennett Johnson, born on the 21st day of Nov, 1904

Name of Father: John Johnson   a citizen of the Chickasaw Nation.
Name of Mother: Emily Johnson   a citizen of the Chickasaw Nation.

Postoffice Milo, I.T.

AFFIDAVIT OF MOTHER.

UNITED STATES OF AMERICA, Indian Territory, }
Southern DISTRICT. }

I, Emily Johnson, on oath state that I am 37 years of age and a citizen by blood, of the Chickasaw Nation; that I am the lawful wife of John Johnson, who is a citizen, by Intermarriage of the Chickasaw Nation; that a male child was born to me on the 21st day of Nov., 1904; that said child has been named Elihu Bennett Johnson, and was living March 4, 1905.

                           Emily Johnson

Witnesses To Mark:
{ Jas T Hill
{ M.F. Moss

Subscribed and sworn to before me this 27th day of March, 1905

                           Notary Public.

AFFIDAVIT OF ATTENDING PHYSICIAN OR MID-WIFE.

UNITED STATES OF AMERICA, Indian Territory, }
Southern DISTRICT. }

I, Dow Taylor, a Physician, on oath state that I attended on Mrs. Emily Johnson, wife of John Johnson on the 21st day of Nov, 1904; that there was born to her on said date a male child; that said child was living March 4, 1905, and is said to have been named Elihu Bennett Johnson

Witnesses To Mark:
{

Applications for Enrollment of Chickasaw Newborn
Act of 1905   Volume I

Subscribed and sworn to before me this 27th day of March, 1905

M F Moss
Notary Public.

BIRTH AFFIDAVIT.

DEPARTMENT OF THE INTERIOR.
COMMISSION TO THE FIVE CIVILIZED TRIBES.

IN RE APPLICATION FOR ENROLLMENT, as a citizen of the Chickasaw Nation, of Elihu Bennett Johnson, born on the 21 day of Nov, 1904

Name of Father: John Johnson   a citizen of the Chickasaw Nation.
Name of Mother: Emily Johnson   a citizen of the Chickasaw Nation.

Postoffice   Milo, I.T.

AFFIDAVIT OF MOTHER.

UNITED STATES OF AMERICA, Indian Territory, }
Southern   DISTRICT.

I, Emily Johnson, on oath state that I am 37 years of age and a citizen by blood, of the Chickasaw Nation; that I am the lawful wife of John Johnson, who is a citizen, by intermarriage of the Chickasaw Nation; that a male child was born to me on the 21 day of Nov, 1904; that said child has been named Elihu Bennett Johnson, and was living March 4, 1905.

Emily Johnson

Witnesses To Mark:
{ *(Name Illegible)*
{ A.E. Ballard

Subscribed and sworn to before me this 29 day of May, 1905

W E Gorbet
Notary Public.

Applications for Enrollment of Chickasaw Newborn
Act of 1905 Volume I

AFFIDAVIT OF ATTENDING PHYSICIAN OR MID-WIFE.

UNITED STATES OF AMERICA, Indian Territory, }
Southern DISTRICT.

I, Dow Taylor , a Physician , on oath state that I attended on Mrs. Emily Johnson , wife of John Johnson on the 21 day of Nov , 1904; that there was born to her on said date a male child; that said child was living March 4, 1905, and is said to have been named Elihu Bennett Johnson

Dow Taylor M.D.
Witnesses To Mark:
{

Subscribed and sworn to before me this 22nd day of May , 1905

Isham Gunn
Notary Public.

J. W. JOHNSON
DEALER IN
Dry Goods, Groceries, Drugs and Notions

MAY 18 1905
Milo, I. T._____190__

Hon. Commissioners To Five Civilized Tribes
Muskogee, I.T.

Gentlemen:-

I W. E. Gorbet, a Notary Public of the Southern District of the Ind. Ter. Do solemny[sic] swear and affirm that on the 21st day of Nov. 1904 that there was a baby boy borned[sic] to John and Emily Johnson, and after wards named, Elihu Bennett Johnson and was living March 4th 1905 and is still alive.

W.E. Gorbet
Notary Public
Milo, I.T.

Applications for Enrollment of Chickasaw Newborn
Act of 1905   Volume I

J. W. JOHNSON
DEALER IN
Dry Goods, Groceries, Drugs and Notions

MAY 18 1905

Milo, I. T._____190__

Hon. Commissioners To Five Civilized Tribes
           Muskogee, I.T.

Gentlemen:-

    I Dr. A. E. Ballard, make oath that I am and was well acquainted with John Johnson father and Emily Johnson mother of the said Elihu Bennett the son of John and Emily Johnson at the time and before the birth of the said Elihu Bennett, borned[sic] Nov. 21, 1904. I do solemly[sic] make oath that the said child was living on March 4th 1905 and is still alive and the land of living.
I am also acquainted with the said Dr. Dow Taylor, whom was the attending physician at the time of the birth of the said Elihu Bennett Johnson
By the request of the said John and Emily Johnson I make the statement on the account of the absence of the said Dr. Dow Taylor whom now in in New York attending medical lectures.

                A. E. Ballard

                Milo, I.T. Mar 21 1905

I, Doctor Dow Taylor, of Woodford, I.T. Solemnly swear and affirm that I am a doctor of medicine and was called on Nov. 21st 1904 to visit one of my patients by the name of Emily Johnson wife of John Johnson of Milo, I.T. and at that time a male child was born to the said Emily Johnson and was named Elihu Bennett Johnson.

                Dow Taylor, M.D.

Subscribed and sworn to before me a Notary Public in and for the Southern District of the Indian Territory. Witness my hand and seal of office this the 21st day of March 1905.

                W.E. Gorbet
                Notary Public.

Applications for Enrollment of Chickasaw Newborn
Act of 1905   Volume I

9-546

Muskogee, Indian Territory, April 1, 1905.

John Johnson,
Milo, Indian Territory.

Dear Sir:

Receipt is hereby acknowledged of the affidavits of Emily Johnson and Dow Taylor to the birth of Elihu Bennett Johnson, son of john and Emily Johnson, November 21, 1904, and the same have been filed with our records as an application for the enrollment of said child.

Respectfully,

Chairman.

9-NB-78.

Muskogee, Indian Territory, May 13, 1905.

John Johnson,
Milo, Indian Territory.

Dear Sir:

There is enclosed you herewith for execution application for the enrollment of your infant child, Elihu Bennett Johnson, born November 21, 1904.

It does not appear from the physician's affidavit, heretofore filed with the Commission, that the applicant was living on March 4, 1905. It is necessary, for the child to be enrolled, that she was living on March 4, 1905. child to be enrolled, that he was living on the above mentioned date. You will, therefore, secure the affidavit of the attending physician to this affect.

In having these affidavits executed care should be exercised to see that all names are written in full, as they appear in the body of the affidavit, and in the event that either of the persons signing the affidavit are unable to write, signatures by mark must be attested by two witnesses. Each affidavit must be executed before a Notary Public and the notarial seal and signature of the officer must be attached to each separate affidavit.

Respectfully,

Chairman.

Applications for Enrollment of Chickasaw Newborn
Act of 1905   Volume I

9-NB-78,

Muskogee, Indian Territory, May 24, 1905.

John Johnson,
  Milo, Indian Territory.

Dear Sir:

Receipt is hereby acknowledged of your letter of May 18, enclosing letters of A. E. Ballard and T. E. Gorbet Notary Public, relative to the birth of Elihu Bennett Johnson, and the same have been filed with the record in this case.

Respectfully,

Chairman.

9-N.B. 78.

Muskogee, Indian Territory, June 5, 1905.

John Johnson,
  Milo, Indian Territory.

Dear Sir:

Receipt is hereby acknowledged of the affidavits of Emily Johnson and Dow Taylor, M.D., to the birth of Elihu Bennett Johnson, son of John and Emily Johnson, November 21, 1904, and the same have been filed with our records to the matter of the application for the enrollment of said child.

Respectfully,

Commissioner in Charge.

Applications for Enrollment of Chickasaw Newborn
Act of 1905   Volume I

Chic. N.B - 79
(Eva Price
Born January 3, 1903)

BIRTH AFFIDAVIT.

DEPARTMENT OF THE INTERIOR,
COMMISSION TO THE FIVE CIVILIZED TRIBES.

IN RE Application for Enrollment, as a citizen of the   Chickasaw   Nation, of Eva , born on the   3   day of   Jan   , 1903

Name of Father: C C Price   a citizen of the by mariage[sic] Nation.
Name of Mother: M J Price   a citizen of the   Chickasaw   Nation.

Post-Office: Lone Grove Ind Ter

AFFIDAVIT OF MOTHER.

UNITED STATES OF AMERICA, ⎫
   INDIAN TERRITORY.   ⎬
   Southern   District.   ⎭

I, M J Price , on oath state that I am 32 years of age and a citizen by Blood , of the Chickasaw Nation; that I am the lawful wife of C C Price , who is a citizen, by marriage of the Chickasaw Nation; that a Girl child was born to me on 3rd day of January , 1903 , that said child has been named Eva , and is now living.

M J Price

WITNESSES TO MARK:

Subscribed and sworn to before me this   13   day of   Jan   , 190 3

S E Drummond
NOTARY PUBLIC.

Applications for Enrollment of Chickasaw Newborn
Act of 1905   Volume I

AFFIDAVIT OF ATTENDING PHYSICIAN OR MID-WIFE.

UNITED STATES OF AMERICA,
    INDIAN TERRITORY.
  Southern   District.

    I, W.J. Brown   , a Physician   , on oath state that I attended on Mrs. M.J. Price   , wife of C.C. Price   on the 3rd day of January , 1903 ; that there was born to her on said date a   Girl   child; that said child is now living and is said to have been named   Eva Price

                                          W.J. Brown M.D.

WITNESSES TO MARK:

    Subscribed and sworn to before me this 13 day of Jan , 190 3

                                      S E Drummond
                                        NOTARY PUBLIC.

BIRTH AFFIDAVIT.

DEPARTMENT OF THE INTERIOR.
COMMISSION TO THE FIVE CIVILIZED TRIBES.

    IN RE APPLICATION FOR ENROLLMENT, as a citizen of the   Chickasaw   Nation, of Eva Price , born on the 3 day of Jan , 1903

Name of Father: C. C. Price   a citizen of the Intermarried Nation.
Name of Mother: Mollie J Price   a citizen of the Chickasaw Nation.

                    Postoffice   Lone Grove I.T.

AFFIDAVIT OF MOTHER.

UNITED STATES OF AMERICA, Indian Territory,
  Southern   DISTRICT.

    I, Mollie J. Price , on oath state that I am 36 years of age and a citizen by Blood , of the   Chickasaw   Nation; that I am the lawful wife of C. C. Price , who is a citizen, by   Intermarriage   of the   Chickasaw   Nation; that a Female   child was born to me on 3 day of Jan , 1903, that said child has been named Eva Price   , and is now living.

                                      Mollie J Price

Witnesses To Mark:

Applications for Enrollment of Chickasaw Newborn
Act of 1905 Volume I

Subscribed and sworn to before me this 13 day of March , 1905.

S E Drummond
Notary Public.

AFFIDAVIT OF ATTENDING PHYSICIAN OR MID-WIFE.

UNITED STATES OF AMERICA, Indian Territory,
Southern DISTRICT.

I, W.J. Brown , a Physician , on oath state that I attended on Mrs. Mollie J Price , wife of C.C. Price on the 3 day of Jan , 1903; that there was born to her on said date a Female child; that said child is now living and is said to have been named Eva Price

W.J. Brown

Witnesses To Mark:
{

Subscribed and sworn to before me this 13 day of March , 1905.

S E Drummond
Notary Public.

9-548.
COPY
Muskogee, Indian Territory, January 21, 1903.

C.C. Price,
Lone Grove, Indian Territory.

Dear Sir:

Receipt is hereby acknowledged of the application for enrollment as a citizen of the Chickasaw Nation of Eva Price, infant daughter of C.C. and M.J. Price, born January 3, 1903.

Your attention is called to section thirty-four of the act of Congress approved July 1, 1902, which was ratified by the citizens of the Choctaw and Chickasaw Nations September 25, 1902, as follows:

"During the ninety days first following the date of the final ratification of this agreement, the Commission to the Five Civilized Tribes may receive applications for enrollment only of persons whose names are on the tribal rolls, but who have not heretofore been enrolled by said Commission, commonly known as "delinquents," and such intermarried white persons as may have

Applications for Enrollment of Chickasaw Newborn
Act of 1905   Volume I

married recognized citizens of the Choctaw and Chickasaw Nations in accordance with the tribal laws, customs and usages on or before the date of the passage of this Act by Congress, and such infant children as may have been born to recognized and enrolled citizens on or before the date of the final ratification of this agreement; but the application of no person whomsoever for enrollment shall be received after the expiration of the said ninety days."

Under the above legislation, the Commission is now without authority to enroll this child.

Respectfully,

SIGNED

Commissioner in Charge.

Chic. N.B - 80
    (Vernie Leader
    Born June 22, 1904)

CERTIFICATE OF RECORD OF MARRIAGE

United States of America, ⎫
   Indian Territory,   ⎬ sct.
     Southern District.⎭

I, C. M. Campbell, Clerk of the United States Court, in the Territory and District aforesaid Do Hereby Certify, that the License for and Certificate of Marriage of

Mr   Wm Leader   and

M   Dott Drawgress

were filed in my office in said Territory and District the 5th day of September A.D., 190 3 and duly recorded in Book G of Marriage Record, Page 394

Witness my hand and Seal of said Court, at Ardmore, this 5th day of September A.D. 190 3

    C. M. Campbell
                Clerk.

Return this License to the United States Clerk at Ardmore, that it may be recorded, when it will be mailed to the proper address.

Applications for Enrollment of Chickasaw Newborn
Act of 1905 Volume I

Indian Territory,
Southern District.

I, C. M. Campbell, Clerk of the United States Court, Southern District, Indian Territory, do hereby certify that the foregoing is a true and correct copy of the Marriage License filed and entered of record in this office and duly recorded in Volume G, Page 394.

IN TESTIMONY WHEREOF, I have hereunto set my hand and official seal, this the 27th day of March, 1905.

C. M. Campbell, Clerk.

By *(Name Illegible)* , Deputy.

No person is authorized to perform the Marriage Ceremony in the Indian Territory unless the proper credentials have first been recorded in the Clerk's office.

MARRIAGE LICENSE.

No. 1190

United States of America ⎫
Indian Territory,   ⎬ ss   To Any Person Authorized by Law to
Southern District.   ⎭   Solemnize Marriage, Greeting:

You are hereby Commanded to solemnize the Rite and publish the Banns of Matrimony between Mr. Wm. Leader of Tishomingo in the Indian Territory, aged 22 years, and M Dott Drawgress of Tishomingo in the Indian Territory, aged 17 years, according to law; and do you officially sign and return this license to the parties therein named.

Witness my hand and official Seal, this 5th day of September A. D. 190 3

C. M. Campbell
Clerk of the United States Court.

Applications for Enrollment of Chickasaw Newborn
Act of 1905 Volume I

Certificate of Marriage.

United States of America ⎫
Indian Territory,   ⎬ ss
Southern District.   ⎭   I,   C. M. Campbell

Clerk U. S. Court,   do hereby certify that on the   5th   day of   September
A. D. 190 3 , I did duly and according to law, as commanded in the foregoing License, solemnize
the Rite and publish the Banns of Matrimony between the parties therein named.

Witness my hand this   5th   day of September   A. D. 190 3

My credentials are recorded in the office of the Clerk of the United States Court,
Indian Territory, Southern District, at Ardmore, Book _____, Page _____

C. M. Campbell.
Clerk U. S. Court.

NOTE. (a)- This License and Certificate of Marriages must be returned to the office of the Clerk of the United
States Court in the Indian Territory, at Ardmore, within sixty days from the date thereof, or the party to whom the License was
issued will be liable in the amount of ONE HUNDRED DOLLARS ($100).

BIRTH AFFIDAVIT.

DEPARTMENT OF THE INTERIOR.
COMMISSION TO THE FIVE CIVILIZED TRIBES.

IN RE APPLICATION FOR ENROLLMENT, as a citizen of the   Chickasaw   Nation,
of   Vernie Leader   , born on the   22   day of   June   , 1904

Name of Father: W M Leader   a citizen of the Chickasaw Nation.
Name of Mother: Elizea Leader   a citizen of the Chickasaw Nation.

Postoffice   Mc Millan

AFFIDAVIT OF MOTHER.

UNITED STATES OF AMERICA, Indian Territory, ⎫
         Southern   DISTRICT.   ⎭

I,   Elizea Leader   , on oath state that I am   19   years of age and a citizen by
blood , of the   Chickasaw   Nation; that I am the lawful wife of   W M Leader   ,
who is a citizen, by Blood   of the   Chickasaw   Nation; that a   Girl   child
was born to me on   22   day of   June   , 1904; that said child has been named
Vernie Leader   , and was living March 4, 1905.

Applications for Enrollment of Chickasaw Newborn
Act of 1905 Volume I

                                              Elizea Leader

Witnesses To Mark:

{

    Subscribed and sworn to before me this   23 day of   March   , 1905

                                              V.J. Howard
                                              Notary Public.

AFFIDAVIT OF ATTENDING PHYSICIAN OR MID-WIFE.

UNITED STATES OF AMERICA, Indian Territory, }
   Southern   DISTRICT. }

    I,   Alice Howard   , a   ———   , on oath state that I attended on Mrs.   Elizea Leader   , wife of   W M Leader   on the 22 day of   June , 1904; that there was born to her on said date a   Girl   child; that said child was living March 4, 1905, and is said to have been named   Vernie

                                              Alice Howard

Witnesses To Mark:

{

    Subscribed and sworn to before me this   23 day of   March   , 1905

                                              V.J. Howard
                                              Notary Public.

                                                                                             80
COPY   9 NB ~~504~~

                                     Muskogee, Indian Territory, April 14, 1905.

W. M. Leader,
      McMillan, Indian Territory.

Dear Sir:

    Referring to the affidavits heretofore forwarded, relative to the enrollment of your infant child, Vernie leader, it appears that you are a citizen by blood of the Chickasaw Nation.

    If this is correct you are requested to state when, where and under what name you were listed for enrollment, the names of your parents and other members of your family

Applications for Enrollment of Chickasaw Newborn
Act of 1905   Volume I

for whom application was made at the same time, and if you have selected an allotment, give your roll number as the same appears upon your allotment certificate.

                Respectfully,

       SIGNED

                T. B. Needles.
                Commissioner in Charge.

                          9 NB 80
                          9--504

            Muskogee, Indian Territory, April 28, 1905.

Billy Leader,
    McMillan, Indian Territory.

Dear Sir:

    Receipt is hereby acknowledged of your letter of April 20, 1905, inclosing your allotment certificate which shows your enrollment number upon the approved rolls of citizens by blood of the Chickasaw Nation to be 1483, forwarded in support of the application for the enrollment of your child, Vernie Leader. The allotment certificate inclosed with your letter is herewith returned.

                Respectfully,

LM 1-28   Chairman.

                          9-N.B. 80

            Muskogee, Indian Territory, May 11, 1905.

W. M. Leader,
    McMillan, Indian Territory.

Dear Sir:

    Referring to the application for the enrollment of your infant child, Vernie Leader, it appears from the affidavits heretofore filed in this office that you and your wife are both citizens by blood of the Chickasaw Nation.

    If this is correct you are requested to state when, where and under what name you were listed for enrollment, the names of your parents and other members of your family

Applications for Enrollment of Chickasaw Newborn
Act of 1905   Volume I

for whom application was made at the same time, and if you have selected an allotment, give your roll number as the same appears on your allotment certificate.

Before this matter can be finally disposed of it will be necessary that you furnish the above information in regard to your self and your wife, Elizea Leader.

Respectfully,

Chairman.

(The letter below typed as given.)

(COPY)

McMillan, I. T.
May 20, 1905.

Hon Daws Comistion

Gentlemen my rol no is 1483 I was enrolled at Ardmore I. T. by my stepfather G. W. McMillan my fahter name was Jim Leader my mother name mcMillan my half sisters and brothers is Milly   Rena   Joseph   Birthie   Lindsey   Lillian   all on McMillan

Please let me know if this all that is needed and

Billie Leader.

---

9 N.B. 80.

Muskogee, Indian Territory, May 26, 1905.

Billy Leader,
   McMillan, Indian Territory.

Dear Sir:

Receipt is hereby acknowledged of your letter of May 20, giving the names of your parents and their roll numbers in the matter of the enrollment of your child, Vernie Leader, and this information has enabled us to identify you upon our records as an enrolled citizen by blood of the Chickasaw Nation.

Respectfully,

Chairman.

Applications for Enrollment of Chickasaw Newborn
Act of 1905 Volume I

9-NB-80.

Muskogee, Indian Territory, June 21, 1905.

Billie Leader,
    McMillan, Indian Territory.

Dear Sir:

    Referring to the application for the enrollment of your infant child, Vernie Leader, born June 22, 1904, your attention is called to the Commission's letter of May 11, 1905, in which you were requested to furnish information by which you and your wife might be identified. In reply to this letter you furnished the desired information concerning yourself, but failed to mention your wife.

    In the affidavits heretofore filed in this office your wife signs the affidavit executed by her as Elizea Leader, while it appears from the marriage license filed on the same date that your wife's maiden name was <u>Dott</u> Drawgress.

    In order that your wife may be properly identified you are requested to state when, where and under what name she was listed for enrollment, the names of her parents and other members of her family for whom application was made at the same time, and if she has selected an allotment of land, please give her roll number as the same appears upon her allotment certificate.

    Please give this matter your immediate attention.

        Respectfully,

                Chairman.

(The letter below typed as given.)

        McMillan I T
                      July   1905
    Hon
Daws Comishion

    Gentlemen

in reply to your letter of June 21 will say it was my mistake in Getting license Dott is a nick name Her name is Listed as Elizer Duroderige her Role no is 1659 her fathers name was Osanta Duroderige her mother name I think was Jane She was Registered with Frank Coones and Mamley Renz

            Res
                Billie Leader

Applications for Enrollment of Chickasaw Newborn
Act of 1905   Volume I

9 NB-80

Muskogee, Indian Territory, July 7, 1905.

Billy Leader,
    McMillan, Indian Territory.

Dear Sir:

    Receipt is hereby acknowledged of your letter of July 1, 1905, giving the name of your wife as Elizer Duroderige and state that you made a mistake in securing the marriage license as Dott is only a nick name.

    In reply to your letter you are advised that this information has been made a part of the record in the matter of the application for the enrollment of your child Vernie Leader as a citizen by blood of the Chickasaw Nation.

                    Respectfully,

                                  Commissioner.

Index

ACKER
  May 50,55
ALDRICH
  Albert Alonzo 155,156
  Albert Nokomis 155,156
  Susan Ann 156
  Susan N 155,156
ALISON
  Will 288
ALLISON
  Nancy 288,289
  Will 288,289
  Willie Laura 287,288,289
ANDERSON
  W H 299
ANGELL
  W H 30
ARPEALER
  Billy 43,44,45,46
  William 43,44,45,46
ASBURY
  Alice 244,245,246
  Allen 247
  Allen S 244,245,246
  Elmer Franklin 244,245,246,247
ASBURY, ... 247
ASHTON
  Bird I 63,64,65,66,67
  Julia V 63,64,65,66
  Mary Mickie 63,64,65,66,67
AUSTIN
  G Y 33
  J E 33
  T J 189,224
  W O 33,34
AUTREY
  D 297
AUTRY
  D 297
  D, MD 297
AYAKATUBBY
  Minnie 32,35

BAKER
  Henry L 45
BALL
  E J 26

BALLARD
  Dr A E 319
  A E 317,319,321
BARLAR
  C T 34,35
BARNES
  Thomas C 310,311
  Thos C, MD 310
BARTLETT
  D G 280,282,283,284,285
BEALL
  W O 227
BELL
  Alta Pearl 241,242,243
  Clara May 241,242,243
  J B 241
  J E 242
  James Edgar 243
  T M 212,213
BINGHAM
  L K 185
BIXBY
  Tams 24,32,36,37,49,54,55,95,172,
  197,223,258,278,312,315
BLACKBURN
  J H 130,131,132
BLANTON
  J T 191,192,254,255,256,257
BLANTON & ANDREWS 263
BOATRIGHT
  J L 142,143
BOND & MELTON 165
BORING
  Jane 91
  Thenie Caraline 91,92
BORRING
  Thenie C 90
BOTTOMS
  C T 178
BOURLAND
  Clemmie 273,274
BRADFORD
  C J 110,111
  C M 142
  M S 23,72,73,74,108,109,110,111,
  141,142,143
  R L 108

BRADLEY
  P C 4,5,7
  P C, MD 4,5,7
BRADSHAW
  Bertha 129
  Berthena 127,128
BRADY
  W T 299
BRAGG
  A H 246,247
  Mrs A H 245,246
BRANUM
  T C 222
  T C, MD 222
BREWER
  Myrtle 198
BROWN
  Adaline 302
  Adeline 301,302
  Affason 157,158,159,161,162,163
  Afferson 158,160,162
  Alice L 81,82,83,85,86,88
  Allice L 81,84
  Emra C 248,249,250
  Lucy 11,12
  M L 33
  Malinda... 162
  Malinda Caely 160
  Malinda Sealey 159
  Malinda Sealy 157,161,163
  Martin 98
  Melinda Caely 158
  Melinda Celia 157,158
  A P 56,58,59
  A P, MD 57,58
  Stephen 252
  T A 304
  Tecumseh...... 157,158,160,161,162,163
  W J 323,324
  W J, MD 323
BURDESHAW
  W H 11,140
BURKES
  Lenoir Gretell 254
BURKS
  Gretell Lenoir 255,256,257,259,261,
    262,263

Gretelle 263
Lenoir 255,256
Lenoir Gretell 254,255,260
Lenori 261
Nora 254,255,256,257,260,261,262
R E 258,259,260,261
Royden 255,256,259,261,263
Royden E 254,255,259,260,262
Roydon 256,257,261,262
BURRIS
  Douglas H Johnson........... 296,297,298
  Duglass H Johnson 296
  G W 141
  Letha................................. 296,297
  Lethia 298
  Melton 296,297,298
BYRD
  B F 140
  Ed 94

CALLAWAY
  James R 264,265
  James R, MD................................. 265
CAMPBELL
  C M 24,25,114,115,172,173,228,
    229,258,259,325,326,327
CAMPELUBE
  Columbus 44
CARLISLE
  J H 237,238
  M A 237
CARNEY
  Burney .. 138,139,140,141,142,143,144
  Cicen 111
  Josephine 138,139,140,141,142,143
  Josiephine....................................... 144
  Lizia 143,144
  Sallie................. 138,139,140,141,143
  Sarah...................... 138,142,143,144
CARTER
  Dorant.. 105
  Gretell Lenoir 260
  Nora...................... 258,259,260,261
CASH
  Albert P 188,189
  Alice 187,188,189,190
  Minnie Ruth 187,188,189,190

334

Index

A P 187,188,190
CHAPMAN
  A A 96,97,98,99
  J C 152
CHILDERS
  A J 150
CHILDS
  J S 248
  J S, MD 248
  Joseph S 249,250
  Joseph S, MD 249
CLARK
  W H 140
CLAYTON
  Julia Rebekah 264,265,266
  Tamsey A 264
  Tansy A 265
  W S 266
  William S 264,265
  Wm S 264
CLEMMONS
  J R 122,123,124
CLOWDUS
  J A 313
COCHRAN
  R M 205,206
COFFEY
  Finis 311,314,315
  Ivy 314,315
  J I 312,313,315
  Stella 314
COLBERT
  Annie 145
  Annie E 144,145,146,147
  E F 147
  Edmon 150,151,152,153,154
  Edmond 152,154
  Edward 154
  Elizabeth E 169,170
  Elizabeth Elnora 171
  Emil F 144,145,146
  Emil F Colbert 147
  Holman 150,151,152,153,154
  James Henry 144,145,146,147
  Joe E 171
  Joseph E 169,170
  Katinka 149

  Louisa 10,11,12
  Martha 150,151,152,154
  Marthy 152,153,154
  Marty 151
  Orva L 148,149
  Oscar 149
  Oscar, Jr 148,149
  Oscar, Sr 148,149
  Walter 10,11,12
  Walton 10,11,12
  William Blanchard 169,170,171
COLLEY
  Ella 71,72,73,74
  Myrtle 71,73,74
  Ruby 71,72,74
  William E 71,72,74
  William H 73
COLLINS
  J P 273,274
COLWELL
  F C 153
COONES
  Frank 331
COOPER
  Zach 124
COPELAND
  J J 60,61,62
COSEN
  Willie 167,168
COWAN
  James A 200
CRAIG
  J R 60,62
  J R, MD 60,62
CRAVATT
  Maggie 26
CRAWFORD
  Jno P 39,89,90
CUMMINGS
  S E 299,300

DALTON
  Mattie C 198
DARKEN
  S J 48
  Sarah J 48
DAVIDSON

Index

Georgia 238,240,241
DAVIS
  A B 160
  J L 102
  Linnie K 101,102
  Minnie K 102
  S C 102
  Samuel C 101,102
  Samuel C, Jr 101,102
DAVISON
  Georgia 240
DAWSON
  E L 202,204,205,206
  E L, MD 202,204,205,206,207
DICE
  R J 288,289
  R J, MD 288
DICKERSON
  Fleda 74,75,76,77,78,79,80
  L D 74,75,78,79,80
  Lillie 74,75,76,77,79
  Lorenzo 79
  Lorenzo D 76,77
DILBECK
  F H 168
  Frank W 167,169
  Luella 167,168,169
  Montelee 167,168,169
  W F 168
DILLARD
  Kinzy 94
DINEBAUGH
  D H 47
DOAK
  D N 309
  Dudley Nail 305,306,307,308
  Lovie Lee 305,306,307,308
  Vivian Nail .. 304,305,306,307,308,309
DOBBS
  E A 185,186
  Earl 183
  Martha Ana 185
  Martha Ann 185,186
  Mary 185
  Mollie 185,186
DODSON
  T B 133

DOUGHTY
  H P 103,104
DRAWGRESS
  Dott 325,326,331,332
DRUMMOND
  S E 322,323,324
DUKE
  Maggie 30,31
DULIN
  Fannie 230,231,232,234
  Fanny 230
  James P 228,230,231,232,233, 234,235
  Marcum 141
  Simpson 228,229,230,231,232,233, 234,235
DURANT
  Eathem Lee 29,30,31
  J B 30,31
  Jacob 29,30,31
  Maggie 29,30
  Mary 30
DURODERIGE
  Elizer 331,332
  Jane 331
  Osanta 331
EARL
  S M, MD 304
EARP
  S N, MD 303
ENFIELD
  J D 134
FERRIN
  F F 173
FERRIS
  W T 110,111
FIELDING
  H W 56,57,58
FILLMORE
  Allice Victoria 117
  H C 117
  Minnie L 117
FILMORE
  Alice Victoria 117
  Allice Victora 116,118

Index

Allice Victoria 113,116,118,119, 120,121
H C 101,114,116,118,119,120
Harry... 120
Henry 117,119,120,121
Henry C 116,119
Minnie L 116,118
FLORENCE
C P 21
J K 173,174,229
FOOSHEE
Geo A 9,10
FOOSHEE & BRUNSON 10
FOYIL
W A 148,149
FRANKLIN
Wirt..29,30,44
FRAZIER
Jim... 108
FRIEND
Douglas H.... 201,203,204,205,207,208
Estella M 201,202,205,206,207
Reta... 208
Retta 202,203,204,205,206,207
Thomas L............ 204,205,206,207,208
Thos L 202,203,204
FRY
Sallie.................................238,240,241
FRYREAR
Burrell S 240,241
Eddie Lee..... 235,236,237,238,239,240
Edie Lee.. 241
Frances 185
Francis 184,186
Rosa...... 235,236,237,238,239,240,241
S B 184,238,240,241
S Burl.........................235,236,238,239
S Burrel 236,237
FULLER
Jno W..88,89

GAFFORD
T156
GARDNER
B S 281,283,285
B S, MD.....................................281,283
GAYLORD

J W 198
GIBSON
Minnie 194,195,197
Rodie 194,195,196,197
Silas......................... 194,195,196,197
GILBREATH
Ida 252,253
W W 252
GILLILAND
J N 102
GILLUM
Ben F 150,151
GIPSON
Thomas M 293
GOOCH
Cora Eugenia...... 216,217,218,219,220
Dean 216,217,218,219,220
Gladys Monnie ... 216,217,218,219,220
GOODEN
Minnie D 114,115,118
GORBET
T E...321
W E 317,318,319
GRAHAM
E F 282,284,285
E F, MD...................................282,284
GRAYSON
James...25
James J 22,23,25,26,27,28
Jas...24
Laura 22,23,25,26,27,28
Leo Mayfield........... 22,23,25,26,27,28
GREENWOOD
Ella 107,108,110,111,112,113
Ellen 111
Eller 108,109,110,112
Hogan ... 107,108,109,110,111,112,113
Hogen 112
Homan..111
Mahala.......................... 107,108,111
Mahaley..112
Mahali 110,113
Mahaly 108,109,111
Maliah 113
GREGORY
O..93
GRIFFIN

337

Index

Laura 24,25
Lou 26,27
Lue 23,28
GUNN
   Isham 318

HACKLEMAN
   W H 34,35
HAINS
   J A 47
HALEY
   Lizzie 91
HALL
   Porter 18,19,20
HAMILTON
   Simeon 96,97,98,99,100
   Zora 96,97,98,99,100
HAMMOND
   John S 115
HANNIN
   C S 221,222
HARDY
   W 286,287
   W, MD 287
HARKINS
   Giles W 9,10
   Giles W, MD 9
HARL
   W B 133
HARLIN
   Delta 300
   Delter 298,299,300
   George 298,299,300
   Pearl 300
   Pearl L 298,299,300
HARRISON
   D P 126,127
   Daniel Peyton 128,129
   Earl Eugene 126,127
   Earle Eugene 128,129
   Laura 130,131,132
   Laura Josephine 129,130
   Lillie 131,132
   Mary 126,127,128,129
   W F 1,2,3,4,5,6,7,18,19,20,127, 130,152
HART

J J 101,102,116,121
HARTIN
   Bill 237
HATCHER
   Lillian 92
   Lillie M 91
   Lillie May 89,90,91,92
   Mary Ellen 89,90,91,92
   Robert E 89,90
   Robert Lee 90,91,92
HATHAWAY
   A H 135,136,137
   R K 135,137
HATTLE
   W C 234
HAWKINS
   Mary 12,13,14,15,16,17
   May 12,13,14,15,16,17
   Morris H 12,13,14,15,16,17
HAYES
   Agnes 38,39,40,41,43
   Carrie 38,39,40,41,42,43
   A H 138,139
   William R 38,39,40,41,42,43
HENDERSON
   Marion 192,193,224
HIGGINS
   Frances 182,183,185
   Francis 184
   Mrs 183
   Thomas H 182,183,184,185
   Thomas Howard 183
HILL
   Jas T 316
HOGUE
   Beulah 251,253
   Bulah 252
   H A 253
   Henry 251,252,253
   Henry A 251,253
   John L W 251,252,253
   John W L 252
HOMER
   Enoch 150
HORTON
   Burruss Andrew 60,61,62,63
   Herbert 60,62,63

Index

Mintie 60,61,62
Mrs Herbert 60
HOTTLE
  W C 230,232
  W C, MD 230,232
HOTUBBY
  Julia 160,162
  Sam 158
  Somie 162
HOUSE
  Emma 81,82,83,84,85,86
HOWARD
  Alice 328
  Eulalia Ruth 201
  Kitty 251,252,253
  Mary I 199,200,201
  Ulalia Ruth 199,200
  V J 328
  William B 199,200,201
HULL
  Belle 221,222
  Belle Langdon 222,223
  Jesse 221,222,223,224,225,226,227
  Mattie ... 221,222,223,224,225,226,227
  William 224
HUTUBBY
  Julia 163
  Some 163

INGRAM
  H P 170

JACKSON
  S W 145,146,147
  S W, MD 145,146
JAMES
  Thomas 21
  W S 304
JEMISON
  Eula E 132,133,134
  May 134
  Vera 132,133
  W P 132,133
  William P 134
JOHNSON
  Ben F 166
  Benjamin Franklin 164,165,166

Cecil Elihu 280,281,282,283,284
Cecile Elihu 285
Elihu Bennett 315,316,317,318,319, 320,321
Emily 316,317,318,319,320,321
Eula 285
Fannie 228,229,235
G L 198
G L, MD 198
Gl 199
H Z 280,281,282,283,284,285
J W 318,319
John 316,317,318,319,320,321
Josephine Olive 164,165
Mamie Olive 164,165
Rella 280,281,282,283,284,285
Ula 280,281,282,283,285
JONES
  Bill 47,48,49,51,52,53,54
  Elmer E 47,48,49,50,51,52,53,54,55
  L T 209,210,211
  Luis 50
  Susan 47,48,49,51
  T W 50,54,55
  W E 50
KELLEY
  C P 200
  Dr C P 200
  A S 174,175,176,181,182,230, 231,232
KELLY
  Annie 122,124,125
  W F 158
KENNEMER
  F E 21
KYLES
  Sallie 275,277,279

LANDETH
  L M 68
  P A 68
LEADER
  Billie 330,331
  Billy 329,330,332
  Elizea 327,328,330,331
  Jim 330

Index

Leah 39,40,41
Melton 41
Vernie ... 325,327,328,329,330,331,332
W M 327,328
Wm 325,326
LEECE
   T O 115
LEGGETT
   Henry P 105
LEWIS
   Galloway 11
   Ihcha 152
   Jackson 11
   Mary 97,98,99,100
   Mintie 61,62
   W M 125
   W N 122,123,124
LILLARD
   Minnie 82,84,85
   Minnie B 83
LINDSAY
   Alice 116
LINEBAUGH
   D H 48
LITTLE
   J C 21,38,40
LOFTIN
   G A 166
LOGAN
   C E 116,117
LOUIS
   Highleatha 153
   Hightealha 154
LOVE
   Buck 247,248,249,250
   Hattie S 247,248,249,250
   John Dean 247,248,249,250

MABERY
   F C 25
McCARY
   G W 153
   W J 153
McCLASKY
   C B 124
McCLUSKY
   C B 123

C G 122
McCOY
   C J 301,302
   Hattie Brown 301,302
   Jerry R 301,302
McCURTAIN
   Edmon 142,143
   Zeno 138,139
   Zeno M 88
McDANIEL
   A 103,104
McDANIELS
   Allen 236
McKEOWN
   Tom D 41
McKINNON
   Edith 293
   G G 293
   Lula 293
McMILLAN
   Birthie 330
   G W 330
   Joseph 330
   Lillian 330
   Lindsey 330
   Milly 330
   Rena 330
McNEILL
   J E 165
MALKEY
   Jas H 277
MANISS
   Seila R 210
   W J 210,211
   W J, MD 211
MANSFIELD, McMURRAY &
   CORNISH 37,55
MARROW
   Jewel 172,173,180
   Rebecca 176
MASSEY
   Jnow 303
MASTERSON
   Stella 312,313,315
MATTHEWS
   H H 295
MAXELL

Index

Malinda 276
MAXWELL
  Alie May 274,275,277
  Allie May 274,278
  Malinda 275,276,277,279
  Malindy 274
  Mrs 275
  Ollie May 274,275,276,277,278,279
  Wisdom 274,275,276,277,278,279
MELLAW
  R M 267
MELOY
  H C 35
  R C 35
  R C, MD 35
MERCHANT
  Clover 309,310,311
  E E 309,310,311
  Malvina 309,310,311
MEREDITH
  H D 169
  N D 168
MILLER
  Geo W 242,243,244
  H C 276,305
MITCHELL
  Douglas Thompson 197,198
  Douglis Thompson 199
  Duglis Thompson 197,198
  Gains A 197,198
  James A 199
  Rilla 197,198,199
MOON
  J D 21
MOORE
  Jessie E 210
MORGAN
  E A 21
MORRISS
  W P 211
MORROW
  J W 178
  Johnnie B 178
  Rebecca 174,175,176,177,178
  Walter J 178
  William F 178
MOSS

M F 316,317
MYERS
  Eula 209,210,211
  Joseph F 209,210,211
  Tommie C 210,211
  Tommy C 209,210
NATION
  W C 195
  W C, MD 195
NEEDLES
  T B 36,88,196,329
NELSON
  Columbus 122,123,124,125,126
  Doss 121,123,124,125,126
  Floy 121,122,124,125,126
  Nellie 45
  Sudie 122,123,124,125,126
  Susie 124,125,126
NICHOLS
  James Luther 212,213
  Jerrel Eugenia 215,216
  Jewel Eugenia 212,214
  Joel Eugenia 213,214
  Luther 213,214,215,216
  T J 306,307,308
  Velary Etta 213,214,215,216
  Velary Etta Colbert 212,213
NOLATUBBEE
  Bessie 92,93,94
  James 92,93,94,95
  Mary Luella 92,93,94,95
NOLEN
  Clemmie 272,273,274
  Robert L 272,273,274
  Tishie Hortense 272,273,274
NORMAN
  William H 72,73,74
  William H, MD 72,73

O'DONLEY
  W J 68,69,70
OLIVE
  Mamie 166
OWENS
  Sarah 109,110,112,113
  Seely 108,111

Index

Soloman 159
Solomon 163

PADEN
G J 299
PANACHA
Lizzie 139
PANTSKY
M M 68,70
Mary M 70
PARKER
W F 57,58
PATTEN
W A 133
PATTERSON
Price 189
Price, MD 189
Pris 188,190
PERDUE
A M 170
PERRY
Eli 68,69,70,71
Emma B 68,69,70,71
Lucrecia Exa 67,68,69,70,71
PHILLIPS
Jos W 313
Joseph W 312
PIKEY
Delila 185
Kate 185
Katie 183,184,185
Mollie 185,186
PIRTH
Kittie 101
PIRTLE
Kittie 116
POTOCH
James 105
PRICE
C C 322,323,324
Eva 322,323,324
M J 322,323,324
Mollie J 323,324
PRIVITT
J B 295
PROCTOR
Wm A 310

PUSLEY
Nannie B 151
Rena 43,44,45,46
Susan 151
PUTTY
Geo T 194,195

RANDOLPH
Ira 151
REAVES
J B 259
REDWINE
H H 133
REED
R H 314
RENA
Mamley 331
REXROAT
U T 94,95,294
RICE
F E 214,215,216,217,218,219,220,
290,291,292,293
O E 103,104,105,106,107
O F 105
Odneal 103,104,105,106,107
Surena 106,107
Surena M 103,104,105
RICHARD
W 160
RICHARDS
W L 157,158,159,160,162
RIDER & KENNEMER 22
ROGERS
A B 128,129
Nora 191
Nora Lee 192
U B 131,132
ROWLEY
H B 145,146,147

SALMON
R H 191
SAXON
Lillian Lucile 129,130
SEALEY
Malinda 162
SEALY

342

Index

Maggie 271
Maggie May 266,267
Sallie 22
SELEY
   Culberson 33
SHELTON
   John 166
SIGLER
   Guy A 288
   Guy H 296,297
SIMPSON
   Joe 315
SLOVER
   G W 65,66,156
   G W, MD 65,156
   Geo W, MD 64
   George W 64
SMALL
   J B 245,246
   R Walter 244,245,246
SMITH
   Joseph P 75,76,77,78
   R B 211
SPEARS
   D A 50,51
   W S 306,307,308
   W S, MD 306
SPENCE
   Alice L 81,82,83,84,85,86,88
   Allice L 81,84
   L W 85,87
   W A 81,82,83,84,85,86,87,88
   William W 83,84,85,87,88
   William Wellington 86,87
   William Willington 80,81,82,83,85
STAMPER
   H M 109
STANDRIDGE
   J H 13
   R A 13,14,16
   Ruth Adlin 15
   Rutha Adlin 17
   U B 13,14
STANTON
   M G 191
   Maggie 268,269,271
   Maggie May 267,271

Marrley 272
Marrley M 266,267,268,269,270, 271,272
Mary A 193,267,268,269,270,271
Mirle D 193
Mirle G 192,193
Missouri D 191,192,193
Nora 191
Nora L 191
Nora Lee 192,193
R D 266,267,268,269,270,271,272
R J 295
W H 44
STATLER
   B 158
   Dacie 134,135,136,137
   Gale 134,135,136,137
   James J 134,135,136,137
   James Johnson 135
   Price 135,136
STEWART
   Charles Claud 56,57,58
   Charley Claud 59
   Charlie Claud 57,58,59
   J W 135
   Minnie 56,57,58,59
   Revie 56,57,58,59
STOVER
   George W 66
SUGGS
   Victor 267,268,269,270
SUMMERS
   Alfred 13,14,15,16
   F 14
   Florence 15,16
TAPLIN
   Mattie 91
TAYLOR
   Andrew J 31,32,33,34,35,36,37
   Dow 316,318,320
   Dow, MD 318,319,321
   Dr Dow 319
   Luther 32,34,35,36,37
   Minnie 32,33,34,35,36
   A S 183,185,186,187,236,238
THACKER

Index

Robert E 170
Robt E 170,171
THOM
  Salena 140
  Selina 141
  Sonelia 140
THOMAS
  C H 273
  Minnie 58
  William 58
THOMASON
  C H 264,265
THOMPSON
  G L 90
  W C 195
TRALLE
  G M 75,76,77,242,243
  G M, MD 75,78,79,243
  Geo M 77
TRENTHAM
  Belle Smith 9,10
  Bessie 8,9,10
  Henderson 9,10
TROSPER
  H G, Jr 34,35
TRUAX
  Dr Geo H 84,88,89
  Geo H 2,3,84
  Geo H, MD 3
  George H 17,18,20,87,88
  George Henry 19
  Go H, MD 2
  Mary C 17,18,19,20
  Opal 17,18,19,20
TRYEAR
  Rosa 239
TRYREAR
  Eddie Lee 239
  Rosa 239
  S Burl 239
TUCK
  W T 304
TURNBULL
  Dick 290,292,293
  John B 289,290,291,292,293
  Maud 293
  Maude 290,291,292,293

Richard 291,292
TYE
  R P 164,165
TYSON
  Ed 15,16
UNDERWOOD
  D F 96,97,98
  Jesse 21
  Jessie 20,21,22
  May 54
  Nancy 21,22
  Sallie 21,22
  Sallie Sealy 20,21
  Wesley 20,21,22
VAUGHN
  T H 187,188
VON KELLER
  Dr F P 93
  F P, MD 93
  Frederick P, MD 94
WADE
  A F 30
WAIDE
  W M 262
WALDBY
  G N 91
  George N 91
WALDON
  Byrd 236
  Sophia 236,239
  Sophie 237
WALKER
  J C 1,2,3,4,5,6,7,8,152
  Lucy 1,2,3,4,5,6,7
  Maimie 1,3,4,5,6,7,8
  T C 41
  T G 242
  Tandy C, Jr 1,2,3
WALLACE
  Mary 26
WALTER
  James T 155
WARD
  Jefferson D 30

Index

W P 246
WATKINS
  Bessie May 286,287
  James 286,287
  Nora 286,287
  Norah 286
WEBB
  J W 109
WEBSTER
  J M 65,66
WELLS
  A J 70
WESTHOFF
  E W 167
  Mrs E W 167
WHITE
  Eugene E 64
WHITEHEAD
  J E 154
WIGGINS
  S T 275
WILBORNE
  R D 202,203,204
WILLIAM
  J E 301
WILLIAMS
  Ella 294,295
  G M 294,295
  J E 286,287,302
  Joe B 45
  Mary A 104,105,106,107
  Ruth 294,295
  W W 295
WILNATI
  Zila 58
WILSON
  J R 295
  R M 47
  Robt 295
  S H 293
  S W 214,215,216,217,218,220,290,
  292,293
  S W, MD 213,214,215,217,218,220,
  291,292,293
WINSTON
  S P 314
  S P, MD 314

WISDOM
  Caroline 96,97,98,99,100
WISEMAN
  E S 289,297,298
WOLFE
  Malinda 111
WOLFENBARGER
  Rella 281,282,283,285
  Rella Johnson 282
WOOLTON
  S H 229
WOOTTEN
  J H 259
WORCESTER
  Lyman 159
  Lymon 163
WRIGHT
  E B 30
  Esau S 111
  Francis 30
  Malinda 111
  Reuben 111
  T L 111
YOAKUM
  G H 178,179
  Geo H 172
  George H 173,174,175,176,177,178,
  179,180
  George W 181,182
  Jewel 174,175,176,177,178,179
  John M 172,174,175,176,177,178,
  179,180
  John T 181,182
  Laura A 181,182
  Minnie A 181,182
YOUNG
  Adalia 303
  Adaline 303
  Adeline 304
  Charles Reuben 304
  Charles Rheuben 303
  Charles Ruben 302,303
  G W 303,304
  Granville Walker 303,304
  J A 255,256
  James A 256,257,262
  James A, MD 255

www.ingramcontent.com/pod-product-compliance
Lightning Source LLC
Chambersburg PA
CBHW020241030426
42336CB00010B/564